WITHDRAWN
UTSA LIBRARIES

**Western European Cities
In Crisis**

Western European Cities In Crisis

Edited by
Michael C. Romanos
University of Illinois

Lexington Books
D.C. Heath and Company
Lexington, Massachusetts
Toronto

LIBRARY
The University of Texas
At San Antonio

Library of Congress Cataloging in Publication Data

Main entry under title:
    Western European cities in crisis.

    Includes index.
    1. Urbanization—Europe—Addresses, essays, lectures. 2. Rural-urban migration—Europe—Addresses, essays, lectures. 3. Urban policy—Europe—Addresses, essays, lectures. I. Romanos, Michael C.
HT131.W47   301.36'094   78-21445
ISBN 0-669-02800-2

Copyright © 1979 by D.C. Heath and Company

All rights reserved. No part of this publication may be reproduced or transmitted in any form or by any means, electronic or mechanical, including photocopy, recording, or any information storage or retrieval system, without permission in writing from the publisher.

Published simultaneously in Canada.

Printed in the United States of America.

International Standard Book Number: 0-669-02800-2

Library of Congress Catalog Card Number: 78-21445

To my parents

Contents

	List of Figures	ix
	List of Tables	xiii
	Preface and Acknowledgments	xv
Part I	Urbanization and Quality of Life: The Unsettled Questions	1
Chapter 1	Forsaken Farms: The Village-to-City Movement in Europe *Michael C. Romanos*	3
Chapter 2	Social-Psychological Problems of Urban Migrants *Harry C. Triandis*	21
Chapter 3	Dimensions of the Quality of Life in an Urban Area: An Analysis of Stockholm *B. Guy Peters*	31
Chapter 4	A Policy Antimony: Public Attitudes versus Urban Conditions in Western Europe *Zeline Amen Ward*	47
Chapter 5	Social Networks in an Urban Context: Network Comparisons among Urbanites, Townspeople, and Villagers in Tirol *Patricia Ward Crowe*	67
Part II	The Urban Challenge: Controlling the Physical and Man-Made Environment	81
Chapter 6	Interactions between Cities and Their Local and Regional Weather and Climate *William P. Lowry*	83
Chapter 7	The Quality of the Residential Environment: European Housing after World War II *Guido Francescato*	103

Chapter 8	Milan and Public Housing Policy: A Case of Municipal Initiative *Alberta Mary Sbragia*	135
Chapter 9	Reorienting Urban Transportation Policy in Social-Democratic Stockholm and Hamburg *Frank C. Colcord, Jr.*	153
Part III	*National Politics and the Emergence of* *Regional Institutions*	163
Chapter 10	Territory and Social Conflict in Belfast *John V. O'Loughlin*	165
Chapter 11	The Lost Center: Dispersing Berlin's Capital City Functions, 1945-78 *Richard L. Merritt*	185
Chapter 12	County and Communal Reorganization in Western Germany *Peter H. Merkl*	203
Chapter 13	Regionalism and the Italian City *Robert H. Evans*	215
	Index	233
	About the Contributors	239
	About the Editor	243

List of Figures

1-1	Urban Growth: Residential Densities and Land Values	10
3-1	Changes in Factor Scores	42
6-1	Distribution of Minimum Temperatures in London	87
6-2	Relation between Population, P, and the Maximum Temperature Difference between the Center and the Boundary of the Urban Heat Island, ΔTm	88
6-3	Examples of Precipitation Totals from One Rainstorm Obtained with a Dense Network of Gauges	90
6-4	Control and Effect Areas in St. Louis	91
6-5	Concentration of Sulfur Dioxide Gas above Ludwigshafen-Mannheim, 3 April 1965: A Vertical Cross Section	93
6-6	Concentration of Sulfur Dioxide Gas above Ludwigshafen-Mannheim, 3 April 1965: A Horizontal Section	94
6-7	Lines of Equal Average Acidity of Rainwater for 1965 in Northwestern Europe	96
7-1	Le Corbusier's vision of high-rise buildings immersed in greenery is executed with monotonous grayness in this Dutch development.	108
7-2	Segregation of functions, one of the architectural tenets of the modern movement, is exemplified in the separation of parking and housing shown here. An elevated ramp connects the garage to the residential buildings.	109
7-3	The "street in the sky" reduced to a parody of the concept: a narrow corridor between elevator and apartment door.	110
7-4	The Aylesbury Road Estate in Southwark, England, was built to replace an old neighborhood of row houses. In this case, the new does not appear to have improved upon the old.	113

7-5	Not many would want to walk home after dark through this tunnel in the elevated walkway system of the Aylesbury Road Estate.	114
7-6	In spite of the noticeable difference in scale, both the old and the new neighborhood are built at the same density.	115
7-7	The beginning of a reaction to functional segregation: a shopping center designed right into a British housing development.	116
7-8	The architectural treatment of this development can be seen as an attempt to introduce variety and complexity in the building facade.	117
7-9	In spite of the designers' intentions, it is doubtful that this type of architectural treatment conveys a "home" message.	119
7-10	In reaction against another tenet of the modern movement, this Swedish development reinstates the continuity of the street by bringing the new buildings up to the plane of the older building facades.	120
7-11	Shopping center and subway stop are integrated into this housing development.	121
7-12	A pleasant rest area for shoppers and residents alike.	122
7-13	As shown by this Swedish example, it is possible to provide open space and play areas without creating expanses of landscaped emptiness.	123
7-14	A concern for variety and relatively intimate scale is evident in the Lillington Street Estate, a development located in Westminster, England.	125
7-15	Pleasant and easily supervised open spaces are created in the open courts of the Lillington Street Estate.	126
7-16	A solution to the parking problem which permits easy access to one's dwelling and offers security from vandalism and theft.	127

List of Figures xi

7-17	An old church is visually related to the new development by using similar materials and by orienting the housing so that it wraps around the older building.	128
7-18	Pubs are an integral part of the Lillington Street Estate.	129
7-19	Small scale, simple means, and respect for traditional forms are in evidence in this successful Dutch development.	130
7-20	Repetition is not objectionable if the size of the development is small.	131
7-21	A restored warehouse in Amsterdam captures some of the qualities people value, albeit at a price not all can afford.	132
7-22	A permanently moored boat converted into a house represents another way in which enterprising Amsterdam dwellers have achieved some of the amenities offered by restoration without incurring its high cost.	133
10-1	Northern Ireland	166
10-2	Sectarian Murders in Belfast, January 1972 to June 1973	168
10-3	Number of Persons Found Guilty of Offenses against the Person in Northern Ireland, 1965-75	171
10-4	Pre-1973 Election Trends in Belfast	175
10-5	Distribution of Belfast's Seats in the Northern Ireland Assembly Election, May 1975	177
10-6	Location of Redevelopment Districts in Belfast	179

List of Tables

1-1	Italy: Population Changes between 1952 and 1971	5
1-2	Urban Growth in Europe, 1800-1960	7
1-3	Distribution of Urban and Nonurban Population in Greece, 1928-71	8
3-1	Classification of Quality-of-Life Indicators	32
3-2	Operational Definitions of Indicators in Stockholm Analysis	38
3-3	Eigenvalues of Factors	40
3-4	Quartimax Rotated Factor Loadings	41
4-1	Index of Satisfaction with Life in General, by Size of Locality of Residence: The Netherlands, Denmark, and Germany, September 1973	48
4-2	Index of Economic and Political Satisfaction in the European Community Nations According to Size and Locality, September 1973	50
4-3	Cluster Analysis of Attitudes toward Change: The Problem of Poverty (European Community Nations, May-June 1976)	54
4-4	Cluster Analysis of Attitudes toward Change: Women's Rights (European Community Nations, December 1975)	55
4-5	Quality and Duration of Holiday Activities for the Economically Active Population, by Size of Locality, Denmark, 1974	58
4-6	Children Registered for Day Care, by Age and by Degree of County Urbanization, Denmark, 1975	61
5-1	Percentage of Respondents Reporting No Friends	72
5-2	Percentage of Respondents Reporting Friends Exclusively Outside Their Place of Residence	73
6-1	Western European Countries as Emitters and Receivers of Airborne Sulfur Compounds	97

6-2	Rank Orders for Two Variables Relating Air Pollution Emitters and Receivers in Western Europe	98
11-1	German and Berlin Occupational Structure, 1933 and 1970	192
11-2	Distribution of Employees and Self-Employed in Selected Economic Sectors, 1970	195
11-3	Distribution of Employees and Self-Employed in Broad Economic Sectors, 1970	196

Preface and Acknowledgments

This collection of essays is based on the fundamental premise that Western Europe is a physical and cultural entity whose national components are so closely interrelated, because of historic, demographic, and economic reasons, that they can be studied as a unified system. Furthermore, this book takes the view that Western European urban areas, because of these very interrelationships, have been and still are today confronted with similar sets of problems, are experimenting with similar solutions, and are learning from one another's experiences. When we talk about European cities in this volume, we do so with a certain bias: rather than identify urban areas in terms of their differences, we compare them based on their similarities. The approach has a special connotation in this book, since several of the contributed chapters use a sample of cities for the development of their arguments but attempt to extend their analysis to much larger sets of urban areas with similar basic characteristics.

This volume refers to Western European cities in crisis. The term *crisis* is used, not to denote a stage of catastrophe or of a major and irreversible conflict, but to connote a *critical point*. The term was used as the title because we believe—and make it evident in several chapters of the volume—that Western Europe and its urbanized areas are reaching a point in their history at which they must recollect, evaluate their present state and their prospects for the future, and make decisions which can be far-reaching not only for the urban areas themselves but for the nonurban regions and the non-Western parts of the Continent as well. This turning point has come about as the result of several factors. The increasing role that Europe is playing in world affairs in recent years, the growing economic power of the European Economic Community and its prospects for further expansion through inclusion of additional country-members, as well as the changing international economic order, with its effects on the supply and prices of key resources such as labor and energy, are perhaps among the most important of these factors. Whatever far-reaching decisions, conscious or unconscious, are taken in the Western European cities, this stage in their development is a fascinating one. While European political, social, and economic affairs have historically attracted more than their share of world attention, the cities where most of the dynamics of these affairs are based have been largely neglected. We hope that our ambition to contribute to closing this gap is partly fulfilled through the publication of this volume.

The present collection of readings was perceived as an effort to provide an interdisciplinary view of contemporary issues and problems confronting Western European cities as well as the approaches taken by these cities in their attempt to cure these problems. The need for a book of this nature became apparent in the fall of 1976 and the spring of 1977, when some members of the University of Illinois faculty, including the editor, organized a series of interdisciplinary courses on the problems and prospects of cities in Western Europe under the auspices of the University Office of West European Studies. The search for relevant topics and related published material revealed that there is little readily accessible information on the subject and that much of what is available is of limited use because it is fragmented, published in different languages, and restricted to specialized areas of expertise. A collection of the viewpoints of different disciplines on a set of key issues and problems characteristic of the urban centers of Western Europe was not available. This book is an attempt to fill at least a part of this need. It was produced through the collaborative efforts of a number of contributors who have a wide range of interests and expertise. The essays have been prepared specifically for this project and are written to address students of European urban problems who are accustomed to interdisciplinary analytical approaches.

The volume has been organized into three parts. The first deals with the social and economic space for urban development, the second addresses issues related to the physical urban space, and the third analyzes the political space at the national and the regional levels. Part I consists of five chapters concerned with two major topics: the movement of rural population to the cities and the quality of life that cities under growth stresses have been able to provide their residents. In the first chapter, Romanos analyzes the phenomenon of rural-urban migration in Europe and discusses the effects of the population movement on both exporting and receiving areas. Triandis's chapter deals primarily with these two categories of effects, emphasizing the social and psychological influences of the urban environment on the rural immigrant as a result of the physical and social differences between the village and the city. The chapter by Peters introduces the complex question of the quality of life in cities and develops a framework for the measurement of the quality of life through objective indicators. Two applications of such measurement and analysis techniques by Ward and Crowe present complementary results. They report heightened levels of dissatisfaction and cynicism among residents of larger communities in spite of the comparatively advantaged position of metropolitan residents (Ward), and despite the fact that social networks of contacts, friendships, and kinship are enhanced and strengthened in urban areas as compared to smaller towns and villages (Crowe).

Part II of the volume deals with a number of urban environmental concerns. The first chapter, by Lowry, discusses the interaction between cities and their climate and presents some exciting aspects of the impact of city functions on their microclimate and the role and importance of microclimate in urban life. Francescato's chapter takes a critical view of the qualitative elements of European housing programs and the role of design and architectural visions in shaping the residential environment. It is followed by Sbragia's chapter on public housing policy, which defines public housing as a national policy concern, identifies the failures of Italian housing programs, and elaborates on the case of Milan and the reasons for the success of that city's housing initiative. The optimistic note in Sbragia's chapter is also apparent in Colcord's discussion of the decision-making process with regard to urban transportation in certain major urban areas of Europe. The major argument is that the political system at the national level and the political freedom enjoyed by local governments are largely responsible for the successful implementation of large-scale public transportation programs.

Part III is concerned with the relationship between national and international politics, the disintegration of major urban centers, and the channeling of power and political control to regional institutions, as opposed to the centralized control of past periods. O'Loughlin's chapter gives an in-depth analysis of the Belfast social conflict in the light of the general political controversy and the nationalistic differences between the two rival groups. In a particularly revealing chapter by Merritt, the internal political pressures, which have prevented Belfast from functioning as a stable central point for Ireland, are contrasted with the external pressures that have disintegrated Berlin, dispersed its activities all over the Federal Republic of Germany, and strengthened an emerging national system of major regional centers. The point is generalized and extrapolated by Merkl, who discusses reorganization of the government, emphasizing this dispersion and the rendering of decision-making power to the communities. The model of regionalization thus developed is subsequently documented by Evans, who presents the implementation of such regional institutions in Italy.

Taken together, it is hoped that these chapters help to establish the nature of the book as an interdisciplinary treatise of the social-economic, physical-environmental, and political issues with which European cities of today are confronted, the diversity of problems associated with these issues, and the range of solutions that have been used in an attempt to provide answers for the future.

A substantial number of acknowledgments are due. I am especially grateful to the University of Illinois Office of West European Studies for the grant that allowed me to complete the project during the summer of 1978, as well as the University's Department of Urban and Regional Planning for its generous financial and moral support during the entire period of the preparation of this volume. I owe thanks to my colleagues Richard Merritt and Marilyn Flynn for their strong encouragement to undertake this project, to Scott Michie who served as a research assistant in the early stages of the work and who was instrumental in streamlining it, to Nancy Munshaw for her dedicated work in organizing the typescript and editing the contributed chapters, and to Ellie Penn for her many hours of assistance with the administration of the project. A particular note of gratitude is due to Marilyn Feenberg Cohen, who, as a research assistant during the summer of 1978, masterminded the strategies that convinced the book's contributors to meet the deadlines, prepared the ground for the final organization of the work, and developed the necessary materials for publisher review.

All the chapters in this volume have been critically read by a panel of reviewers. Although they are not responsible for the data presented and the positions held by the authors, they nevertheless contributed significantly to the improvement of the papers and the final format of the collection. Their valuable assistance is gratefully acknowledged.

Part I
Urbanization and Quality of Life: The Unsettled Questions

1

Forsaken Farms: The Village-to-City Movement in Europe

Michael C. Romanos

Rural Labor Shifts and Urban Concentrations

Population growth in European countries during the first three quarters of the twentieth century has been most apparent in the cities. Despite a relative deceleration of this trend in recent years (Vining and Kontuly, 1978), major urban areas of Europe are still experiencing steady urbanization which affects entire regions and reduces the significance of political boundaries between cities (Gallion and Eisner, 1975, p. 457). Irrespective of the rate and direction of change in European urbanization trends, however, both the urban and the rural areas of the Continent have experienced enduring economic pressures and strains caused by rural-urban labor shifts. The examination of these economic forces and their repercussions for both moving and stationary populations is the objective of this study. More specifically, the chapter discusses the most prevailing patterns in European migration throughout the nineteenth and twentieth centuries and the resulting urban population concentrations. Subsequent sections deal with the land use and housing impacts of such population concentrations in urban areas and the strains imposed on rural communities because of the depopulation of their regions. Finally, it looks at some of the positive aspects of European migration and the emerging issues on migration policy.

Large increases in the size of cities are not a new phenomenon in Europe. The entire continent has been organized into a system of cities since the medieval period, and many of these centers survived the transition from an artisan to a mercantilistic economy during the fourteenth and fifteenth centuries when major cities experienced a sudden and unprecedented boom. A characteristic example of the magnitude of this change is Paris, which grew in population from sixty thousand to well over a hundred thousand people within the fourteenth century (Gutkind, 1970).[1]

With the end of the Renaissance period, however, came some painful experiences for European urban centers, as the baroque city of the eighteenth century endured social and economic revolutions and the replacement of handcraft production methods by the machine. The industrial city that emerged

---

The author is grateful to Professor T. Kontuly for making the Italian data available to him, and to Professors B. Checkoway, A. Guttenberg, and G. Hewings for helpful comments on earlier versions of this chapter.

from this radical change maintained very few of the economic and social-cultural characteristics of its preindustrial predecessor, but it had all its problems increased many times over (Higgins, 1968, pp. 150ff).

With industrialization, a wide range of employment opportunities became available, producing an enormous flow of workers from the rural hinterlands to the urban centers. This labor, largely unskilled, moved mainly to the industrial cities of Central, Northern, and Western Europe,[2] driven by these employment opportunities and the desire to taste and experience different life-styles and social opportunities unavailable in the nonurban areas. Throughout the nineteenth and twentieth centuries, this migratory movement to the cities of Europe took three forms: from rural areas to cities within a national region, from rural to urban regions within a country, and from underdeveloped to industrialized areas across national boundaries.

In the first two forms of rural-to-urban migration, farm and nonfarm workers moved initially from the rural areas of the region containing the urban center and later from the entire country to the cities and were employed in factories or in supporting urban activities. This *internal* migratory movement occurred over a period of more than a hundred years and, by the early twentieth century, had changed the map of Europe in terms of population distribution.[3] Countries that experienced this movement during the whole nineteenth century (such as the United Kingdom, France, and Germany) were able to absorb the additional population without considerable time lags. In some instances, however, due primarily to limited information and lack of transportation, countries such as Italy and those of Central Europe did not enter the period of migratory movement until the beginning of the twentieth century. In such cases, this delayed activity occurred suddenly and abruptly, and in some instances it reached critical dimensions. For example in Italy the migratory movement to the cities reached totally unexpected proportions (table 1-1), finding the country unprepared to deal with the problems involved (Baglioni, 1964, p. 35).

In Italy the migratory movement included not only farmers but also a diverse assortment of labor moving consistently from southern to northern regions. That is, this exodus expanded to regions other than those traditionally considered economically depressed and therefore took dimensions other than those of the simple worker exportation case. Apparently, the nonregional movement was not exclusively economic in nature but had a social component. A clear indication that this is true is that rural workers have been moving to the urban centers from the rural areas of the North, despite the fact that unskilled labor in industry earned (and is still earning) less than farm labor in the North of Italy.[4] It appears then that migratory movement is caused to a large extent by a preference of farm workers for employment in the secondary and tertiary sectors, as well as by their desire to live in an urban area where recreational and social opportunities are more available. Since the urban centers of the North have offered the most opportunities for employment in industry, that is also where the movement has consistently terminated.

Table 1-1
Italy: Population Changes between 1952 and 1971
(thousands of inhabitants)

	1952-1961			1962-1971		
Regions	Natural Growth	Actual[a] Growth	Emigrational (−) or Immigrational (+) Movement	Natural Growth	Actual[a] Growth	Emigrational (−) or Immigrational (+) Movement
Northwest	331.4	1,428.6	+1,097.2	563.0	1,629.5	1,066.5
Northeast	573.4	92.0	−481.4	599.0	526.8	−72.2
Center	608.6	733.2	124.6	711.6	903.1	191.5
South and Sicily	2,677.8	901.3	−1,776.5	2,487.4	306.3	−2,181.1
Total	4,191.2	3,155.1	−1,036.1	4,361.0	3,365.7	−995.3

Source: *Annuario Statistico Italiano*, 1951 to 1971. Rome: Instituto Centrale di Statistica.
[a]Includes both interregional and international migration.

In addition to internal migration, an *international* flow of workers has also developed, which has been channeling labor to the European metropolises of economic power, from the industrially dependent colonies outside Europe, as well as from underdeveloped European regions, mainly from the East and the South. These regions, however, have also been experiencing internal migratory movements for many years. Besides Italy, others belong to this group: Greece, Portugal, Spain, and Turkey. The combined effect of these two trends has been a tremendous degree of urbanization throughout Europe (table 1-2) and a deterioration of the agricultural population in its economically weaker regions. An illustration of this dual trend is shown for Greece in table 1-3, which shows a 1971 urban population of 4,666,060 out of a total of 8,768,649 for the country, making urban residents represent over 53 percent of the national population. Between 1951 and 1971 this urban population grew by 29.2 percent and, combined with outmigration ranging yearly between 40,000 and 75,000 workers, caused a real draining of manpower from the rural areas.

Population movements did not occur at the same time in all parts of Europe. The first countries to experience depopulation of their rural areas and higher urban concentrations—as well as a considerable flight to the United States—were those of Northern and Western Europe. Beginning at the end of the eighteenth century and continuing through the nineteenth century, these movements occurred in Germany, the United Kingdom, Ireland, and the Scandinavian countries. Their migratory flows were very large early in the nineteenth century but had diminished to small numbers by its end. On the other hand, the countries of Eastern and Southern Europe (Poland, Hungary, Turkey, Greece, Italy, Spain, Portugal) did not experience population and labor migratory movements until the midnineteenth century, and even then in very small numbers. Outmigration from these countries toward the more industrialized regions of Europe and the United States expanded rapidly around the end of the nineteenth century and reached phenomenal dimensions by the early twentieth century (Ward, 1971).

The considerable variations in both migratory patterns and the time periods in which they occurred make it necessary to study cross-national migratory movements in Europe not as an isolated phenomenon but in conjunction with internal migratory trends in the labor exporting countries. Only then can the repercussions of this massive movement be fully assessed. Indeed, both types of movements have had a number of direct and indirect effects, some experienced by the regions exporting labor and some by the receiving urban areas.

Population and Land Use Impacts of Rural Migration on the Receiving Urban Areas

The strains imposed on urban areas by the massive influx of rural labor had serious short- and long-range effects on urban land use and the overall structure

Table 1-2
Urban Growth in Europe, 1800-1960
(population in thousands)

	1800	1860	Percentage Change 1800-1860	1900	Percentage Change 1860-1900	1930	Percentage Change 1900-1930	1960	Percentage Change 1930-1960
England									
London[a]	1,117	3,227	188.9	6,586	104.1	8,216	24.7	8,172	−0.5
Edinburgh	83	203	144.6	394	95.6	439	11.4	468	6.6
Manchester	90	339	276.7	645	90.3	766	18.8	661	−13.7
France									
Paris	547	1,696	210.1	2,714	60.0	2,891	6.5	2,790	−3.5
Toulouse	50	113	126.0	150	32.7	195	30.0	324	66.2
Marseille	111	261	135.1	491	88.1	610	24.2	778	27.5
Bordeaux	91	163	79.1	257	57.7	263	2.3	250	−4.9
Germany									
Berlin	172[b]	548	218.6	1,889	71.0	4,243[c]	124.6	3,261[d,e]	−23.1
Cologne	50	121	142.0	373	208.2	757	102.9	809	6.9
Hamburg	130	134	3.1	706	426.9	1,129	59.9	1,832	62.3
Munich	40	148	270.0	500	237.8	735	47.0	1,085	47.6

Source: B.R. Mitchell. 1975. *European Historical Statistics, 1750-1970*. New York: Columbia University Press; and London: Macmillan, table B4, pp. 76-79. Reprinted with permission.

[a]Refers to the Greater London Area.
[b]Data for Germany are from 1816.
[c]Data for Germany are from 1933.
[d]Data for Germany are from 1964.
[e]Includes both East and West Berlin.

Table 1-3
Distribution of Urban and Nonurban Population in Greece, 1928-1971

	Total	Urban[a]	Percentage of Total	Semiurban[b]	Percentage of Total	Rural[c]	Percentage of Total
1928	6,204,684	1,931,937	31.1	899,466	14.5	3,373,281	54.4
1940	7,344,860	2,411,647	32.8	1,086,079	14.8	3,847,134	52.4
1951	7,632,801	2,879,994	37.7	1,130,188	14.8	3,622,619	47.5
1961	8,388,553	3,628,105	43.3	1,085,856	12.9	3,674,592	43.8
1971	8,768,640	4,666,060	53.2	1,019,680	11.6	3,082,900	35.2
Percentage Change							
1928-40	18.4	24.8		20.7		14.0	
1940-51	3.9	19.4		4.1		−5.8	
1951-61	9.9	26.0		−3.9		1.4	
1961-71	4.5	28.6		−6.1		−16.1	

Sources: 1928-61: National Statistical Service of Greece. 1964. *Results of the Population and Housing Census of 19 March 1961*, vol. 1: *Population*. Athens. 1971: National Statistical Service of Greece. 1972. *Population of Greece: Census of 14 March 1971*. Athens.
[a]Population residing in municipalities containing at least one town of 10,000 inhabitants or more.
[b]Population residing in municipalities containing at least one town of between 2,000 and 9,999 inhabitants.
[c]Population residing in counties or municipalities containing settlements below 2,000 inhabitants.

of cities. Predominant among these effects were the impacts on urban densities and housing and the resulting outward urban expansion, accompanied by the appearance of squatter settlements.

Urban Concentration and Population Densities

Since the beginning of the industrial revolution, European cities have had a rapid and continuous increase of their populations as seen in table 1-2. This increase reached record heights in certain periods but was not as a rule accompanied by equivalent increases in the land used by urban functions—at least not without a considerable time lag between population increase and the corresponding urban land expansion. Instead early population increases during the eighteenth century were accommodated by filling in the built-up areas and by building on available open space. When the cities of Europe finally began to extend their boundaries, congestion of movement increased because of the need to connect the distant urban fringe areas with the numerous activities concentrated in central business districts. During the entire nineteenth century, the dual effects of filling in for residential use in the inner city and of the tremendous concentration of economic activity around the central business district caused the appearance of unparalleled urban densities. Paris, to cite only one example, went from approximately 77 persons per acre in the beginning of the century to over 140 persons per acre by 1870. During the same period London had reached a density of 265 persons per acre (*American Cyclopedia*, 1882; Gutkind, 1970, p. 257; Bastié, 1975, p. 57). These densities were caused largely by and in turn resulted in booming land prices. Even when the expansion of cities to the suburbs began, land speculation largely guided the process of urban growth and controlled land prices. The circular pattern that this cause-and-effect relationship produced is illustrated in figure 1-1.

Urban Housing

Most prominent among the results of this urbanization was the European tenement. Tenements were the response of the Northern and Central European cities to the pressing demand for housing by the rural newcomers. They were residential structures of extremely high densities, plagued by unsanitary conditions and with limited space per family. To a certain extent, they resembled the housing conditions of the seventeenth century but without the picturesque appearance of the narrow winding streets and the variety of building design of that period. These structures, characteristically described and criticized by writers such as Dickens and Zola, created extensive slums, parts of which are still evident today. Little variation existed from country to country in the production of the tenements. In the nineteenth-century factory towns of England, the two-story row house predominated, built in long rows with small backyards and narrow streets. In Holland the construction layouts are similar, but the buildings often have three stories and small, crowded flats. Even the various housing policies adopted in the midnineteenth century by European governments were similar in conception and were designed to inhibit the worst type of slum housing (Fuerst, 1974).

Appearance of Illegal Settlements

Housing conditions were drastically altered during the twentieth century. Although many of these buildings still exist, most have disappeared, some owing to demolition and replacement, others to the destructive effects of the two world wars, and others to the progressive housing policies adopted by most European governments during the last half of the century. However, many housing-related problems still exist today, mainly caused by three market factors: soaring land prices within the boundaries of the cities and their suburbs, the slow pace of construction of new housing units relative to the increase in demand, and the frequent strictures of housing mortgage policies, which make the establishment of credit and the receipt of loans a cumbersome procedure. Such constraints have forced many urban newcomers to search for shelter

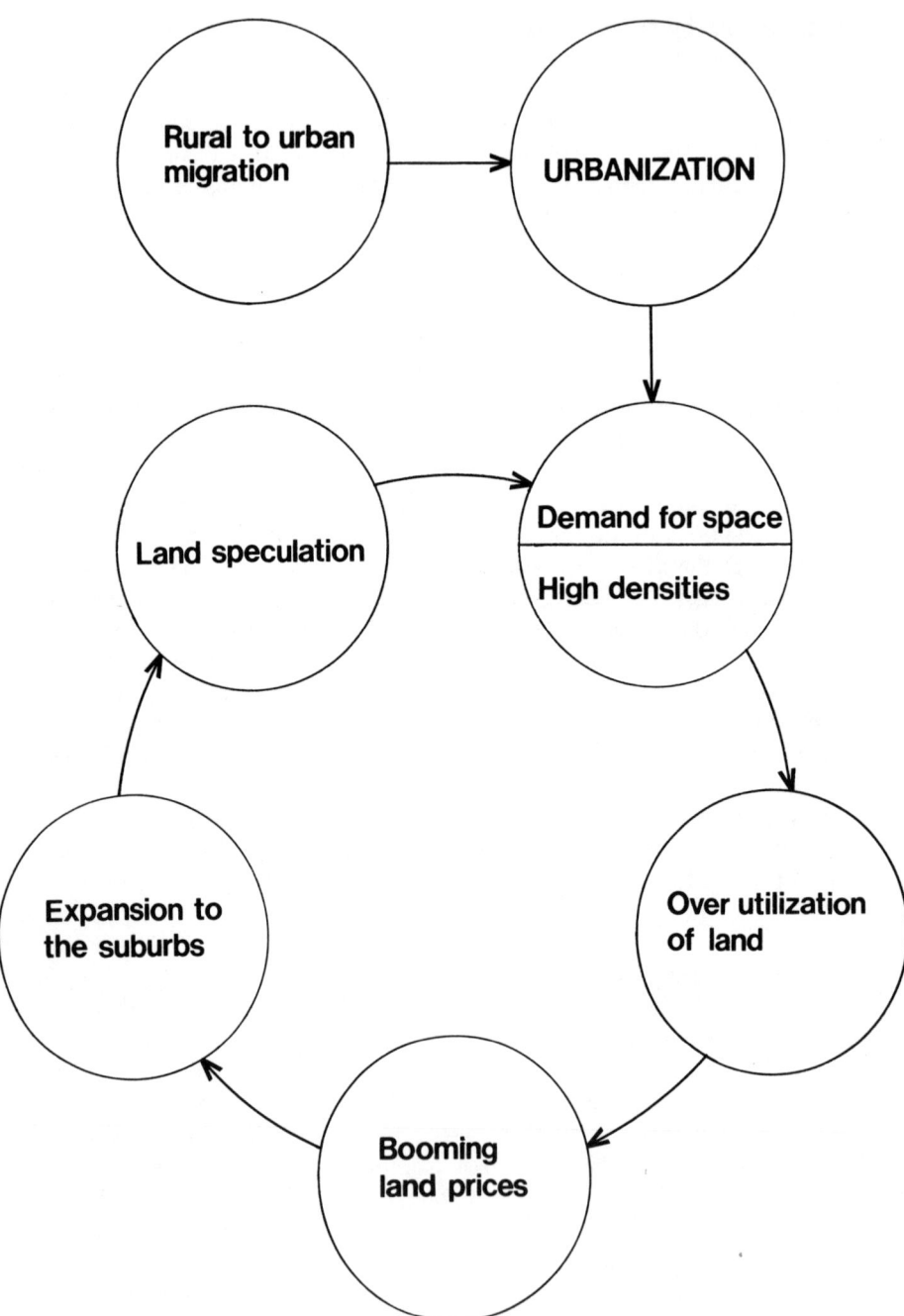

Figure 1-1. Urban Growth: Residential Densities and Land Values.

outside the legal boundaries of urban-suburban jurisdictions, a search which has often resulted in the appearance of illegal peripheral settlements.[5]

Illegal settlements is a term used to characterize housing enclaves constructed without a building permit in parts of the urban periphery where construction is either prohibited altogether—because of land banking reserves, open space preservation, or planned nonresidential development—or allowed under very low density restrictions. They are characteristically present in these European nations which have antiquated or inadequate housing policies and supporting legislation and are usually the subject of political exploitation and maneuvering.[6] New urban residents often settle there because of lack of residential alternatives, and they consider this a temporary solution to their housing problem. Over the years, however, these settlements have expanded, their inhabitants have turned into stationary populations, and their living conditions have become reminiscent of the eighteenth- and nineteenth-century tenement house neighborhoods.

The appearance of such squatters is most apparent around larger metropolitan areas. Greece can perhaps be cited as one of the most characteristic examples. It is estimated that the greater Athens area gained between 320,000 and 390,000 illegal residents outside its metropolitan boundaries in the 1945-66 period, representing about 50 percent of its total growth for that period (Romanos, 1969 and 1970). In Salonica six thousand illegal residences were constructed during the first six months of 1976 alone (Kouvelas, 1976).

Most analyses of the illegal settlement problem agree on a central set of causes for the emergence of the phenomenon. Dominant among them are the following:

1. The land in the area where these settlements are established is at a low price when compared to the soaring land values within the legal urban boundaries. This is usually underutilized farm or grazing land that has been speculatively sold after having been segmented into relatively small plots. Seldom, if ever, are any facilities, utilities, or public services provided to the residents as part of the land purchase transaction.

2. Building contractors are willing to do the construction work because of excessive profits justified by the risks they take in undertaking illegal construction.

3. There is a sizable housing shortage, especially of residential units for low-income households, within the confines of the urban or metropolitan entity.

4. The state is unable or unwilling to cope with the rural immigrant housing problem by preventing land speculation, expanding official land use plans rapidly enough to prevent unplanned sprawl, initiating extensive housing construction and housing financing programs to meet growing housing demand, and adopting regional development policies designed to reverse the rural-to-urban movement (Vlachos, 1976).

Products of an absent social and housing policy, such illegal settlements have serious repercussions for both the host cities and the resident population. Cities experiencing this population growth suffer a loss of revenues that would regularly be produced by real estate taxation of these residents and building permits for the construction of new housing. Large amounts of investment are also wasted in the effort to bring utilities, schools, and other facilities to these settlements, which are legalized by the state *after* the entire settlement has been established firmly. Land speculation is encouraged, causing increases in the value of land and impeding the application of preventive land measures, such as regional zoning, control of development rights, and land banking. Finally, the possibilities for orderly and controlled urban growth and development are diminishing, as expansion policies become virtually impossible to implement, given the levels and rates of illegal construction outside the city.

Residents of these settlements, on the other hand, are forced to live under legal and financial risks and be at the mercy of the political interests of the municipal government which can exercise police power, force residents to vacate their self-styled homes, and demolish the structures as illegal, unhealthy, and unsafe. Their living conditions are substandard, and the lack of social services helps to perpetuate these conditions for the younger generations as well.

Very little has been done to eliminate this problem, other than the exercise of police power for the demolition of some structures and the occasional passage of new laws legalizing existing conditions. Housing construction programs have existed in Europe for several decades, as several other chapters in this volume document, but often their progress has been slow, their productivity low, and their quality questionable. Measures that have been suggested to improve on these weaknesses cover a wide range of options, from the allocation of authority to local governments for study, planning, and construction of housing to more efficient, imaginative, and diversified design. But the problems still exist in all their magnitude, and they become pressing.

Need for Social and Cultural Adjustment

Whether the rural migrants to the cities settled in illegal settlements or found a residence within the existing housing stock, they were still subject to a cultural shock caused by the sharp differences between their rural origins and the urban environment where they chose to live. This shock and its elements are discussed by other authors in the volume (Triandis, 1979). It is, however, useful to mention here that the adjustments that these people have had to make generally fall into two categories: (1) psychological adjustments, in order to adapt to the urban environment and life-styles; and (2) cultural adjustments, including learning a foreign language, in order to become part of the foreign country in the case of cross-national migration. The problems associated with these adjustments have included acceptance by urbanites, an understanding of the institutional mechanisms, and the interactions with the work environment where immigrants were employed. Many foreign workers chose to adjust culturally only to the extent necessary to survive in the new environment, while others were able to adjust more fully. Yet another segment of the foreign worker population chose to keep this cultural adjustment away from their families, thus causing the appearance of national or racial enclaves in the industrialized metropolitan areas of Europe.

The mentality of the rural worker and the ways in which he reacts to changing living and working conditions have attracted the attention of many European countries with different degrees of involvement and effectiveness. Some countries, such as Austria and Germany, deal with the problem informally. Officials and members of the labor unions seem to believe that, as a whole, social and cultural distances have been bridged historically and that individuals with adjustment problems should be handled as special cases (Barkin, 1966, pp. 5-6). In the Scandinavian countries and Holland, on the contrary, many public services are available to make the transition of the rural worker and perhaps his family as smooth as possible, both psychologically and financially. Yet another group of countries, including France and England, considers the problem of their relatively small group of aliens seeking employment as one of racial tensions, since the largest percentage of their foreign labor force comes from Africa or from the countries of the Commonwealth. In these nations, the native population has shown an intolerance to foreign workers, and discrimination in both work and social opportunities reached such levels in the recent past that special legislation was necessary to guarantee certain basic rights to aliens.

Irrespective of the official government policies toward immigrant workers, however, labor unions in the industrial countries of Western Europe have favored keeping foreign workers apart and restricting their entry to jobs requiring skilled labor. Because of this attitude, foreign workers are confined mostly to unskilled labor employment, various inferior jobs not sought by the national labor force, and undesirable work locations. It was only recently, during the economic crisis of 1974-75, that foreign worker groups became actively involved in union activity in Western Europe, largely because the national unions realized for the first time that foreign workers represented a sizable population with a considerable potential for support of the union demands.

Effects of Migration on the Exporting Rural Communities

All three types of outmigration have the same impact on exporting rural areas. Whether the departing labor moves to the nearby city, one of the major cities of the country, or to one of the industrial centers of Western Europe, the effects on the rural community are the same, although the economic repercussions for the nation as a whole are quite different. Primary among these negative effects are the losses in labor force, the resulting social disintegration of the community, and the deterioration of the local economic base.

Farm Labor Losses

The migratory movement from the rural hinterlands to the urban centers of Europe was initiated as an intraregional push-pull phenomenon—an overspill of labor from agrarian areas and a pull by large cities with nonfarm employment opportunities and higher living standards (Schöller, 1975). It soon spread across regional boundaries to engulf the entire nation. Outmigration was directed primarily to the United States. After the Second World War, however, migration among European countries intensified as the major industrial centers of Central and Northern Europe began to attract largely unskilled workers from the rural areas of Eastern and Southern Europe, as well as countries beyond the Mediterranean. Under the migratory urge workers moved out of rural areas *en masse*, followed by their entire families. Over a period of years, and through correspondence, word of mouth, or visits by the immigrants to their villages, the attractiveness of the city as a locus of opportunities infiltrated the remaining rural population and helped to accelerate the outgoing migratory wave.

This phenomenon of rural depopulation reached its peak intensity in Italy from 1881 to 1931. During this fifty-year period 3.1 million people left the rural South to move to the urban areas of the Mezzogiorno (the southern part of peninsular Italy, including Sicily and Sardinia) and the industrialized North. Between 1871 and 1951 Sicily alone lost 1.2 million inhabitants. At the end of that period, however, the Mezzogiorno as a whole supported approximately 7 million more inhabitants than at its beginning, indicating that the largest percentage of the population remained within the region. This trend did not change in subsequent periods. Indeed, in the 1951-61 decade, the active labor force in agriculture in the region declined by nearly 863,000, while it increased by 694,000 in the nonagricultural sectors (Franklin, 1969, p. 129).

Such massive and unselective migration to the cities has had a number of major economic and social ramifications for the exporting rural areas. Perhaps the most critical among these effects is the draining from the less developed, peripheral regions of their main potential, the young segment of the labor force. This segment, primarily males between the ages of eighteen and forty years of age, caused dramatic distortions of the age and sex ratios in the population pyramids and undermined the hierarchical structure of rural communities.

Community Disintegration

The far-reaching repercussions of these distortions have been evident in the weakening of family ties and the extremely small number of new households established in the villages. Families that lived in temporary separation, with the head of the household abroad, have usually been reunited either in the host country or in a major urban center within the exporting region. Seldom is there a return to the village. The skills acquired abroad and the adoption of urban life-styles have made it difficult for immigrants to return to old traditions, customs, and working habits. The population of the villages has thus become dominated by women and old people. Beyond a certain threshold, depopulation has made it impossible for the villages to sustain a viable population. Public services such as schools close down, retail businesses lose their financial base, and rural life becomes increasingly unattractive.

Deterioration of Community Economic Base

The economic repercussions of the rural movement to the cities are no less important. The major results of this depopulation are the abandonment of the rural farmland and the reduction in agricultural product. In areas of rural Italy and Greece, considerable tracts of farmland suitable for cultivation remain idle today because of owner absenteeism, unavailability of local or migratory farm workers, and lack of governmental policies that would allow idle land to be used by landless rural residents. A considerable percentage of the potential agricultural product is thus lost, and its impact on the regional and national economy is often sizable. Food must be imported to make up for these losses, and valuable foreign currency that could be obtained through farm product exports is also lost.

It is often claimed that the exported labor force contributes significantly to the local economy by sending foreign currency back to the villages of origin in order to support relatives or simply as savings. While it is true that this influx of money helps to make up for foreign exchange lost through reduced exports, it is also a fact that this situation helps to prolong the status of dependence of exporting regions on the industrialized-urbanized areas from which this currency springs. Thus substituting worker remittances for local production and development perpetuates the underdevelopment of peripheral regions.

Even for the remaining farmers and their land, the potential for economic survival diminishes. The small number of available farm workers and the lack of farming support services in the rural areas hinder the appearance of positive externalities (Hall, 1977, p. 67). Mechanization, irrigation, and systematic farming become more expensive, while organized marketing of fertilizer, animal food, and farm products remains problematic. The available rural labor force cannot stay competitive with the massively producing agribusiness practiced in the fertile areas of Western Europe and is losing its positive expectations for the future. It is clear that the peripheral regions of Europe exporting labor to the industrialized areas of the Continent are losing socially and financially on all fronts and have become unable to even invest in their own future. Their economic status and condition is one of rampant deterioration, and there can be no market solution to the loss of productivity and the waste of available resources.

European Migration in Perspective

Although both internal and external migration have severely taxed the labor-exporting areas of Europe and have imposed considerable demands on the receiving nations and their urban centers, these two types of labor movement have also had several positive effects. In addition to the clear benefits that they offered to the receiving areas by increasing their labor potential, exporting areas have also benefited from outmigration. Major among these benefits is the provision of employment to people from underprivileged areas where subsistence agriculture was the principal activity and unemployment was running high. Another occasional benefit was the formation of large farms, which are amenable to mechanized cultivation and the use of advanced farming methods, in the exporting rural regions, through abandonment or sale of property by departing farmers.

Migration has often been used by exporting countries as a safety valve. Exporting workers can have three immediate results; it can reduce national unemployment, provide quick on-the-job training for industrial work, and produce an inflow of cash from workers' wages sent home. All three classes of benefits, however, can turn into major problems if national policies are not carefully drafted by the exporting country in order to minimize the negative impacts of such export. Thus to the extent that outmigration constitutes a temporary and not a permanent draining of the labor force of a nation, policies guaranteeing full employment need to be implemented early enough to make the national economy able to absorb both new and returning workers. Second, workers' training may not produce any benefits for the exporting country if workers do not return to their places of origin or if they return without any new skills acquired. The exporting nation should therefore establish its own training programs. Last but not least, the inflow of foreign currency sent home by immigrants is creating an artificial purchasing power in the rural communities, while it renders the exporting country economically dependent on the economic activity of the host countries (Paine, 1974) and is therefore seriously impeding regional development efforts. Minimization of this economic dependence should then be an urgent priority for exporting countries, to insure their independent economic development.

Another aspect to the European immigration issue requires attention because it could have serious consequences for the economy of the weaker European nations. Since 1971, Western European nations have begun a reexamination of their immigration policies. In 1971-72 France imposed the first quotas on the number of Portuguese and Algerian workers to be admitted to the country yearly. Germany tightened its quotas in 1973, while Britain and Switzerland began a stricter enforcement of laws instituted as early as 1962-63. There were three main reasons for the stricter enforcement of these policies: (1) the anticipation of the economic recession of 1973-75, (2) the expectation of a considerable increase in the rate of growth of the labor force in the European Economic Community, from 0.27 percent in 1970-75 to 0.67 percent in 1975-80 and 0.74 percent in 1980-85 (Yiannopoulos, 1978), and (3) the concern over the large numbers of foreign workers and their families who, over the years, decided to settle in the host countries, thus creating large minority populations with all the associated needs for social services and facilities. The migratory movement to the urban centers of Western Europe seems therefore to have reached a ceiling and is gradually reversing itself. Already countries such as Turkey are regaining more workers than they export yearly. In a very few years, the migratory solution to the unemployment problems of developing European countries may not be a possibility, and it may no longer be possible to postpone the long-overdue need for comprehensive national policies emphasizing the utilization of each country's labor potential.

Notes

1. Such large increases of urban populations throughout continental Europe and England caused deterioration of living conditions in cities and towns. High densities and the lack of sanitary conditions were responsible for high infant mortality, low average life expectancies, and terrible epidemics such as the plague, which represented a constant threat during the medieval period (Rörig, 1975, pp. 111-119).
2. A large percentage of the migrating population landed on American soil, mainly in the United States. Between 1800 and 1900, over 16 million Europeans entered the United States. By 1920 fully 75 percent of these were urban residents, making up slightly more than 50 percent of the entire urban population (Ward, 1971, pp. 52-57).
3. Between 1821 and 1936, the rural population of Germany dropped from 23 million to 19 million, while its urban population increased from 2 million to 48 million. Similarly, England went from 10 million to 9.5 million in its rural areas, while it gained from 4 million to 37 million people during the same period (Gallion and Eisner, 1975, p. 81).
4. In the Po Valley, for example, agricultural productivity ranks among the highest in Europe, with pay for agricultural work well above that of unskilled industrial labor.
5. The term *illegal settlement* has been adopted here, because it is considered more descriptive of these residential concentrations. Other terms with similar connotations are squatter settlement, spontaneous settlement,

shanty town, or barriadas. In Europe a term often used to describe these complexes is *gecekondu* after the Turkish for squatter (Suzuki, 1964).

6. In Greece, for example, illegal settlements have been systematically used by the governing party as a preelection device for the collection of votes, by becoming subject to presidential decrees which legalize them every three to four years (always during preelection periods) under conditions of no further expansion of their boundaries. The latest in this series of "legalization of the illegal" occurred during the spring of 1977, when the Republican party in power legalized all the settlements established before 1953. The public law passed on the issue was signed only months before the November 1977 general elections (Technical Chamber of Greece, 1977).

References

American Cyclopedia. 1882. Miscellaneous Articles. New York: D. Appleton.
Annuario Statistico Italiano. 1951 to 1971. Rome: Instituto Centrale di Statistica.
Baglioni, G. 1964. "Trade Union Assistance to Workers Migrating from the South to the North of Italy." In OECD, *International Joint Seminar on Geographical and Occupational Mobility of Manpower, Final Report,* pp. 35-40. Paris: OECD, Manpower and Social Affairs Directorate.
Barkin, S. 1966. "Trade Union Policies and Programmes for National Internal Rural Migrants and Foreign Workers." *International Migration* 4:3-20.
Bastié, J. 1975. Paris: "Baroque Elegance and Agglomeration." In *World Capitals: Toward Guided Urbanization,* ed. H.W. Eldredge. Garden City, N.Y.: Anchor Press.
Franklin, S.H. 1969. *The European Peasantry: The Final Phase.* London: Methuen.
Fuerst, J.F. 1974. *Public Housing in Europe and America.* New York: John Wiley and Sons.
Gallion, A.B., and Eisner, S. 1975. *The Urban Pattern: City Planning and Design,* 3rd ed. New York: D. Van Nostrand Co.
Gutkind, E.A. 1970. *Urban Development in Western Europe: France and Belgium.* New York: Free Press.
Hall, P., ed. 1977. *Europe 2000.* New York: Columbia University Press.
Higgins, B. 1968. *Economic Development: Problems, Principles, and Policies,* rev. ed. New York: W.W. Norton and Company.
Kouvelas, S. 1976. "Public Discussion on Salonica's Illegal Settlements." *Technica Chronica* 46:41-42.
Mitchell, B.R. 1975. *European Historical Statistics, 1950-1970.* New York: Columbia University Press.
National Statistical Service of Greece. 1964. *Results of the Population and Housing Census of 19 March 1961.* Athens: NSSG.

———. 1972. *Population of Greece: Census of 14 March 1971.* Athens: NSSG.
Paine, S. 1974. *Exporting Workers: The Turkish Case.* Cambridge: Cambridge University Press.
Romanos, A. 1969. "Illegal Settlements in Athens." In *Shelter and Society: New Studies in Vernacular Architecture,* ed. P. Oliver. London: Bassie and Jenkins, pp. 137-155.
———. 1970. "Unauthorized Settlements and the Housing Problem." *Architecture in Greece* 4:25-30.
Rörig, F. 1975. *The Medieval Town.* Berkeley and Los Angeles: University of California Press.
Schöller, P. 1975. "The Problems and Consequences of Urbanization." In *Essays on World Urbanization,* ed. R. Jones, London: G. Philip and Son, pp. 37-46.
Suzuki, P. 1974. "Encounters with Istanbul: Urban Peasants and Village Peasants." *International Journal of Comparative Sociology* 5:208-216.
Technical Chamber of Greece. 1977. "Legalization of Illegal Settlements of the Period 1955-73." *News Bulletin,* no. 954, July 16, pp. 20-22.
Triandis, H. 1979. "Social-Psychological Problems of Urban Migrants," chapter 2 of this volume.
Vining, D.R., Jr., and Kontuly, T. 1978. "Population Dispersal from Major Metropolitan Regions: An International Comparison." *International Regional Science Review* 3:49-73.
Vlachos, D. 1976. "Illegal Settlements: Technical or Socioeconomic Problem?" Newspaper *Vema,* August 22 (in Greek).
Ward, D. 1971. *Cities and Immigrants.* New York: Oxford University Press.
Yiannopoulos, G.N. 1978. "Immigrants: The Tenth *'Invisible Country-Member'* of the Common Market." British Broadcasting Corporation series of lectures, *The Crisis and Southern Europe.*

2 Social-Psychological Problems of Urban Migrants

Harry C. Triandis

In many parts of Europe there is significant migration from rural to urban environments. This can be seen particularly in the case of rural populations from the South of Europe—Spain, Italy, the Balkans—moving to the cities of Northern Europe—Belgium, Germany, Switzerland. There is also a good deal of internal rural-to-urban migration, for example in Italy from the rural South to the urban North and in Greece from rural or island environments to Athens or Salonica.

People who move from a rural to an urban environment encounter differences in the physical and social environments. To illustrate these differences it is useful to consider the extreme case of moving from an isolated village to a large city.

Changes in the Physical and Social Environment

A striking aspect of isolated villages is the lack of communication with the outside world. There are still villages without electricity, whose only connection with the outside is a road suitable for mountain goats. For example, the Greek electrification system is not yet able to cover all the country. In communities without electricity there may or may not be one telephone or one battery-operated radio as the only link with the outside, and goods are transported by animals in and out of the village.

Another striking factor is size. Typically, such villages are very small, with perhaps fifty to two hundred inhabitants. The contrast with the large city is obvious and needs no elaboration, since most readers of this paper will be familiar with such physical environments.

As a consequence of the isolation, the lack of communication, and the small size, the social environment of the village is very intimate. People know everybody; most are fully aware of the social patterns, the sexual relationships, the quarrels and alliances among the villagers. Typically people have very strong feelings about other people: they either love them or hate them.

In contrast, city residents feel quite indifferent about most other people. One may have a few friends and perhaps one or two enemies, but the typical interpersonal relationship involves anonymity. Anonymity has distinct consequences; people who feel anonymous feel less concerned with social norms. They feel free to behave as they please rather than as the social group deems correct. They also feel less responsible for what happens to others. There are specialized agencies—police, social workers, firemen—who are supposed to help those who need help, so that one feels no concern for the fate of others. The result is a great deal of behavior that can be described as anomic, having no laws.

Numerous experimental demonstrations of the effects of anonymity can be provided. These include experiments by Zimbardo (1969), Latané and Darley (1970), and Milgram (1965). Among the most important findings of these studies are the following:

1. In one experiment "teachers" who corrected "learners" who made mistakes by shocking them gave stronger electric shocks when the students were made anonymous by having hoods placed over their heads.

2. When a car was abandoned in a rural environment, it was undisturbed for weeks. A similar car abandoned in a dense urban environment, with the hood open to indicate mechanical problems, was approached by thieves within minutes. The thieves removed tires, batteries, and other useful components within minutes after it was left unattended by the owner. Zimbardo and his students photographed the thieves and timed the sequence of events in both kinds of environments.

3. People do not get involved in helping others in urban environments. There is a diffusion of responsibility, and people are unlikely to help even when a victim desperately asks for assistance. Darley and Latané carried out a series of studies inspired by the famous Kitty Genovese case, in which a girl who was attacked and shouted for help was heard by dozens of people who did nothing. They showed that the greater the number of people who are present, the *less* responsible a person feels and the less likely he or she is to help.

4. People asked to administer electric shocks to others, who were not known to them, followed the instructions of the experimenters, even when the victims (actually confederates of the experimenter) protested that they had a heart condition, pretended to be quite sick as a result of the shocks, and begged them to stop the shocks. The shocks were more intense when the subject and the victim were separated by a wall and at a considerable distance from each other than when they were close together.

In sum, people who feel anonymous, who feel that there are many people around them, and who feel a social or physical distance from others behave in more indifferent or even hostile ways toward others. Thus the city environment is conducive to indifference or even hostility. However, one should not assume that the village is not hostile. Because of the great intimacy in a village, one may often have resources to divide or strong expectations about receiving a resource from someone else that are not fulfilled. In such cases hostility is just as severe. One can simply distinguish the indifferent hostility of the city from the involved hostility of the small village.

A good analogy is the situation in extended versus nuclear families (see Whiting and Whiting, 1975). Members of extended families—particularly young married couples—receive a lot of help and support. If they are sick or unemployed, they are protected. However, they have to deal with a complex set of interpersonal relationships and often must conform to demands made by the older members of the family; as a result, intense hostilities develop. When the parents are too demanding and unyielding, young people in such situations have been known to commit suicide, as in traditional China. By contrast, in the nuclear family the individual is free and can control his or her own life and have privacy. But the individual also experiences loneliness. In extreme cases depression and other psychopathology are associated with life in the nuclear family, but such problems are not found as frequently in the traditional extended family (Tseng and Hsu, 1979).

Another possible difference between village and city is crowding. *Crowding* refers to the situation where there is more social interaction than is desired (Altman, 1975, p. 192). *Density* refers to the number of people per unit of area (for example, hectare) and is not necessarily highly correlated with crowding. Laboratory studies suggest that the effects of high density are only mild. That is, high density produces little change in interpersonal feelings, anxiety, stress, and feelings toward others (Altman, 1975, p. 193). However, most of this research used short periods of time, and it is not certain that it is applicable to long periods. Most studies of crowding have also not provided strong evidence of detrimental effects, although again the short duration of the studies makes generalization difficult. Further, it is not clear how villages and cities differ on crowding, while it is certain that large cities are more dense. In a rural environment one can avoid interaction with others by simply walking a few miles away from the village, but when one is in the village there may be more intrusions from others, and hence more crowding, than in a large, anonymous environment.

A third dimension of difference is heterogeneity. Obviously the social environment of the city is more heterogeneous than that of the village. A villager has to learn to interact with a relatively narrow range of human social types. The urban dweller, by contrast, has to learn to relate to a rather broad spectrum of social types. The more cosmopolitan the city, the broader the range. Almost the full range of human cultural variation may be found within cities such as New York and London. Furthermore, there is more heterogeneity in occupations, educational levels, and political, religious, communicative, and other structures in the city than in the village.

The greater the complexity of the social environment, the more complex and difficult the social relationships. People have to learn more and become more flexible in relating to others in the more complex social environments.

In addition, time becomes a factor of special significance in the city. Activities are usually regulated according to tight time limits. People are expected to arrive and leave at regular intervals and at predetermined times. Village life is much less regimented on the temporal dimension.

While the preceding discussion has emphasized the problems of moving from village to city, in reality a number of mechanisms develop that reduce the impact of variables such as anonymity, crowding, heterogeneity, complexity, and time pressure. In many cities neighborhoods are essentially replications of the village. Such ethnic enclaves have important functions in reducing the detrimental effects associated with anonymity and complexity. They help the migrant adjust to the new environment, provide a set of social relationships similar to those found in the village, and protect the individual from the impact of the city. They are used as social supports that help in the adjustment of the migrant to the new environment.

The extent to which this is likely to happen can be suggested by an observation that surprised the author. While interviewing factory workers in Chicago, a number of ethnic Italians in one neighborhood mentioned that they have never been to the Loop (center of Chicago). At first it was thought that there was a communication difficulty, but further investigation showed that there are indeed people in Chicago who have lived all their lives ten miles from the center of town and have never had the courage to visit the center. Their enclaves provide everything they need—jobs, housing, food, clothing, lawyers, and doctors. Most of their friends are there. The social aspects of that environment are similar to those of a village.

Attitudes Associated with Urban Life

Extensive research reported by Inkeles and Smith (1974) suggests that a set of attitudes characterizes modernity. The major antecedents of this syndrome are education, exposure to communications, and factory experience. The more educated a person, the more years spent in cities, and the more years spent in factories, the more likely this person is to have attitudes described as modern. These attitudes are characterized by openness to new experience, greater attendance at movies, greater exposure to the mass media, independence from parental authority, and involvement in civic affairs (for example, political action, revolutions, demonstrations). Finally, modern attitudes are associated with greater concern for time. Since cities offer more educational facilities, on the whole one finds more modern attitudes in the city.

Another aspect of life in the city is the presence of anomic attitudes. A major aspect of anomie is powerlessness. The person feels unable to control the environment. In a small village each inhabitant has an important voice in what goes on and has a more or less direct impact on the environment. In a vast city one feels less powerful. Most people have little influence on city hall. Seeman (1959) analyzed anomic responses along several dimensions, such as powerlessness or normlessness. In cities norms may not be imposed by anyone, or a person may feel cut off from the mainstream of society or have goals that are inconsistent with those of the society. In the city one is more likely to find people who have such experiences.

Interpersonal attitudes are also different in the city. In the village people are likely to hold traditional attitudes and to view interpersonal relationships differently, depending on whether the person is a member of the *in-group* (family and friends and other people concerned with one's welfare) or *out-group* (everyone else). Triandis and Vassiliou (1972) analyzed the interpersonal attitudes of Greeks and Americans and found that core-culture Greeks (people who migrated recently from villages) had relatively narrow in-groups. Americans tended to have broad in-groups, consisting of those whom they see as similar to themselves. Others were viewed as similar as long as they had the same beliefs. The American in-group is thus very broad, since it includes millions of persons who think alike, while the Greek in-group is limited to persons having good face-to-face relations.

Within the in-group there is much cooperation, even self-sacrifice. By contrast, when a person relates to an out-group member, competition, indifference, and unwillingness to help are appropriate.

The Greek concept of *philotimo* is a key to understanding Greek interpersonal behavior. It refers to a person behaving as the in-group expects him or her to behave. A person who is *philotimos* is a paragon of virtue—reliable, self-sacrificing, helpful, cooperative, and honest. Vassiliou and Vassiliou (1973) found that rural Greeks have a very clear concept of *philotimo,* but the urban Greeks' concept of *philotimo* becomes less clear the longer they live in large cities. In the city people relate to a greater number of others, but on a superficial level. They feel less obliged to behave as required by the *philotimo.*

It makes sense that people will have less *philotimo* in the city. In the village interpersonal relationships are stable and last long periods of time. Those who behave in a helpful and self-sacrificing way know that the other person is likely to return the favor. But in the city one relates to constantly changing constellations of people. Relationships do not last as long. It may not be as useful to behave in a self-sacrificing way, since the other person may not have a chance to return the favor.

Empirically, then, according to Vassiliou and Vassiliou, traditional Greeks hold a clear view of *philotimo,* but urban Greeks do not. People with a strong *philotimo* behave as they are expected to behave by their in-group. As the *philotimo* weakens, behavior is controlled more by private, personal factors and less by the social group to which the person belongs.

Much behavior is controlled by the self-concept. People behave in ways that validate their conceptions of themselves. (See, for review, Triandis, 1977, pp. 211-212.) People who are socialized in an extended family, or in a tightly organized society, often develop very positive self-concepts (Ziller et al., 1968). People with such self-concepts usually behave honestly and correctly in the process of validating their self-concept. By contrast, people raised in anomic social environments have less positive self-concepts; thus deviant, delinquent, or even criminal behavior may be consistent with their self-concepts. Most major cities experience crimes at higher levels of frequency and severity than rural environments in the same country, with the exception of rural environments in which deviant groups such as gypsies are present in substantial numbers. Crime in cities is related to both the anonymity and the heterogeneity of the environment. In Western European cities the influx of people from different cultural backgrounds, mostly from the South, has produced substantial increases in crime rates.

In short, the attitudes and behaviors found in cities tend to be different from the attitudes and behaviors found in rural environments of the same country, and this has numerous consequences.

Differences in the Opportunity Structure

Opportunities for careers are very different in cities than they are in the country. This may be one of the major reasons that rural dwellers migrate in large numbers to the city. In addition, the city offers a way of life, including entertainment, that is often more stimulating and agreeable than that found in villages. The gap between village and city is greater in countries of lower economic development than in the more developed ones. For example, a Swiss living in a village is likely to be only minutes away from a city that offers educational and recreational opportunities and has access to television, radio, and newspapers. He is likely to live in a house with running hot and cold water and have access to most of the luxuries found in the city. This is not always true for a Greek villager. In fact, in less developed countries the gap between city and village is very great. Even relatively large cities may offer little in the way of concerts, theaters, or educational opportunities, so that the large city is often seen as much more cultured or civilized than the small town. These gaps in development contribute to the pressures to migrate to the large city. In many less developed countries the one large city is already polluted, too dense, too expensive, and too difficult to live in; yet it continues to attract thousands of migrants each year.

The Norwegian political scientist Galtung (1974) has argued that some regions of the world are central (North and West Europe, the United States, and Japan) and other regions are peripheral (African countries). Some cities (Paris) are central and other cities (Marseilles) are peripheral. The important difference between countries, according to Galtung, is that in central countries the difference between central and peripheral cities is relatively small, while in peripheral countries the difference between central and peripheral cities is very large.

In very advanced countries, such as the United States or Sweden, one can maintain a similar life-style anywhere in the country. In peripheral countries, however, one can have such a life-style only in the central city. Thus the attraction of Cairo or Jakarta can be irresistible.

A host of attitudes is associated with living in the central city, particularly in countries that have not changed their traditional attitudes toward the central city. For example, Paris is overvalued relative to other cities in France. This is not as true in Italy, where Rome is not as much ahead of Milan, Turin, Venice, Florence, or Naples as Paris is ahead of Marseilles. The result of such differences in attitudes can sometimes be comical. For instance, a study by Crozier reported in Adams (1965), which tested the job satisfaction of employees in Paris banks, found that workers who came from Paris were less satisfied than those who came from the provinces. The explanation, according to the researcher, is that those who came from Paris had a very good opinion of themselves because they are Parisians. They expect their income to be high, since they have such splendid qualities. Those who are provincials expect less. For a particular level of job in a bank, these two groups of employees earn identical salaries, but the Parisians find their income inadequate and are dissatisfied while the provincials feel well-paid and satisfied.

Differences in the real opportunity structure correspond also to differences in access to particular goals. In the village goals are specific and accessible. Another goat or another fruit tree will improve one's life-style. This is concrete and accessible. In the city goals are often diffuse and difficult to attain. City dwellers are often exposed to movies and television shows that suggest that most people have very high standards of living. When they compare what they have with what they see in the media, they feel most frustrated. The powerlessness mentioned earlier is characteristic of the large city, particularly among those who are economically unsuccessful. Attaining the goals that are developed by viewing movies is difficult. When the goals of the opportunity structure seem impossible to attain, a person may give up—by becoming an alcoholic, a drug addict, or a dropout. The cities are competitive. Dropping out of this competition is more prevalent in cities than in villages.

Satisfaction with life is a function of how much one gets relative to how much one expects. The city provides greater opportunities for acquiring wealth and other resources. At the same time, however, it increases expectations. The result is that satisfaction may not be greater in the cities, despite higher standards of living and more glamorous life-styles.

In sum, cities offer many advantages—better health and educational facilities, more recreation and stimulation. People have a chance to earn more and to live in better environments. Life-styles can be more glamorous. On the other hand, cities also create problems. People are more likely to become frustrated, to feel powerless, and to become dissatisfied with their life. Divorce, suicide, and crime statistics suggest higher levels of social problems in many urban as compared to rural environments of the same country.

Problems of Adjustment to Change

When a person moves from the rural to the urban environment, the probability of adjustment depends on a number of factors, including differences in physical and social environments. First, the greater the difference between the two physical environments, the more difficult the adjustment. Second, the greater the difference between the two social environments, the more difficult the adjustment. Each of the differences mentioned earlier must be considered. Much depends on the attitudes and values of the migrant. If the migrant has modern attitudes, is well educated, and has highly valued skills, adjustment is likely to be easy.

Further complications arise when the skills developed in the rural environment are useful in one kind of occupation but not in another. For instance, a person who does not learn how to follow orders and adjust to tight time requirements may have great difficulties in a job that requires following orders and meeting deadlines. On the other hand, such a person may have no trouble adjusting to an academic job, where following orders is of little importance and where temporal demands are relatively minor. In different societies people raise their children so that they acquire attributes that maximize their chances of occupational success in the environments familiar to the parents. For example, lower-class Italians as well as Americans want their children to be obedient, clean, and reliable. Upper-middle-class Italians and Americans, by contrast, are less concerned about those attributes and more concerned about creativity, imagination, individuality, and ability to work independently (Kohn, 1969). This is a predictable pattern because the children of most blue-collar workers become blue-collar workers, and the children of most professionals become professionals. A blue-collar worker who is reliable and obeys the boss is likely to advance. But physicians or research scientists are less likely to be supervised and do not find obedience to be a concomitant to professional advancement. An individualistic blue-collar worker is likely to be considered a troublemaker, but a research scientist who works independently is likely to be successful. In short, there is a match between the way people raise their children and the occupational demands that these children are likely to encounter.

Similar analyses can be done in examining the way rural and urban parents raise their children and the occupational requirements that these children are likely to encounter when they become adults.

The adjustment of the migrants to their new environment is highly dependent on the match between the way they were raised in the rural environment and the occupational demands of the city environment. The controls of social behavior that develop in the rural environment may be consistent or inconsistent with the demands of the new environment. A person who learns to be controlled by following orders from only those who are much older may have trouble following orders from a young executive. In addition, adjustment depends on the attitudes and values that develop in the village and the extent to which they fit the needs of the urban environment. A person who learns to be competitive is likely to survive in the city much better than a person who is unable to compete with others. A person who values achievement is more likely to succeed in the city than a person who emphasizes affiliation.

The extent to which a person is similar to those who live in the city is also relevant to adjustment. If there is already a group that is like the newcomer in ethnicity, religion, race, and other characteristics, adjustment will be much easier.

Summary

Villages differ from cities in the degree of isolation, size, intimacy levels, and degree of anonymity. Furthermore, they are less anomic, less crowded, more homogeneous, less complex, less indifferent, less exploitative, more helpful, and less concerned with time.

An attitudinal syndrome called modernity is associated with high levels of education, access to the mass media, and factory life. One finds more modern people in cities and more traditional people in rural environments, particularly in the less economically developed parts of the world. Anomic attitudes, including powerlessness, are more likely to be found in the city. In the village people often have narrow in-groups and behave to conform with norms developed by these groups. Self-concepts tend to be more positive in rural environments, and behavior tends to be more honest and less deviant from group norms. Alcoholism, dropping out, suicide, and crime are more widespread in cities than in villages.

This chapter discussed the factors that contribute to the ease with which a person adjusts when moving from a rural to an urban environment and concludes that the match between a person's rural upbringing and the occupational demands of city life is an important factor in ease of adjustment.

References

Adams, J.S. 1965. "Études Experimentales en Matière d'Inégalités de Salaires, de Productivité, et de Qualité de Travail." *Synopsis* 7:25-34.
Altman, I. 1975. *The Environment and Social Behavior.* Monterey, Ca.: Brooks/Cole.
Galtung, I. 1974. Private communication.
Inkeles, A., and Smith, D.H. 1974. *Becoming Modern.* Cambridge, Mass.: Harvard University Press.
Kohn, M.L. 1969. *Class and Conformity: A Study in Values.* Homewood, Ill.: Dorsey.

Latané, B., and Darley, J.M. 1970. *The Unresponsive Bystander: Why Doesn't He Help?* New York: Appleton-Century-Crofts.

Milgram, S. 1965. "Some Conditions of Obedience and Disobedience to Authority." *Human Relations* 18:57-75.

Seeman, M. 1959. "On the Meaning of Alienation." *American Sociological Review* 24:783-791.

Triandis, H.C. 1977. *Interpersonal Behavior.* Monterey, Ca.: Brooks/Cole.

Triandis, H.C., and Vassiliou, V. 1972. A Comparative Analysis of Subjective Culture. In *The Analysis of Subjective Culture,* ed. H.C. Triandis. New York: Wiley.

Tseng, W., and Hsu, J. 1979. "Subclinical and Minor Psychological Disturbances." In *Handbook of Cross-Cultural Psychology,* vol. 6, ed. H.C. Triandis and J. Draguns. Boston: Allyn and Bacon.

Vassiliou, V., and Vassiliou, G. 1973. "The Implicative Meaning of the Greek Concept of Philotimo." *Journal of Cross-Cultural Psychology* 4:326-341.

Whiting, B.B., and Whiting, W.M. 1975. *Children of Six Cultures: A Psychocultural Analysis.* Cambridge, Mass.: Harvard University Press.

Ziller, R.C., Long, B.H., Ramana, K.V., and Reddy, W.E. 1968. "Self-Orientation in Indian and American Adolescents." *Journal of Personality* 36:315-330.

Zimbardo, P.G. 1969. "The Human Choice: Individuation, Reason, and Order versus Deindividuation, Impulse, and Chaos." In *Nebraska Symposium on Motivation.* Lincoln, Nebraska: University of Nebraska Press, pp. 237-307.

3 Dimensions of the Quality of Life in an Urban Area: An Analysis of Stockholm

B. Guy Peters

The concept of the quality of life is difficult to delimit theoretically, operationally, or even in practice for individuals (Peters, 1973). Rather this analysis proceeds from the basic assumption that the quality of life is essentially a multifaceted amalgam of societal conditions, governmental policies, and public responses to those conditions and policies. Further, unlike Allardt in his definition and operationalization of the concept (1975, pp. 2-3), I will focus on the objective as opposed to the subjective components of the concept, so that this might be termed a level-of-living study of an urban area. That is, I will look primarily at objective indicators of the goods, services, and opportunities available to the population, although I will also show some indicators of the reaction of the population to those objective conditions.

Issues of the quality of life have been of increasing importance in European politics in recent years. Several analysts have noted the decline in traditional economic issues as a basis of politics and the concomitant surge of post-bourgeois, or quality-of-life, issues (Inglehart, 1977). The latter issues are difficult to isolate with these types of objective indicators, but the use of health, education, equality, and participation indicators may to some degree touch on the ability of citizens to live a good life. This study, however, will also have a substantial interest in the economic dimensions of the quality of life, as these are obviously both for politicians and for citizens, and will include indicators of a number of the universal wants enumerated by Maslow (1943) and later by Peretz (1978).

This study is an attempt to further specify just what the quality of life may mean empirically rather than conceptually. It will use a variety of indicators, all of which are partial measures of one or more dimensions of the quality of life—or level of living—and will attempt to determine just what empirical dimensions exist among these indicators. Thus, this study will develop some inductive generalizations about the nature of the quality of life. These may be used to specify more thoroughly the significant sources of variation of the manner in which people live in an urban area. Further, the results of the dimensional analysis can then be employed to test hypotheses about the timing,

---

The author gratefully acknowledges research support from the Ford Foundation through a grant to Emory University, and the assistance of John C. Doughtie, Thomas A. Hoy, George Peery, and Robert Snow.

sequencing, and convertibility of factors in the quality of life, especially as they are related to the social, economic, and political environments. Cities are important as shapers and focusers of these environments. As Europe and the rest of the world become increasingly urbanized, they will be increasingly important as defining agents of the quality of life for citizens. Without this initial exploration of the data and the indicators of concepts, there is little objective means of comprehending the sources and dimensions of variation in the quality of life in European cities.

Measurement

The first step then is to apply a dimensional analysis to the set of indicators selected as measuring aspects of the quality of life. In the selection of those indicators we had some implicit hypotheses about which indicators were related to selected dimensions of the quality of life. These indicators are categorized in table 3-1 along two dimensions. The first is a dimension of proximity to the

Table 3-1
Classification of Quality-of-Life Indicators

Functions	Output	Service	Impact
Education, culture	Education expenditures Cultural expenditures	Percentage of age group in school Pupil-teacher ratio Cultural seats Cinema seats	?
Welfare	Welfare expenditures	Number receiving assistance	Divorce (−) Illegitimacy (−) Crime data (−)
Health	Health expenditures	Doctors per capita Dentists per capita Hospital beds per capita	Infant mortality (−) Life expectancy Morbidity (−) Man days lost due to illness (−)
Housing	Housing expenditures	Public housing units	Rooms per unit Multifamily dwellings Crime (−) Divorce (−)
Economic security and redistribution	Total expenditures Revenue Structures		Unemployment rate Income inequality
Urban amenities	Public works expenditures	Green space Roads Recreational facilities	Health indicators (?) Pollution index

population. There are three categories: outputs, services, and impacts.[1] Outputs are considered to be measures of the activities of the government or the private sector directed at some goal, as for example public expenditure for some purpose. Outputs are then a measure of a purposive behavior on the part of individuals or groups directed toward some goal. This goal may not be specified precisely by the actor(s) involved, but one must assume, for example, that expenditures for education are directed toward improving education.

Services, as the name implies, are measures of the quantity of service actually being rendered by public and private entities in an area. So, for example, in the policy area of health care, expenditures by the public sector for health care may be a measure of the outputs for this policy objective, while the number of hospital beds, doctors, and nurses would be measures of the services. In general, measures of outputs will be more closely related to governmental activity, while the service measures will contain both public and private service provision. Finally, the impacts are measures of the effects that those services and outputs have for the population. To return to the health care example, measures such as infant mortality, gross mortality, morbidity, and life expectancy would all be measures of impacts (Peters, 1970).

The second dimension of classification is functional areas, such as health, education, and social services. The majority of these classifications were rather obvious; the only real difficulties were in general measures of impacts such as divorce, alcoholism, suicide, and so forth, which indicate some general social reaction to life conditions. These are classified as just that—social impacts—to indicate something of their summary nature as indicators of the impact of general social conditions on individuals.

The use of dimensional analysis—in this case factor analysis—makes it possible to determine whether these implicit hypotheses about the classification of variables included in the analysis have any validity (Campbell and Fiske, 1959, pp. 81-105). If variables assumed to be similar in terms of both functional area and relationship to the population do indeed cluster together, then the measurements have been at least partly validated. This would receive even stronger confirmation if they were to behave similarly in a number of social and cultural settings. This study will work with only a single urban area, but if the results here can be replicated elsewhere, there would be some assurance that the patterns found have some theoretical usefulness and importance. This is not to say that we do not expect important differences in the quality of life across countries and cities—we certainly do—but rather that we hope there will not be significant differences in the dimensions of the concept across those units.

There is also a very strong probability that these dimensions will change over time. In particular, in relation to the Maslow hierarchy of needs, it seems likely that there will now be greater emphasis on wants such as esteem and self-actualization rather than on material needs, as found in the 1930s, 1940s, and 1950s (Maslow, 1943; Peretz, 1978; Inglehart, 1977). This might not affect the dimensionality of the concept but would affect the relative predictive powers on dimensions for an overall subjective evaluation of the quality of life. On the other hand, the dimensionality could be affected if economic conditions ceased to be related (as one would assume in a materialist culture) to indicators of social unrest and anomie.[2]

The Use of Factor Analysis

The use of dimensional analysis as an analytic device has come under attack as being at best a method of barefoot empiricism, and as being of little or no utility in theoretical inquiries (Coan, 1964). However, this method is important in this analysis for two reasons. First, if one seeks to determine as a theoretically meaningful question whether there are underlying dimensions in a set of indicators, all of which are assumed to be related to some broader concept, then factor analysis is a most appropriate method (Rummel, 1970, pp. 29-32). Second, factor analysis can also be employed as a means of data reduction and index construction (Rummel, 1970). Factor analysis can be used to create summary measures of dimensions found in the data. These summary measures can in turn be related to other factors to assess the degree to which there is spillover and convertibility—and to measures of social, political, and economic conditions to attempt to measure factors related to changes in the quality of life. Factor analysis provides an excellent means of creating such summary measures to simplify and clarify further analysis.

The factor analysis of longitudinal data does, however, present a number of problems as a result of the methodological difficulties in time series (Anderson, 1963). In the first place there is a tendency for the values of the correlation coefficients included in the initial matrix to be extremely high. This is frequently the result of general trends across time rather than *true* relationships among the variables. This autocorrelation is a difficult problem because unreliable estimates of the correlation coefficient are included in the analysis. The second difficulty is multicollinearity, the inability to differentiate between relationships because all the intercorrelations are so strong. This makes the results of the factor analysis unreliable and in some cases indeterminate.

There are unfortunately no ready-made solutions to these problems, but one can attempt to reduce them by employing change rates rather than raw data in the analysis. This greatly reduces the levels of intercorrelation and allows the reliable estimation of factors. One must be aware, however, that an analysis of rates of change must be given an interpretation slightly different from an analysis of absolute values of indicators. In addition, some methodological problems are involved (Horn and Little, 1966). An analysis using the intercorrelations of rates of change is assessing the degree to which indicators of the quality of life change at the same rate. These rates of change may be affected more by the history before the analysis than will analyses of absolute values. This is especially true when variables having some real upper or lower bounds, such as infant mortality or the proportion of the school-age population attending school, are being used. As such boundaries are approached, the rates of change will tend to decrease, with variations becoming perhaps more random than systematic (Anderson, 1963).

Furthermore, the results of a time-series analysis may be confounded by the fact that changes in indicators may not be timed coterminously (Anderson, 1963). That is, certain variables may react more quickly to changes in external events and resources than other variables even though these indicators may be the consequences of identical changes in the environment of the decision-making system. For example, given the annual budget cycles of most political systems— and even the ability to react more rapidly if the need should arise—it is possible for policy outputs to react rather rapidly to changes in environmental conditions or to changes in priorities and programs of different governments. Services, on the other hand, may be expected to respond more slowly to such changes. In addition to policy statements by government and the authorization of expenditures, there may be any number of time-consuming stages that must be gone through before services can actually be rendered; for example, in education, a pronouncement that the current pupil-teacher ratio is too high and that a program to train more teachers may take up to four years before the first new teachers are ready to take teaching positions. Therefore there may not be coterminous changes in outputs and services, although they both may be related to the same program statements.

This problem is even more complex when the impacts of these outputs and services on society are taken into account. For some programs such as education the results are far in the future and quite diffuse. Again, one may not always expect the changes in these three types of measures of the quality of life to occur at the same time with the distinct possibility that results will thereby be confounded. However, this exercise does provide one test for the hypotheses about the existence of meaningful dimensions of this concept of the quality of life.

Data and Methodology

The exploration of the dimensionality of quality of life will begin with an examination of annual data for the city of Stockholm in the time period 1938 to 1972. This is of course only a single case and therefore can only partially answer questions concerning the validity of the hypothesized dimensions. However, there are excellent data and subjective evidence of a high quality of life in this city, so it serves as a good standard of comparison (Anton, 1975; Calmfors, Rabinovitz, and Alesch, 1968). The data used here are rates of change—first differences—for the thirty-six indicators of the quality of life on which there are reasonably complete data. These indicators are listed in table 3-1 with operational definitions in table 3-2.

The rates of change of these thirty-six indicators were used in a principal-components factor analysis using a quartimax rotation. The quartimax rotation was used instead of the more common varimax because it tends to concentrate the loadings of variables on a single factor rather than having relatively high loadings on several factors (Rummel, 1970, pp. 390-392).[3] This type of solution was appropriate for these data since there tended to be considerable overlap of variables on factors, some of which persisted in the quartimax rotation.

One methodological problem was the selection of the number of factors to be considered meaningful and therefore to be rotated for the final solution. There are several criteria on which to base a decision (Rummel, 1970, pp. 349-367; Cattell, 1958). One of the most common is to choose every factor with an eigenvalue greater than 1.0 (indicating that the factor explains more variance than any single variable). A second is to determine a point at which there is a significant drop in the eigenvalues and then choose all factors above that (Rummel, 1970, p. 364). In this case the former solution to the problem of the number of factors would have resulted in the use of thirteen factors (see table 3-3), which would have been something more than a parsimonious solution. The latter solution to the problem offered natural cutting points at five and at ten factors. Both of these solutions were tried, and an examination of the results showed that the five-factor solution was by far the best choice. This is true not only because of the relative simplicity of the results but also because the results appeared to make more sense theoretically.[4] It is judged in this case that the five-factor solution—explaining 52.5 percent of the variance in the set of indicators—is the most appropriate at this stage of the investigation.

Results of the Analysis

The results of the five-factor solution are presented in table 3-4. These five factors appear to make sense theoretically and have been labeled to describe their apparent content. It is obvious that the use of the quartimax rotation was not entirely successful in eliminating the overlap of variables on several factors, but the principal loadings of each variable will be used as the primary means of locating a variable and in naming the factors.

The first factor extracted can be labeled *size of output*. The principal leaders on this factor are total expenditures and revenue, revenue from income taxation (the primary source of revenue for the city of Stockholm), the total number of housing units, and the total number of policemen. This then obviously measures the total output of the city government, as well as some of the other variables related to the general size of the city. In this way this factor is related to a common result of many factor analyses of national and subnational units of governments, namely, that the first factor found is a size factor measuring total population, size of the government budget, total GNP, and so on (Cattell, 1949; Russet, 1968; Wood, 1969, p. 233). Size may be an especially important element in Stockholm, since its population increased over 40 percent from the beginning of the time period (1938) to its largest size in the early 1960s. This influx of people, largely from the rural and traditional parts of the country, meant a significant reordering of values and life-styles for many citizens (Källberg, 1969). Likewise, this influx placed strains on the public service delivery systems, especially in housing and transportation.

The second factor extracted is *economic services and impacts.* The defining variables for this factor are the rate of unemployment and the proportion of the working-age population receiving assistance. Other high loadings (negative) are found for public expenditures for housing and for the general administration of the city government. This factor might then be considered a hard-times factor relating unemployment and reliance on public assistance to slowdowns in public spending for certain services. Also loading strongly on the second factor are the divorce rate—perhaps a general indicator of the social impacts of hard-times—and the robbery rate. It is important that robbery, a crime against property, should be related to this largely economic factor, while crimes against the person are all related to another factor. It is especially interesting that such a factor would emerge in an analysis of a Swedish city, where there is perhaps the best recent record of economic management and the reduction of the cyclical dislocations of the private market.[5] One might therefore expect this factor to emerge even more strongly in subsequent analyses of other societies that have not been so successful in managing their economies.

The third factor is clearly defined by a cluster of *housing* indicators, all designed to measure the availability and spaciousness of housing if not the actual quality of the accommodations. Also loading strongly on this factor, although not for readily explicable reasons, is the size of total local government employment. This was originally intended to be an indicator of the outputs of government, being the total number of people available for the delivery of public services, but it appears now that it is related to the delivery of a particular service—housing—which has both public and private components. Housing has been a problem of special importance in the politics of Stockholm because of the rapidly growing population and it has forced a number of creative solutions (Anton, 1975).

The fourth factor that emerged in this analysis is a composite of four seemingly unrelated sets of indicators, made up mainly of *health, education, and crime* indicators. The three variables having the highest loadings on the factor are measures of public outputs: spending for public works, education, and public welfare. Three measures of health-related services and impacts also load on factor four: the number of doctors and nurses per capita and the infant

Table 3-2
Operational Definitions of Indicators in Stockholm Analysis

Variables	Definition
Total expenditures	Per capita total operating expenditures of city government
Expenditures, government	Per capita expenditures for general governmental administration
Expenditures, public works	Per capita expenditures for roads, sanitation, public buildings, and so on
Expenditures, welfare	Per capita local expenditures for social welfare
Expenditures, education	Per capita local expenditures for educational services
Expenditures, health	Per capita local expenditures for health care and facilities
Expenditures, housing	Per capita local expenditures for housing (subsidies and facilities)
Total revenue	Total local revenue from all sources
Revenue, income tax	Revenue from local income tax
Revenue, fees	Revenue from fees for local services and licenses
Government employment	Total employment by local government
Doctors per capita	Number of physicians in city per capita
Nurses per capita	Registered nurses per capita
Hospital beds per capita	Total number of hospital beds in city per capita
Mental beds per capita	Number of beds devoted to psychiatric care per capita
Infant mortality	Deaths in the first year of life per thousand live births
Gross mortality	Total deaths per thousand population
Turnout, national	Percentage of qualified electors voting in national elections for lower house (nonelection years interpolated)
Turnout, local	Percentage of qualified electors voting in elections for city council (nonelection years interpolated)
Murder	Number of murders per capita
Assaults per capita	Number of assaults per capita
Rapes	Number of rapes per capita
Robbery per capita	Number of robberies per capita
Police per capita	Number of police officers per capita
Unemployment	Percentage of work force actively seeking employment
Public assistance	Recipients of public assistance per capita
Gini index	Gini index of income inequality based on taxable income
Divorce	Number of divorces per capita
Suicides	Number of suicides per capita
Multi-family units	Percentage of housing units occupied by more than one family

Table 3-2 continued

Variables	Definition
Rooms per unit	Mean number of rooms per housing unit
Units per building	Mean number of housing units per building
High school attendance	Secondary students as a percentage of population fourteen to seventeen years of age
Alcoholism	Alcoholism convictions per capita
Illegitimacy	Ratio of illegitimate births to total live births

mortality rate. Likewise, the proportion of the teenage population attending secondary school and all crimes except robbery load strongly on this factor. These crime indicators were intended primarily as indicators of the impacts of outputs and services on general social conditions and secondly as a measure of the safety of the population as a component of the quality of life. In this latter meaning the relationship to the health variables might be understood as a safety factor or as an indication of a general lessening of anxiety due to natural or human threats to one's safety.[6] However, despite the broad assortment of indicators included on this one factor, they all are related in predictable directions so there is apparently some coherence to the data. The output measures and the health- and education-related measures load positively, while the crime measures all load negatively. This appears to mean that the increased output of government and the increases in services may be related to the reduction of crime in the city across time.[7]

Finally, the fifth factor found in this analysis contains several measures of the *redistributional* component of the public budget, of economic inequality. It also contains several of the general measures of diffuse social impact of the quality of life and measures of participation. On the budget side are expenditures for health and education, revenue from income taxation, and (negatively) the proportion of revenues coming from fees, all related to this factor. These measures all indicate something of the extent of redistribution of income coming about through the public budget, with revenue from fees—being a regressive means of finance—being negatively related to the other variables. Also loading on this factor is the Gini index of income inequality as a measure of the existence of inequality which may need to be redressed through the public budget. As I noted with the preceding factor (and to a lesser extent with factor two, housing), these results appear to indicate that there is an intimate connection between the output of public services in a city and the general social conditions within that urban area. For the fifth factor, this relationship could be expressed in terms of economic class, so that the existence of social and economic inequality is related to a variety of social ills. Again, the direction of the causation is not clearly determinable, and any number of other variables may intervene, but there is clearly a relationship between the activities of government, the services provided through public or private means, and general

Table 3-3
Eigenvalues of Factors

Factor	Eigenvalue	Percentage of Variance
1	5.545	15.4
2	4.137	11.5
3	3.280	9.1
4	3.189	8.9
5	2.735	7.6
6	2.163	6.3
7	1.951	5.4
8	1.842	5.1
9	1.769	4.9
10	1.712	4.8
11	1.504	4.2
12	1.482	4.1
13	1.115	3.1

indicators of societal reactions. Since these latter indicators may be taken as reactions to the overall quality of life in the area, it appears that public services indeed have a large role in the quality of life, at least in Stockholm and Sweden.

The location of the participation variables on this factor is an anomaly, at least from the point of view of those who regard participation as an issue different from economic redistribution. The participation measured here, however, is different from the forms of participation envisioned by theorists of postbourgeois society (Inglehart, 1977). However, this may indicate that in Stockholm at least the more traditional forms of participation have been associated with bringing about changes in economic stratification in the city.

Our findings to this point have been that there are five significant factors in this set of indicators for Stockholm that can explain over half the variance in those indicators. These factors appear to have considerable theoretical coherence as well as statistical significance and can be used to describe the circumstances and conditions of the quality of life in that city over time.

Variations across Time

Factor scores for each of these factors were computed for each year, and these were in turn graphed by year in order to determine the temporal patterns of development for each of the dimensions (figure 3-1). For the first four factors—size, property and economy, housing, and crime and health—the pattern of development across time was clearly curvilinear. The quality of life along each of these dimensions appears to have reached a peak during the decade of the

Table 3-4
Quartimax Rotated Factor Loadings

	Factors				
	(1)	(2)	(3)	(4) Health,	(5)
Variable	Size	Economy	Housing	Crime	Redistribution
Total revenue	0.905	−0.046	−0.029	0.242	−0.072
Total expenditures	0.906	−0.044	−0.026	0.241	−0.069
Revenue income tax	0.474	0.295	−0.163	0.239	0.425
Police/capita	0.665	0.097	0.045	−0.224	0.055
Unemployment	−0.179	0.879	0.176	0.202	0.063
Public assistance	0.047	0.572	−0.029	−0.081	−0.162
Housing expenditures	0.062	−0.518	0.160	−0.327	−0.189
Govt. expenditures	0.112	−0.468	0.166	0.126	−0.139
Robbery/capita	−0.189	0.480	−0.352	−0.073	−0.083
Divorce	0.237	0.468	0.149	0.162	0.219
Hospital beds	−0.308	0.541	0.327	0.197	−0.297
Multifamily	0.329	−0.268	0.984	0.141	−0.037
Rooms/unit	0.025	0.360	0.574	0.120	−0.145
Units/bldg.	0.346	−0.153	0.484	−0.003	−0.464
Govt. employment	0.036	−0.014	0.467	−0.170	0.290
Gross mortality	−0.179	−0.066	0.427	0.255	−0.012
Exp. pub. wks.	0.196	−0.160	−0.029	0.636	0.102
Exp. welfare	0.336	−0.067	−0.249	0.726	−0.211
Exp. education	0.220	0.141	−0.182	0.552	−0.451
Nurses/capita	−0.504	−0.196	−0.391	0.612	0.139
Infant mortality	−0.248	0.113	−0.058	−0.402	−0.170
H.S. attendance	0.091	0.123	0.202	0.512	0.139
Murder	−0.180	−0.161	−0.230	−0.424	0.254
Assaults/capita	0.164	−0.173	−0.026	−0.582	0.068
Rapes	−0.001	0.206	−0.272	−0.373	−0.017
Doctors/capita	−0.359	0.210	0.381	0.488	−0.021
Gini Index	−0.055	−0.051	−0.097	0.114	−0.424
Revenue fees	0.079	0.087	0.041	−0.163	−0.378
Exp., health	−0.020	0.313	−0.052	0.132	0.580
Suicide	0.209	0.286	−0.380	0.038	0.494
Alcoholism	−0.312	0.075	−0.068	0.129	0.435
Illegitimacy	−0.220	0.131	0.037	−0.043	0.601
Mental beds	−0.336	0.033	−0.378	0.015	−0.529
Turnout, national	−0.186	0.149	0.101	−0.110	0.616
Turnout, local	−0.222	−0.049	0.275	−0.097	0.584

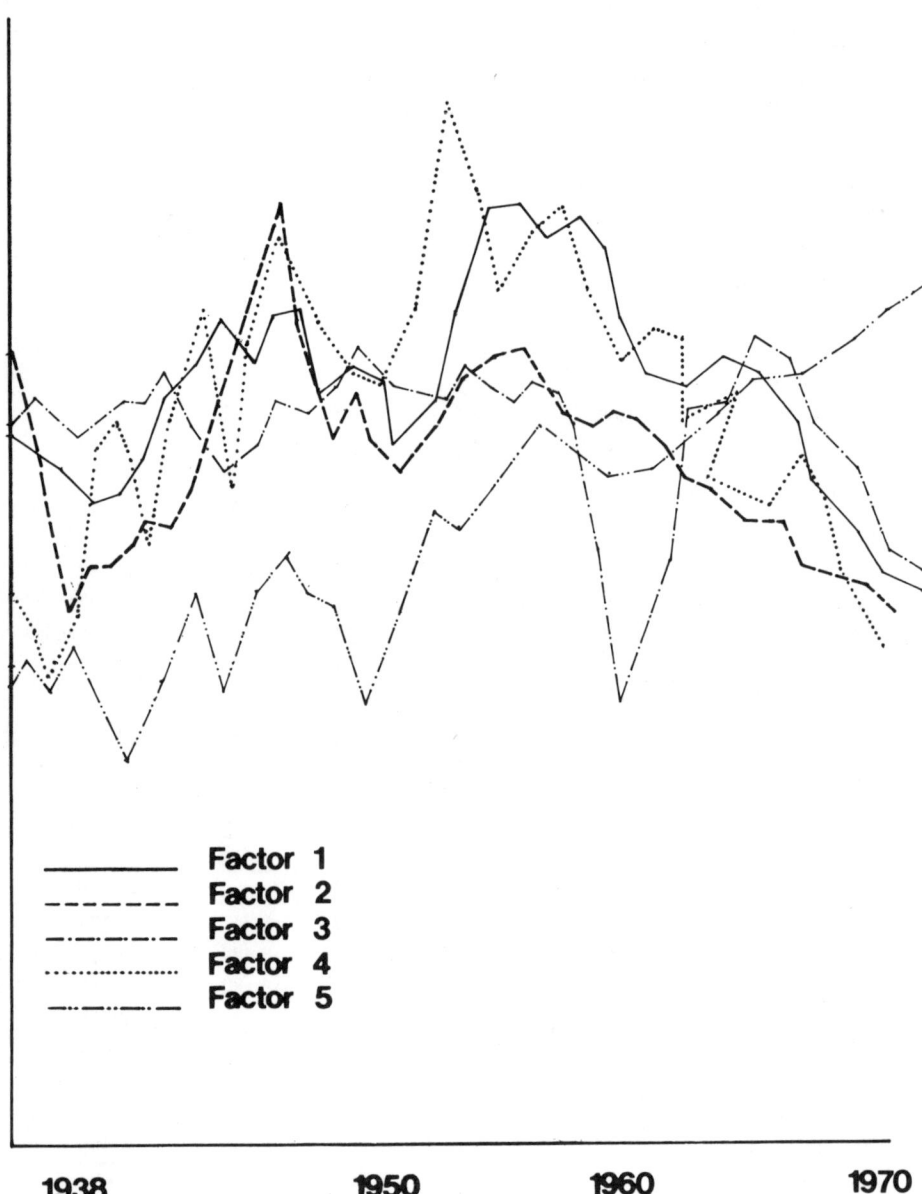

Figure 3-1. Changes in Factor Scores

sixties and then to have begun a gradual downward movement. This pattern is especially pronounced for factors two and four (property-economy and crime-health) but is also clear for size and housing. The redistributional factor, however, is generally linear, increasing across time, and it appears that the expenditure component of public activity in Stockholm is increasing rapidly, but the services and impacts are not increasing so rapidly. Further, the redistribution factor in this analysis also contains a number of measures of social impacts—alcoholism, illegitimacy, and suicide—which are also increasing in this period.

A variety of interpretations can be made of the general increases in both expenditures and measures of social impact. One ideological camp might argue that it was indeed the increase in redistributional effort of government that led to increased social unrest and would therefore argue for lower taxes and less public involvement in the lives of citizens. This viewpoint had few champions in Sweden in this time period. It was well received in nearby Denmark, and the victory of bourgeois parties in Sweden in subsequent elections indicates some greater acceptance (Borre, 1975). Others might argue exactly the opposite, that the increase in these indicators of social ills is evidence of a need for further public action and involvement. No attempt will be made to add to that long-standing ideological struggle, only a comment that there is indeed such a relationship and common pattern of change, that it is important for the future of modern societies and governments as they seek to achieve welfare-oriented goals, and that the causal mechanisms need to be explored further in these data and in other similar data sets.[8]

Summary and Conclusions

One purpose of this exercise was to determine whether there were significant dimensions in a set of quality-of-life indicators and whether such dimensions corresponded to the dimensions hypothesized to exist. While there certainly are dimensions, they do not appear to correspond exactly to the six dimensions thought to exist. Actually, there is a tendency for the hypothesized dimensions to collapse into a smaller number. For example, the fourth factor contains much of the content of the health and education function categories. On the more positive side of the results, the housing factor emerged clearly, and although the location of the variables is somewhat different from that expected, so are the economic security and the welfare factors. The first factor labeled *size* is the major unexpected finding.

Allardt's findings of factors in survey and attitudinal data in the Scandinavian countries are similar on some points to the findings of the study. One of the important factors extracted in Allardt's analysis is stratification, and both the economy-property and redistribution factors of this study appear to be related to questions of economic stratification (Allardt, 1975). However, these factors also contain some measures that Allardt located on his *being* factor, such as measures of personal alienation (suicide). Allardt (1975) also reports an employment and health factor in his data, and this factor has an obvious partial overlap with the study's health (or crime and health) factor. Finally Allardt also found a dissatisfaction factor. Although these variables do not themselves constitute an independent factor in the change data reported here, the tendency of measures of social dissatisfaction, as reflected in alcoholism, suicide, illegitimacy, and crime, to form rather tight clusters within these data indicates some support for the dimension of dissatisfaction as basic to the measurement of the quality of life. It is obviously indicative of negative reactions to conditions within the society and therefore of a low quality of life (everything else being equal). The degree of congruence between these factor analyses is far from perfect, but important similarities exist and bear further investigation both within the context of this single city and in more broadly comparative analyses.

A second purpose of the study, perhaps less adequately fulfilled, was to investigate the quality of life as something other than a slogan in European social and political life. In this case it appears that the concern for economic success and equality, redistribution, and participation may not be as mutually exclusive as they are sometimes thought to be. In fact, it appears from some results that participation may be an instrument in achieving greater economic satisfaction. There is no hard evidence of this causal statement, but the association of the two types of variables may be indicative of such a pattern. These findings may be peculiar to Sweden, and form particularly strong materialist element in the political culture, but they are findings that also bear further investigation.

Thus this article has shown that indeed significant dimensions of the quality of life exist. These are significant not only statistically but substantively. One of the most important findings in this analysis is that the outputs and services provided in a city are related to measures of popular reaction to living conditions. The dimensions that were found have varied over time, with a tendency to peak in the late 1960s. These findings indicate a need for further investigation into the generality of dimensions of the quality of life and their relationships to the social, economic, and political environments.

Notes

1. For a similar type of categorization see Sharkansky, 1970, pp. 61-79.

2. Despite the American conceptualization of Sweden as a socialist economy, a strong element of the free market remains, and economic success is highly valued.

3. In this case the tendency toward one common factor in quartimax rotation did not emerge.

4. As Rummel points out (1970, p. 367), the selection of the number of factors to be accepted remains largely a matter of judgment without any specific rules for decision.

5. For a discussion of economic management in Sweden during this period, see Samuelson, 1971.

6. This is therefore similar to Bay's concept (1958, p. 74) of objective security. It is easy to see how these might be joined psychologically, but the policy dynamics involved are somewhat more difficult to conceptualize.

7. There were significant correlations of the output and crime factors in the raw data. The loadings of these variables together on the same factor seem to substantiate this finding. No correlations of factors in orthogonal factor analysis are possible, but oblique rotations did not show a correlation between the size or distribution factors and the crime-health factor.

8. Some of the implications are discussed in Peters, 1976.

References

Allardt, E. 1975. "A Comparative Study of Need-Satisfaction, Alienation and Discontent in the Scandinavian Countries." Paper prepared for the Conference on Recent Political Trends in Scandinavia, American Enterprise Institute, in Washington, D.C.

Anderson, T.W. 1963. The Use of Factor Analysis in the Statistical Analysis of Multiple Time Series." *Psychometrika* 28:1-25.

Anton, T.J. 1975. *Governing Greater Stockholm.* Berkeley and Los Angeles: University of California Press.

Bay, C. 1958. *The Structure of Freedom.* Stanford, Cal.: Stanford University Press.

Borre, O. 1975. "Recent Trends in Danish Electoral Behavior." Paper presented to Conference on Recent Political Trends in Scandinavia, American Enterprise Institute, in Washington, D.C.

Calmfors, H., Rabinovitz, F.F., and Alesch, D.J. 1968. *Urban Government for Greater Stockholm.* New York: Praeger.

Campbell, D.T., and Fiske, D.W. 1959. "Convergent and Discriminant Validation by the Multitrait-Multimethod Matrix." *Psychological Bulletin* 56:81-105.

Cattell, R.B. 1949. "The Dimension of Culture Patterns by Factorization of National Characters." *Journal of Abnormal and Social Psychology* 14:189-214.

———. 1958. "Extracting the Correct Number of Factors in Factor Analysis." *Educational and Psychological Measurement* 18:791-837.

Coan, R. 1964. "Facts, Factors, and Artifacts: The Quest for Psychological Meaning." *Psychological Review* 71:123-140.

Horn, J.L., and Little, K.B. 1966. "Isolating Change and Invariance." *Multivariate Behavioral Research* 1:219-228.

Inglehart, R. 1977. *The Silent Revolution: Changing Values and Political Styles among Western Publics.* Princeton, N.J.: Princeton University Press.

Källberg, S. 1969. *Report from a Swedish Village.* Harmondsworth, Middlesex: Penguin.

Maslow, A.H. 1943. "Theory of Human Motivation." *Psychological Review* 50:379-396.

Peretz, P. 1978. "Universal Wants: A Deductive Framework for Comparative Policy Analysis.." In *Comparing Public Policies: New Concepts and*

Methods, ed. D.E. Ashford. Beverly Hills, Ca.: Sage Publications, pp. 113-130.

Peters, B.G. 1970. "The Development of Objective Security: A Longitudinal Analysis of Infant Mortality." Paper presented at Midwest Political Science Association Convention, in Chicago, April.

_____. 1973. *Considerations on the Quality of Life in the Urban Setting.* Working Paper No. 1, Center for International Studies, Emory University.

_____. 1976. "The Pressure of Public Expenditure." Paper presented to Conference on Crisis and Choice in the Welfare State, at Studly Priory Manor, Oxfordshire, January 12-14.

Rummel, R.J. 1970. *Applied Factor Analysis.* Evanston, Ill.: Northwestern University Press.

Russet, B.M. 1968. "Delineating International Regions." In *Quantitative International Politics,* ed. J.D. Singer. New York: Free Press.

Samuelson, K. 1971. *From Great Power to Welfare State.* London: George Allen and Unwin.

Sharkansky, I. 1970. "Environment, Policy, Output and Impact: Problems of Theory and Method in the Analysis of Public Policy." In *Policy Analysis in Political Science,* ed. I. Sharkansky. Chicago: Markham, pp. 61-79.

Wood, R.C. 1969. *1400 Governments.* Cambridge, Mass.: Harvard University Press.

4

A Policy Antimony: Public Attitudes versus Urban Conditions in Western Europe

Zelime Amen Ward

The quality of life in urban areas may be viewed from two perspectives: that of the urban resident and that of the statistician. Indeed the perceptions of urban residents may corroborate the statistical evidence. Even in cases of uniformity between the two perspectives, however, the personal assessments of city dwellers frequently include a qualitative dimension that is not perfectly mirrored by objective measures of policies in the public sector.

This study represents a preliminary exploration of the conflicts and problems inherent in the relationship between citizens' satisfaction in the Western European city on the one hand and their objective circumstances on the other. Attitudes of urban residents in the nine nations of the European Community are compared with specific examples of urban conditions, such as the benefits available to urban residents in Denmark. Although no sunny pattern of urban harmony can be sketched at this point, the analysis of public attitudes versus urban conditions may help to elucidate the policy problems as well as to provide guidelines and caveats for the future.

Attitudes toward the Quality of Life: Divergent Levels of Satisfaction-Dissatisfaction

Public satisfaction with life in general, and with economic and political conditions specifically, ranks markedly low among residents of large cities. In addition, the size of locality determines contrasts between political versus economic satisfaction, as well as between levels of satisfaction for the five small versus the four large European Community nations.

Among the nine nations of the European Community, it is in the Netherlands, Denmark, and West Germany that town size plays a dominant role in determining the degree of satisfaction with life in general. The fact of city residency in these three nations directly impinges on personal judgments about the overall quality of life, whereas in other nations factors such as the regional

---

Research for this article was funded by a grant from the Earhart Foundation and supported also by the generous assistance of Jacques-René Rabier, Special Advisor to the Commission of the European Community, and of Rudolf Wildenmann and the Lehrstuhl fuer Politische Wissenschaft at the University of Mannheim. The author is responsible for the analysis and conclusions.

culture, political preference, religion, and family income weigh more heavily as determinants of public satisfaction (Rabier, 1974, p. 19).[1]

In the Netherlands and Denmark residents of large urban centers express less satisfaction with life in general than do residents of smaller towns and rural communes. In West Germany, where satisfaction is considerably lower in all categories, the populations of rural communes as well as of large centers of over 1 million rank lowest in satisfaction. Residents of small towns of 10,000 to 20,000 rank highest in satisfaction (table 4-1).

For the European Community as a unit, differences based on town size are

Table 4-1
Index of Satisfaction with Life in General, by Size of Locality of Residence: The Netherlands, Denmark, and West Germany, September 1973

Size of Locality	N	Percentile of the Representative National Sample	Percentile of Those Who Are Satisfied
The Netherlands			
Rural villages[a]	329	23.9	95.0
10,000-20,000 inhabitants	187	13.6	93.0
20,000-100,000 inhabitants	388	28.2	97.2
100,000-500,000 inhabitants			
500,000-1 million inhabitants	474	34.4	88.2
Capital agglomeration			
Total	1378	100.0	93.0
Denmark			
Rural villages	419	35.2	97.1
10,000-20,000 inhabitants	106	8.9	93.4
20,000-100,000 inhabitants	203	17.0	93.6
100,000-500,000 inhabitants	103	8.6	95.1
Capital agglomeration	360	30.2	89.7
Total	1191	100.0	93.8
West Germany			
Rural villages	628	32.8	76.9
10,000-20,000 inhabitants	170	8.9	85.9
20,000-100,000 inhabitants	448	23.4	79.2
100,000-500,000 inhabitants	372	19.5	82.0
500,000-1 million inhabitants	133	7.0	79.7
Over 1 million inhabitants	161	8.4	77.0
Total	1912	100.0	79.4

Source: Jacques-René Rabier, *Satisfaction et Insatisfaction Quant Aux Conditions de Vie dans les Pays Membres de la Communauté Européene* (Brussels: Commission of the European Communities, June 1974), p. 29. The Rabier general-satisfaction index is derived from the summed proportions of satisfied versus dissatisfied responses to five questions, assessments of (1) the life one leads, (2) personal income, (3) the work situation, (4) the type of society, and (5) the functioning of democracy in that society.

[a]Rural villages constitute those with fewer than 10,000 inhabitants.

more muted than in the case of specific nations. In a 1975 public opinion survey, expressions of *general satisfaction* as well as of *happiness* with life were dispersed at various levels regardless of the size of locality. There were, at most, slight distinctions between the proportions of the *very satisfied* respondents in villages and small towns (20 to 21 percent) and in the large cities (17 percent) (Rabier, 1975, pp. 75, 153). In a 1976 European Community survey, however, responses pointed somewhat more definitively toward a low level of general satisfaction in the cities and a moderately high level in small and medium-size towns. With respondents ranking general satisfaction between a high of 10 points and a low of 1 point, village residents averaged 6.64, small-town residents 6.75, and large-city residents 6.43. If the average ranking for the total European Community (6.60) is equated with an index base of 100, small-town residents would score 102 on the index and large-city residents would score 97 (Rabier and Riffault, 1977, p. 46).[2]

Beyond the issue of satisfaction with life in general to issues of satisfaction with the economic level exclusively, the size of locality acts as a significant predictor. The Rabier economic-satisfaction index, (Rabier, 1974, p. 49), constructed on the basis of three questions concerning degree of satisfaction with income, with work, and with standard of living, yields interesting results for the European Community nations. With the exception of Italy and the Netherlands, the fact of residence in an urban area provides an indication of the degree of individual economic satisfaction. The relation between town size, as one of eleven predictor variables, and degree of economic satisfaction is particularly strong in Luxembourg ($\beta = 0.176$), Ireland ($\beta = 0.111$), and Denmark ($\beta = 0.161$), and moderately strong in West Germany ($\beta = 0.135$) and Great Britain ($\beta = 0.119$) (Rabier, 1974, pp. 56-57).[3]

The distribution of degree of economic satisfaction according to size of locality varies from one nation to another. However, in all nine European Community nations, satisfaction with economic conditions ranks low (although not uniformly lowest) among large-city residents (table 4-2).

The Rabier political-satisfaction index (Rabier, 1974, p. 58), based on replies to two questions concerning satisfaction with the form of society and with the functioning of democracy, also yields notable results. Popular satisfaction with political conditions is determined in part by the size of the locality in which the respondent resides, although the strength of the relationship is weaker than that for economic issues.[4] Town size, among eleven other variables, is a significant predictor of political satisfaction in Luxembourg ($\beta = 0.200$), France ($\beta = 0.107$), Italy ($\beta = 0.102$), the Netherlands ($\beta = 0.097$), and Belgium ($\beta = 0.092$) (Rabier, 1974, pp. 63-64).[5]

The relation between town size and the level of political satisfaction is striking. By contrast with the more irregular pattern for economic satisfaction, political satisfaction is uniformly the lowest within the largest urban centers of each nation, with the exception of Luxembourg (table 4-2).

Table 4-2
Index of Economic and Political Satisfaction in the EC Nations According to Size of Locality, September 1973

Size of Locality	Economic	Political	Difference[a]	Economic	Political	Difference[a]	Economic	Political	Difference[a]
	Belgium			France			West Germany		
Rural villages[b]	2.76	3.17	0.91	3.64	3.98	0.84	3.81	3.99	0.68
10,000-20,000	2.73	3.28	1.05	4.00	4.33	0.83	3.42	4.09	1.17
20,000-100,000	2.64	3.17	1.03	3.88	4.53	1.15	3.61	4.13	1.02
100,000-500,000	2.69	3.45	1.26	3.77	4.38	1.11	3.64	3.94	0.80
500,000-1 million	2.59	3.25	1.16	3.49	4.24	1.25	3.87	3.85	0.48
Over 1 million	2.93	3.65	1.22	4.01	4.71	1.10	3.63	4.23	1.10
Total	2.76	3.38	1.12	3.78	4.32	1.04	3.69	4.03	0.84
	Denmark			Great Britain			Ireland		
Rural villages[b]	2.32	3.91	2.09	3.69	4.28	1.09	3.06	3.56	1.00
10,000-20,000	2.40	4.08	2.18	3.29	4.15	1.36	3.05	3.35	0.80
20,000-100,000	2.49	3.79	1.80	3.27	4.19	1.42	3.41	3.83	0.92
100,000-500,000	2.59	4.07	1.98	3.51	4.14	1.13	2.73	3.97	1.74
500,000-1 million				3.12	4.19	1.57			
Over 1 million	2.97	4.10	1.63	3.47	4.36	1.39	2.86	4.06	1.70
Total	2.57	3.97	1.90	3.43	4.21	1.28	2.99	3.72	1.23
	Italy			Luxembourg			The Netherlands		
Rural villages[b]	4.28	4.61	0.83	2.91	3.20	0.79	2.72	3.65	1.43
10,000-20,000	4.23	4.95	1.22	3.17	3.00	0.33	2.77	3.69	1.42
20,000-100,000	4.35	4.93	1.08	2.91	4.08	0.67	2.63	3.88	1.75
100,000-500,000	4.26	5.00	1.24	2.78	3.72	1.44			
500,000-1 million	4.04	5.00	1.45	3.19[a]	3.64[a]	0.95	2.93	4.08	1.65
Over 1 million	4.42	5.24	1.32						
Total	4.29	4.87	1.08	3.02	3.45	0.93	2.78	3.87	1.59

Source: Jacques-René Rabier, *Satisfaction et Insatisfaction Quant Aux Conditions de Vie dans les Pays Membres de la Communauté Européne* (Brussels: Commission of the European Communities, June 1974), p. 87.

[a]The arithmetic difference has been measured at a base of 0.5 to account for the neutral point falling at 4.5. (In these indices, the score of maximum satisfaction is measured at the value 1 and the score of minimum satisfaction at the value 8. The neutral point falls therefore at 4.5.)
[b]Rural villages constitute those with fewer than 10,000 inhabitants.

In West Germany, France, and Britain, (three of the four large European Community nations), among inhabitants of rural communes (West Germany and Britain), and of small towns with 10,000 to 20,000 (France), economic dissatisfaction is as high or higher than in the most urban areas. West Germany and Britain, as the most densely populated large nations, also represent exceptional cases. West Germany reflects moderately high economic satisfaction for the large urban centers of over 1 million, in contrast with low economic satisfaction in urban communities of 500,000 to 1 million as well as in rural communes. Britain has low levels of economic satisfaction not only in rural communes and urban centers over 1,000,000 but also in cities of 100,000 to 500,000. Yet in the six other European Community nations except for Ireland, dissatisfaction with economic conditions is overwhelmingly strongest in the large urban centers. Whereas political satisfaction is lowest in the large urban centers of all nations, it appears that economic satisfaction is lowest in large urban centers only in the small nations.

There is a second facet to the comparison between economic and political satisfaction. For all nine nations, political satisfaction ranks consistently lower than economic satisfaction (an average of 3.98 for the former and 3.26 for the latter on a scale from 1 to 8, with the median at 4.5). The difference between levels of political and economic satisfaction is especially strong in the rural communes and small towns of Denmark, where a distinct sense of political discontent is aligned with strong economic satisfaction.

Differences between large and small nations are also evident.[6] The variance in both economic and political satisfaction is explained more completely in the small European Community nations by the size of locality than in the large nations. In a 1973 public opinion survey, the beta coefficient for town size as a *predictor* of economic satisfaction in the five small European Community nations averaged 0.140, versus 0.104 in the four large European Community nations. The corresponding beta coefficients for political satisfaction were 0.109 in the five small nations versus only 0.081 in the four large nations (Rabier, 1974, pp. 56, 64, 89).[7]

Conjointly, the *level* of satisfaction—both economic and political—is lower in the four large nations than in the five small ones. Level of political satisfaction (measured as 1 for maximum satisfaction and 8 for minimum satisfaction, with the neutral point at 4.5), averaged 4.39 among the four large nations versus 3.68 among the five small nations. Economic satisfaction averaged 3.80 versus 2.82, respectively (Rabier, 1974, p. 87).[8]

In sum, public attitudes toward the quality of life demonstrate marked consistencies:

1. The size of locality, particularly in the Netherlands, Denmark, and West Germany, affects personal judgments about satisfaction or dissatisfaction with life in general. In addition, levels of general satisfaction tend to be lowest among the residents of large cities.

2. Town size is a significant predictor of both economic and political satisfaction in a majority of the European Community nations. Moreover, in all nine nations satisfaction with economic conditions, as well as with political conditions, ranks low among residents of large cities.

3. For all nine nations, political satisfaction falls consistently lower than economic satisfaction—and the size of locality is a major predictor of these differences.

4. Public attitudes toward both the economy and the political system are more positive in the small than in the large European Community nations. Moreover, these attitudes are more completely explained in the small than in the large nations by town size.

Attitudes toward Social Change:
Poverty and Women's Rights

Beyond the question of broad public attitudes toward the quality of life lies the more volatile problem of attitudes toward social change. Town size plays a significant role in this area also. The perception or nonperception of poverty in a community, as well as personal beliefs about the causes of poverty, for example, are related to the size of locality. The perception versus nonperception of poverty is based primarily on the individual's nationality (as a measure of predictive strength, $\beta = 0.323$) and on the size of the town in which the respondent resides ($\beta = 0.153$). Beliefs about the causes of poverty also are derived from the size of locality ($\beta = 0.086$) as well as from six other background indicators (Rabier and Riffault, 1977, p. 90).[9]

Rural populations have lower average incomes than people living in cities, yet rural residents are comparatively oblivious to conditions of poverty (or less generous in their individual definitions of poverty). City dwellers, by contrast, have a heightened sense of awareness of poverty. Regardless of economic status, they more readily perceive poverty than do rural residents. The image of poverty is an urban image.

The perception of poverty as a critical social condition increases in tandem with an increase in the size of locality: 41 percent for inhabitants of rural communes, 49 percent for small-town residents, and 55 percent for residents of large urban communities. Of striking significance, however, is the higher degree to which residents of large urban communities attribute poverty to basic flaws in the social structure. Among the residents of large urban centers, 32 percent attribute poverty to social injustice, whereas only 24 percent to 25 percent of village and small-town residents hold these attitudes. Similarly, 62 percent of the residents of large urban communities, versus 51 percent to 52 percent of the inhabitants of other areas, are critical of public authorities for "doing too little" (Rabier and Riffault, 1977, p. 79).

Public attitudes toward the problem of poverty cluster at seven attitude poles: cynical egoists, noncynical egoists, the passive, the well-intentioned, the pessimists, the optimists, and the militants. Although residents of small towns constitute a stable proportion of all seven groups, residents of rural villages and of large towns reflect exceptional levels of membership in the passive, optimist, and militant categories (table 4-3).

For the question of poverty, residents of rural communes assume a more recalcitrant stance toward social change than do inhabitants of larger communities. Thirty-eight percent of the population of the European Community resides in a village, yet village inhabitants constitute 45 percent of the passive groups (that is, those who lack involvement in social change) and only 30 percent to 32 percent of the militant and optimist groups (that is, those who are actively seeking social change). Conversely, large-city residents, who comprise 25 percent of the European Community sample, constitute only 20 percent of the passive group but 31 percent to 33 percent of the optimist and militant groups.

The impact of town size on attitudes toward social change is also apparent in the area of women's rights. There is, however, a wide variance across nations in the predictive strength of town size. In West Germany, Italy, Ireland, and Belgium, positive attitudes toward change, as reflected in a supportive stance toward women's rights, are heavily reliant on the size of the community in which the respondent lives (Rabier and Riffault, 1977, p. 191).

Specific attitudes toward the issue of women's rights follow a stable and theoretically insignificant pattern for residents of small towns. For residents of rural villages and cities, however, attitudes toward change are somewhat tied to the size of locality (table 4-4).

For residents of small towns, the distribution of attitudes among change-supportive and change-adverse groups roughly parallels the distribution of the national sample, that is, the small-town residents constitute 31 percent to 34 percent of each attitude cluster. By contrast, residents of rural villages reflect a proclivity toward antichange attitudes (42 percent) and indecision (42 percent), toward satisfaction with the prospects for future solutions (41 percent) and support for moderate change (41 percent), juxtaposed with a disinclination toward critical militant change (34 percent). Inhabitants of large cities project the reverse tendencies. They disproportionately support critical militant change (31 percent) and shun, in particular, stand-pat attitudes of satisfaction with the prospects for future solutions (25 percent). It is, in fact, the category composed of supporters of critical militant change that is most clearly tied to the level of urbanization. The critical militants may be characterized exclusively as respondents who are well educated and from urban areas.[10]

In sum, for the issues of poverty as well as women's rights, large-city residents are more open to, and more solicitous of, social change than are their rural compatriots.

Table 4-3
Cluster Analysis of Attitudes toward Change: The Problem of Poverty (European Community Nations, May-June 1976)
(in percent)

	Total European Community	Village (38 Percent of European Community)	Small Town (37 Percent of European Community)	Large Town (25 Percent of European Community)	Total
Cynical Egoists[a]	14	37	39	24	100
Noncynical egoists[b]	6	35	38	27	100
Passive[c]	13	45	35	20	100
Well-intentioned[d]	39	41	35	24	100
Pessimists[e]	7	39	36	25	100
Optimists[f]	11	32	37	31	100
Militants[g]	10	30	37	33	100
	100				

Source: Jacques-René Rabier and Helène Riffault, *The Perception of Poverty in Europe* (Brussels: Commission of the European Communities, March 1977), p. 87.

[a]Cynical egoists are social reactionaries who hold attitudes such as "the poor are responsible for their situation." For them, "poverty—what's that?"
[b]Noncynical egoists do not recognize the problem and believe "it has nothing to do with me."
[c]The passive perceive poverty but remain uninvolved.
[d]The well-intentioned do not perceive poverty, yet they are not against social reform in that area.
[e]The pessimists also do not perceive poverty and are unwilling or too despairing to act.
[f]The optimists recognize the problem of poverty, yet feel the course of events, *of itself*, will provide solutions. They prefer reform to revolution.
[g]The militants recognize the severity of the problem. They are activists who contest the type of society in which poverty is allowed to exist.

Table 4-4
Cluster Analysis of Attitudes toward Change: Women's Rights (European Community Nations, December 1975)
(in percent)

Levels of Support for Change	EC Nations in toto	Locality: Village	Locality: Small Town	Locality: Large City	Totals[a]
Militant supporters of change					
Critical of inadequate opportunity structures	20.3	34	33	31	98
Perceive adequate opportunity structures	13.4	38	34	27	99
Support moderate change	18.3	41	31	27	99
Satisfied with present conditions					
View prospects for future change as adequate	10.2	41	33	25	99
View future change as unnecessary but acceptable	10.7	37	34	28	99
Anti-change	18.2	42	31	27	100
Undecided	8.5	42	31	25	98
Total	100				

Source: Jacques-René Rabier, *European Men and Women: A Comparison of their Attitudes to Some of the Problems Facing Society* (Brussels: Commission of the European Communities, December 1975), p. 182.
[a]Most totals fall under 100 percent due to the exclusion of "no response; undecided" replies.

Objective Indicators of the Quality of Life: Urban Conditions in Denmark

Personal assessments of the quality of life in urban areas, as expressed in terms of economic and political satisfaction, of satisfaction with life in general, and in attitudes toward social change, may be juxtaposed with specific indicators of urban quality of life. In this respect, Denmark, due to its representativeness both as an urbanized European Community nation and as a postindustrial model, provides a notable case study. The fact of urban versus nonurban residency plays an unusually dominant role in Denmark. It was noted at the outset of this study that town size in Denmark is a significant determinant of satisfaction with life in general. Table 4-1 detailed the effect of town size on general satisfaction, that is, that capital-area residents express less general satisfaction than do residents of other areas, with inhabitants of rural communes reflecting the highest level of general satisfaction. It is also in the rural communes and small towns of Denmark that the difference between levels of political versus economic satisfaction is greatest: strong economic satisfaction is paired with a distinct sense of political discontent.

In terms of "objective" measures of urban conditions in Denmark, there is a variance in quality according to the size of locality. It is striking that precisely in the large metropolitan areas, where discontent is usually highest, the analysis of leisure pursuits, health care, family structure, and the educational system indicates a comparatively advantageous position. In general, structural measures of the quality of life in Denmark reflect a stepwise rise of benefits in the public sector as the town size increases. An overview of the process of urbanization in Denmark will help place later structural data in perspective.

Between 1921 and 1970, the proportion of the Danish population residing in rural districts declined from 46 percent to 21 percent. Coterminous with the rural decline was the growth of the urban population—a rise from 9 percent to 18 percent for inhabitants of small towns, and from 24 percent to 33 percent for residents of provincial towns and their suburbs. For Copenhagen, there was growth in the central city until the 1950s, with a decline thereafter (from 21 percent of the national population in 1921 to 23 percent in 1950, declining to 16 percent in 1970), coupled with the ongoing growth of the inner suburbs of Copenhagen (from 0 percent in 1921 to 12 percent in 1970).

In 1970, 28 percent of the population resided in the Copenhagen metropolitan area; 30 percent in other urban areas with 10,000 inhabitants or more; 9 percent in urban areas of at least 2,000 inhabitants; 13 percent in towns of between 200 and 2,000 residents; and 20 percent in rural areas (Kjerkegaard and Munck, 1976, pp. 42-43). By 1975, the proportions of arable land continued at fairly stable levels (the proportion of arable land in a county demonstrated a relation to the degree of county urbanization only in the two largest municipal counties). Proportions of arable land ranged from 0 percent in the municipalities of Copenhagen and Frederiksberg, to 21 percent and 47 percent, respectively, in Copenhagen and Frederiksberg counties, thereafter ranging between 65 percent and 69 percent in most other Danish counties.[11] By contrast, Danish counties (excluding Copenhagen and Frederiksberg) ranged between 66 percent and 34 percent urban, on the basis of 2,000 inhabitants as the minimal indicator of urbanization, and between 58 percent and 25 percent, based on a population of 10,000 as the minimal urban indicator (*Statistiske Efterretninger*, 1972, No. 52, table 4).[12]

Leisure pursuits in Denmark are stratified according to town size. Sports as a spare-time activity is selected by 35 percent to 36 percent of the residents of minor towns and the inner suburbs of Copenhagen (due probably to more economically advantaged life-styles), by 28 percent to 30 percent of the residents of central Copenhagen, major towns and villages, and by only 23 percent of the rural population. Other leisure activities that are associated with an urban environment also follow a pattern based on the size of locality, with the usual exception that the inner suburbs of Copenhagen rank higher than the central city. Attendance at movies gradually drops from a high of 14 percent in the Copenhagen inner suburbs to a low of 6 percent in rural districts. Similarly theater attendance ranges from 29 percent to 9 percent and concert attendance from 22 percent to 3 percent. Attendance at art exhibits and individual musical activities runs the gamut from a high of 23 percent to a low of 15 percent and from a high of 34 percent to a low of 11 percent, respectively, as the size of the locality declines from central Copenhagen to rural districts. Church attendance, by contrast, demonstrates no significant relationship with the size of locality (Kjerkegaard and Munck, 1976, p. 230).

Participation in leisure activities related to reading and study is also influenced (although not so strongly as is participation in the foregoing set of leisure pursuits) by town size (table 4-5). Again, the highest proportions of involvement are usually found in the inner suburbs of Copenhagen, followed by the central city itself and thereafter declining uniformly with town size. The reading of more than one newspaper ranges from a high of 24 percent in the inner suburbs of Copenhagen to a low of 13 percent in rural districts; making use of the library from 52 percent to 21 percent; and participation in continuing-education courses from 22 percent to 11-13 percent in the two least urbanized groupings. Reading a book varies directly according to the size of the residential community, from 52 percent in central Copenhagen to 28 percent in the rural districts (Kjerkegaard and Munck, 1976, p. 233).

An overview of leisure pursuits involving information-gathering, self-improvement, or the traditional spectator activities demonstrates a direct relation to the size of locality (with the exception of church attendance and the reading of a single newspaper). These activities are pursued most heavily largely by residents of the inner suburbs of Copenhagen, followed by residents of the central city and followed finally, on a declining scale, by residents of other areas according to town size.

In both quality and duration, holiday activities follow a similar pattern. Residents of rural areas are the most disadvantaged, with a gradual increase in advantages as town size expands. Again the inner suburbs of Copenhagen, rather than the central city itself, represent the most advantaged area. Only 7 percent of the large metropolitan populations have no holiday, in contrast to 35 percent of the inhabitants of rural areas. Fifty percent to 53 percent of the residents of highly urban areas enjoy holidays of four weeks or more, whereas this is paralleled by only 27 percent of the populations of rural districts. In terms of quality, 27 percent to 30 percent of the two more rural groups spend the

Table 4-5
Quality and Duration of Holiday Activities for the Economically Active Population, by Size of Locality, Denmark, 1974
(in percent)

	Central Copenhagen	Inner Suburbs of Copenhagen	Major Towns	Minor Towns	Other Urban Settlements	Rural Districts	Denmark: Total
Duration of Holiday							
No holiday	7	7	8	13	14	35	14
Under four weeks	38	37	39	39	42	35	39
Four weeks and more	51	53	50	46	40	27	44
No response	4	3	3	2	4	3	3
Total	100	100	100	100	100	100	100
Type of Holiday							
At home	12	20	24	26	30	27	23
Summer cottage in Denmark	17	11	9	5	4	1	8
Other vacation in Denmark	28	25	33	27	26	19	27
Foreign country	28	34	21	22	13	11	21
No holiday	15	9	12	19	26	41	20
No response	—	1	1	1	1	1	1
Total	100	100	100	100	100	100	100

Source: Else Marie Kjerkegaard, and Henrik Munck, eds., *Levevilkar i Danmark: Statistisk Oversigt 1976* (Copenhagen: Danmarks Statistik and Socialforskningsinstituttet, 1976), pp. 237 and 240.

holidays at home, in contrast to 12 percent among residents of central Copenhagen, and 20 percent to 26 percent among other city dwellers. Passing the holidays beyond the boundaries of Denmark is heavily weighted toward those in the inner suburbs of Copenhagen (34 percent) as well as toward other urban areas (21 percent to 28 percent) and against inhabitants of rural districts and villages (11 percent to 13 percent).

Among the fourteen Danish counties, residents of the less urbanized counties tend to have a more abbreviated period of schooling than do residents of the more urbanized counties.[13] Of counties that are 44 percent or more urban, 21 percent to 28 percent of the population has received a maximum of ten years of schooling, as opposed to a range of between 15 percent and 19 percent for counties that are less than 44 percent urban. Concomitantly, 55 percent to 65 percent of the inhabitants of the less urban counties have received a maximum of seven years of schooling, by contrast with 31 percent to 54 percent for the more urban counties. Four of the five counties that are at least 49 percent urban demonstrate comparatively high population proportions for those who have completed eleven years or more of schooling, that is, 6 percent to 14 percent. The same level of schooling was attained by only 3 percent to 4 percent of the other ten less urbanized Danish counties (Kjerkegaard and Munck, 1976, p. 108).

The dominance of the Copenhagen region (the municipalities of Copenhagen and Frederiksberg and the counties of Copenhagen, Frederiksberg, and Roskilde) is particularly strong in the upper secondary schools, where 25 percent of the sixteen-year-old population of the Copenhagen region is in attendance. This compares with 21 percent for the two next most urbanized counties (Arhus, which is 58 percent urban, and Vejle, which is 54 percent urban); with 16 percent to 19 percent in the next eight counties (which range from 44 percent to 25 percent urban) and with 14 percent in the least urbanized county, Southern Jutland.

The distribution of age cohorts in the Danish population has two notable characteristics: a lower proportion of the under-fourteen group in the Copenhagen metropolis and in urban areas with populations of over 10,000 (20 percent to 22 percent of these urban residents fall in this youngest grouping) and a higher proportion in the rural villages, small towns, and urban communities under 10,000 (with 25 percent to 26 percent of the under-fourteen-year-olds). For the age cohorts between twenty and twenty-nine, the reverse is true, that is, a higher proportion (18 percent) in the urban areas over 10,000 and a very low proportion in rural villages (12 percent). The breadth of employment opportunities is probably the primary factor contributing to this rural versus urban alignment among young adults.

In terms of nuclear family structure, the only notable urban-rural differences fall in the categories of households with (1) single persons without children living with them, and (2) married couples with one or more children under eighteen living with them. Proportions for the former category decline with a decline in town size. Forty-one percent of households in the Copenhagen metropolitan area are constituted of single persons without children, in contrast with 38 percent of households in other urban areas with 10,000 inhabitants or more; 31 percent of households in urban areas with populations between 2,000 and 10,000; 28 percent in areas of between 200 and 2,000 inhabitants; and 27 percent in rural districts. For the latter category (married couples with one or more children under eighteen, there is the reciprocal upward trend as the size of locality declines. This category constitutes 25 percent of households in the Copenhagen metropolitan area; 30 percent of households in other urban areas with populations of at least 10,000; and 37 to 38 percent of households in all other areas.

Specifically for families with children, the trend is similar: as town size increases, there is a rise in the proportion of families with only one or two children coupled with a decline in the proportion of families with three or more children (Kjerkegaard and Munck, 1976, p. 56). Families in urban areas tend to have not only fewer children but also the advantage of a greater availability of day-care facilities. Although day-care indicators, as measured strictly against town size, are not available, inferences may be drawn on the basis of day care by county, when ranked according to the level of county urbanization. There appear to be three gross levels of stratification: Copenhagen county, the five next most urbanized counties, and the eight least urbanized counties (table 4-6).

Although most of the age-by-urbanization day-care groupings contain an exceptional case (and, in several instances, two exceptional cases), the broad perspectives are of expanded day-care opportunities in urban areas, with Copenhagen county ranking exceptionally high in its proportion of day-care registrations. It is also notable that, regardless of the level of urbanization, day-care registrations show a continual rise through the four-year-old group and begin a gradual decline thereafter. It appears therefore that the differing rhythms of rural versus urban life-styles (such as public schooling, work, recreational activities) have no effect on changes in the family structure *over time* in terms of day care.

At the other pole of the age spectrum, care for the aged follows a similar pattern. In the six most urbanized counties (including Copenhagen), the proportion of full-time staff engaged in care for the aged in 1975 ranged, with one exceptional county, between 19 percent and 24 percent per county population aged seventy-five or more. The range of proportions (again, with one exceptional county) for the eight least urbanized counties was 15 percent to 18 percent (Kjerkegaard and Munck, 1976, p. 282).

However, the availability of physical facilities for the aged only partially mirrors that trend. Measures of the capacities of homes for the aged and nursing homes during 1975 rank the least urbanized county (Southern Jutland) at a total capacity of 16 percent of the county population aged over seventy-four. The

Table 4-6
Children Registered for Day Care, by Age and by Degree of County Urbanization, Denmark, 1975

Age	Copenhagen County[a]	Range among the Five Next-Most-Urbanized Counties[a]	Range among the Eight Least-Urbanized Counties[a]
Under 1 year	198	117-167 (one exception)	63-102 (one exception)
1 year old	297	158-221 (one exception)	83-150 (one exception)
2 years old	373	206-264 (one exception)	104-179 (one exception)
3 years old	519	298-406 (one exception)	183-285 (one exception)
4 years old	601	359-488 (one exception)	215-347 (one exception)
5 years old	561	330-453 (one exception)	208-331 (one exception)
6 years old	369	245-302 (two exceptions)	147-223 (one exception)
7 years old	244	101-154 (two exceptions)	52-101 (no exceptions)
8 years old	207	67-112 (two exceptions)	25-55 (no exceptions)
9 years old	154	54-81 (two exceptions)	16-40 (no exceptions)
10-13 years old	53	9-28 (no exceptions)	7-15 (no exceptions)

Source: Else Marie Kjerkegaard, and Henrik Munck, eds., *Levevilkar i Danmark: Statistisk Oversigt 1976* (Copenhagen: Danmarks Statistik and Social forskningsinstituttet, 1976), p. 261; data on county urbanization are drawn from *Statistiske Efterretninger 1972*, no. 52 (Copenhagen: Danmarks Statistik).

Note: "Registered for day Care" consists of children registered in day institutions and for approved day nursing in private households.

My criterion for the ranking of counties by level of urbanization is based on the proportion of the county population that resides in communities of at least 10,000 inhabitants (1970).

[a]These comprise the proportion registered per 1,000 county population in the age group.

seven least urbanized counties after Southern Jutland range between 18 percent and 22 percent per county population aged over seventy-four. Yet the remaining six counties, which are more urban, do not present a unified image but fall rather into groupings above and below the range for the less urbanized counties. Three of the six more urban counties rank between 20 percent and 24 percent, and three rank between 15 percent and 17 percent, with Copenhagen placing lowest among all counties in capacity for homes for the aged.

Prospects for the Future

The problems of the Western European city, in particular those of the large urban metropolis, abound. Residents of large urban centers view their quality of life from a more discontented perspective than do residents of smaller communities. The metropolitan residents, by comparison with other groups, are less satisfied with the quality of life and more solicitous of social change. As the case of Denmark exemplifies, these attitudes present a striking contrast to the comparatively advantaged position of the metropolitan residents: higher incomes, longer and more variegated holidays, as well as more diversified and personally fulfilling leisure activities, unequaled educational opportunities, smaller families, and more extensive child-care facilities.

Are urban problems, consequently, only problems of perception? Many would agree with this conclusion and thereby perhaps wish the problem out of sight. Cities such as Bremen commission reports, such as *Leisure Time in Bremen* (Institut fuer Angewandte Sozialwissenschaft, 1974), to improve their images, not only in order to encourage possible immigrants but also to heighten allegiance to the city among its present occupants. Within the past three years, Mannheim and Stuttgart have transformed small sections of the inner city into pleasant park areas in order to participate in the *Bundesgartenschau*—again evoking the question whether the parks represented the beginnings of inner-city reforms or were merely a one-time token change for purposes of image-building through the manipulation of public perceptions.[14]

A corollary to these considerations is the question *who* constitutes a dissatisfied or change-directed metropolitan resident. Due to the aggregate nature of the data presented in this study, it is not possible to determine whether those large-city residents who are discontented constitute wholly, in part, or not at all, the same group of metropolitan respondents who are highly advantaged in objective measures of living conditions.

If indeed it is, at least in part, the more advantaged urban residents who also are the most discontented, changes must be made in the current measures of urban quality of life to account for the disjuncture between conditions and attitudes.[15] This is a dichotomous issue.

1. Are present measures of citizen satisfaction adequate? A survey question regarding satisfaction (either in general or in a specific area of concern) may be interpreted differently by respondents of divergent economic and cultural backgrounds. In addition, there remains the enigma of respondents "objectively" assessing their own living conditions, including the evaluation of trade-offs of possible advances in one area of the public sector made in exchange for improvements in another area.

2. Are present structural measures of the quality of life actually "objective"? The choice of criteria for assessing the quality of life reflects an inherent value bias. The issue whether numerous structural criteria (for example, leisure pursuits, educational opportunities, and patterns of distribution for housing and health care) can be comparatively weighed and result in some ultimate objectivity is problematic.[16]

The heightened levels of satisfaction in the less agglomerated areas may point to the fact that "small is beautiful." How then is the large urban metropolis to be made "small"? The solution certainly cannot rely on utopian and unrealistic visions of vast population shifts that will institute greater parity among sizes of communities. Yet small need not be a measure of quantity but may refer instead to quality; the positive qualities of the less populated communities must be transferred to the large urban complexes. Perhaps the key to the future lies in the establishment within the large urban centers of a sense of public allegiance to a community within a community.[17] This consideration evokes, in turn, a pivotal issue: will image-building provide adequate support for the development of a new sense of community allegiance—or is a radically different policy orientation necessary?

Notes

1. The coefficient beta, as a measure of the impact of each predictor variable in relation to the other eleven variables, has varying distributions among the nine nations. The principal (strongest) predictor of general satisfaction within each nation ranges from a high of 0.212 and 0.185 for the impact of profession as a predictor in Ireland and Belgium, respectively, to a low of 0.119 for party identification as the strongest predictor in Denmark. Total explained variance, on the basis of the twelve variables, ranges from 8.7 percent in France and 7.3 percent in Italy to 3.7 percent in Denmark and 4.0 percent in Ireland. Town size, as a predictor of general satisfaction, has somewhat more weight in the small European Community nations (average $\beta = 0.100$). For the three nations in which town size has a strong influence on attitudes of general satisfaction, the beta coefficient for town size ranges from 0.122 in the Netherlands to 0.107 in Denmark and 0.105 in West Germany. (Beta coefficients below 0.075 are of little or no significance.)

2. The specific question was worded as follows: "We have talked about the various parts of your life. *All things considered,* how satisfied or dissatisfied are you with your life as a whole these days?"

3. Beta coefficients below 0.075 are of little or no significance.

4. The average beta is 0.096 for town size as a determinant of political satisfaction and 0.124 as a determinant of economic satisfaction (compare 0.095 as a determinant of satisfaction toward life in general).

5. Beta coefficients below 0.075 are of little or no significance.

6. The four large European Community nations are Britain, France, Italy, and West Germany; the five small European Community nations are Belgium, Denmark, Ireland, Luxemburg, and the Netherlands.

7. Of eleven predictor variables that were investigated and measured comparatively as beta coefficients, town size emerged as one of the stronger predictors. (Beta coefficients below 0.075 are of little or no significance.) Total explained variance, based on the eleven-variable model, ranged between 7.9 percent and 15.4 percent for economic satisfaction and between 2.9 percent and 30.5 percent for political satisfaction.

8. Differences between large and small nations toward satisfaction with life in general (e.g., 92 percent for small nations, 73 percent for large nations on the 1973 poll) also appear to remain stable over time. Note Rabier's comments (1975, p. 138) on the almost perfect stability between the polls of September 1973 and May 1975. On the latter poll, the level of general satisfaction dropped

most heavily in the Netherlands (93 percent in 1973 to 85 percent in 1975) and Italy (65 percent in 1973 to 59 percent in 1975) as well as slightly in Ireland (92 percent in 1973 to 88 percent in 1975) and West Germany (82 percent in 1973 to 79 percent in 1975). Denmark continued to reflect the highest level of general satisfaction (95 percent in 1973 and 92 percent in 1975) and Italy the lowest level.

9. Twelve predictor variables are measured. Total explained variance for the perception versus nonperception of poverty is 17.6 percent, and for the respondent's choice between social injustice or laziness as the cause of poverty, 18.7 percent.

10. On specific women's rights issues, however, town size has little impact on the European Community as a unit. Note, for example, in Rabier (1975, p. 75), the lack of urban-rural stratification among public attitudes toward the employment of women.

11. The exceptions also place near these proportions, that is, Bornholm (63 percent), Funen (71 percent), Storstrom-Zealand portion (73 percent), and Southern Jutland (75 percent). These data were supplied with the generous assistance of Henrik Munck, Chair, Editorial Board, *Levevilkar i Danmark*.

12. These data were also provided through the assistance of Henrik Munck.

13. My criterion for the level of county urbanization is the proportion of the county population that resides in communities of at least ten thousand inhabitants (1970). Data on county urbanization are found in *Statistiske Efterretninger*, no. 52, table 4.

14. The difficulty—if not impossibility—of radically transforming the core of the city also must be recognized. By contrast with Canadian and American cities, the structural environment of European cities is based on narrow spatial limits. Street patterns and lot outlines are fixed and inhibit the freedom for major development. See, for example, Vance (1977, pp. 377-382) and Elkins (1973, pp. 43-48). Yet these restrictions are muted by the fact that inner-city reform constitutes a problem not only of physical development but also, and perhaps more importantly, of social change. Structural development alone will not assuage metropolitan tensions.

15. For a further theoretical exploration of the divergence of urban conditions from public attitudes toward quality of life, see Ward (1979).

16. An incisive analysis of the sometimes conflicting facets of the problem of expanded leisure needs in the city is presented by the West German Bundesforschungsanstalt fuer Landeskunde und Raumordnung (1974).

17. The problem of community allegiance has become particularly visible in France in the wake of the "personality" failure of the new towns. French planners today, decrying their own sterile architecture of the past decade, are placing new emphasis on ways to *retrouver la ville*; see Huxtable (1978). At the other end of the spectrum lies the issue of forcible resettlement, exemplified perhaps most dramatically by the contract between the state government of

North Rhine-Westphalia in West Germany and a mining cartel to resettle the total populations of approximately fifty communities that presently are located on what is to be "the largest hole in the world," (Ulrich, 1977). Whether viewed from the perspective of major population shifts *to* "new towns" or *away from* traditional communities, the problem of community allegiance is becoming more expansive as well as more acute.

References

Bundesforschungsanstalt fuer Landeskunde und Raumordnung. 1974. "Freizeit zurueck in die Staedte?" No. 9, 1974, of *Informationen zur Raumentwicklung*. Bonn.
Elkins, T.H. 1973. *The Urban Explosion*. New York: Macmillan.
Huxtable, A.L. 1978. "Cold Comfort: The New French Towns." *The New York Times Magazine*. November 19, pp. 164-169.
Institut fuer Angewandte Sozialwissenschaft (INFAS). 1974. *Freizeit in Bremen*. Frankfurt.
Kjerkegaard, E.M., and Munck, H., eds. 1976. *Levevilkar i Danmark: Statistisk Oversigt 1976*. Copenhagen: Danmarks Statistik and Socialforskningsnstituttet.
Rabier, J.-R. 1974. *Satisfaction et Insatisfaction quant aux Conditions de Vie dans la Communauté Européene*. Brussels: Commission of the European Communities.
_____. 1975. *European Men and Women: A Comparison of their Attitudes to Some of the Problems Facing Society*. Brussels: Commission of the European Communities.
Rabier, J.-R., and Riffault, H. 1977. *The Perception of Poverty in Europe*. Brussels: Commission of the European Communities.
Statistiske Efterretninger. 1972. No. 52. Copenhagen: Danmarks Statistik.
Ulrich, K.L. 1977. "Doerfer auf dem Rueckzug." *Frankfurter Allgemeine Zeitung*. June 25, p. 7.
Vance, J.E. 1977. *This Scene of Man: The Role and Structure of the City in the Geography of Western Civilization*. New York: Harper & Row.
Ward, Z.A. 1979. *The Urban Question in Western Europe: An Elusive Quarry*. Studies in Politics, series 2. Austin: University of Texas.

5

Social Networks in an Urban Context: Network Comparisons among Urbanites, Townspeople, and Villagers in Tirol

Patricia Ward Crowe

Traditional studies of urbanization and urbanism took essentially two forms: the first developed abstract typologies of urban and nonurban qualities (Redfield, 1947; Childe, 1969; Wirth, 1938), while the second explored social problems in urban settings. The various typologies, though differing somewhat in their specifics, presented a fairly uniform picture of cities as being large, densely settled, heterogeneous, literate, organic,[1] impersonal, achievement- or success-oriented, and progressive or nontraditional. Urbanites were more dependent on others because of higher division of labor, but at the same time they were more isolated socially, had weaker kinship ties, were more self-seeking, and generally less securely anchored to society (here Gesellschaft) than rural persons, who were in general more securely embedded in the Gemeinschaft of a small local community, where kin and other personal ties dominated interactions, and where the moral community was relatively homogeneous and close knit. As a result of the relative flux, impersonality, heterogeneity, and isolation of the city, urbanites became alienated: norms weakened, social deviance flourished, and the individual grew apathetic or hostile, miserable and perhaps depraved as well. Both the historic interests of many of the typologies (which led to much abstract speculation) and the polar quality of ideal typologies in general (which exaggerate in order to intensify contrast) contributed to this very negative portrayal of urban life. Such studies acknowledged the progressive and creative deviance of cities among a small elite (such as artists, governors, the highly educated), but they assumed that the negative deviance of cities (such as higher crime rates, more immoral behavior, anomie) had more effect on the ordinary citizen than did its culturally valued qualities, and this assumption was extended to contemporary cities as well as to remotely historical ones.

The research reported here began as dissertation fieldwork in anthropology for Stanford University. It was supported in part by the Social Science Research Council, the American Council of Learned Societies, and the National Science Foundation. I am also particularly indebted to Bernard J. Siegel and George D. Spindler for their encouragement and advice. The conclusions, opinions, and other statements presented in this chapter are those of the author, however, and not necessarily those of either my advisors or the supporting institutions.

Such a view was supported by most urban research, which was not comparative and focused on social problems in urban settings. To the degree that comparisons were made, they were usually from the assumed qualities of an idealized rural life (both Americans and Western, non-Mediterranean Europeans tend to idealize rural life) (Fischer, 1973; Spindler, 1973; Pfeil, 1972) or from the comparison of rural and urban studies performed by different researchers for somewhat different purposes in different places and among different socioeconomic groups. In addition, the typologies persisted to some degree because researchers refused to define as cities any that failed to meet the criteria set out by them; thus, for example, Lloyd was able to argue in 1959 that Yoruba cities (traditional central places[2] in Nigeria with populations up to 150,000 and with population densities at times in excess of that of New York City even at the time of first European contact) were not in fact cities because kinship was too important to the organization of social life. Generally, the negative stereotypes (Wirth, 1938; Simmel, 1970) have remained more or less untested, impressionistically supported by the focus of much of social science research on problems, by new media reports of urban troubles, and by popular idealizations of rural life.

The research reported in this paper set out to test some of the negative stereotypes of urban life. Indeed, there is some reason to suppose that urban life, defined egocentrically (that is from the point of view of the individual), is actually more socially creative on the average than town or village life and not isolated, apathetic, alienated, or disorganized. First, cities are central places serving as nexuses in the social and economic system, and it is individuals who are the contacts between sectors. These contacts can be viewed as social resources, which the individual can manipulate within certain limits to his own advantage. The multiplicity of contacts of any given type and the variety of types of contacts can therefore be interpreted as socially advantageous. In addition, they create broadened knowledge of the social system, and this knowledge presumably increases individual ability to negotiate social interactions successfully. Second, not only will the urbanite have certain instrumental advantages over the nonurbanite, but he may well have personal ones as well, as a result of his more numerous and diverse contacts. The recruitment and replacement pool for friends and acquaintances will be larger; thus, the individual has greater selection.[3] Although the relationships formed may not be transient in fact, the knowledge that they can be replaced would presumably reduce the personal risk involved in forming the relationships in the first place. Third, the relative anonymity of urban life means that the individual has greater control over information flow about himself and over social contact with specific others. These two considerations should also reduce the personal risk of involvement, as unsatisfactory relationships can usually be shed and new relationships added without dramatic reverberations throughout the entire social network of the individual. In addition, the individual can better regulate his involvement with others in a setting where contact and information are better controlled by him, so that transitions (and the lack thereof) in the level and type of involvement should become logistically less problematic.

On the basis of these considerations, various research hypotheses were made, chief among them are the following: (1) More urban persons will have larger, more functional networks, not only at the periphery and midrange of the network, but also at the core. (2) In this regard, higher class (using income, education, and job status) will have the same type and direction of effect as urbanness. That is, (3) social and geographic centrality will positively affect network structure and function, each form of centrality operating in the same direction.

Network studies are still in the developmental stage; yet networks promise a theoretical and strategic link between the egocentric concerns of psychology and the more sociocentric concerns of structural-functional analysis with its focus on institutions. Networks have proved useful in family studies (Bott, 1971) and political studies (Barnes, 1968) in both rural and urban contexts (Boissevain and Mitchell, 1973, and Mitchell, 1969, for selected readings), so that it is reasonable to assume that they would prove a useful tool for rural-urban comparisons. In addition, they have the advantage of being the medium through which the ordinary person most intensely experiences society. *Personal network* or *network* here designates the aggregated relationships of the individual to other persons and the structure and content of those relationships. Because of the logistical problems of studying whole networks and because many of the properties of the peripheral and midrange network segments can be relatively safely postulated based on observable conditions of rural and urban life (for example the greater impersonal instrumental options of cities as reflected in services provided by different level central places), the present study focuses primarily on the network core, that is, on relationships to friends, closer acquaintances, and kin.

The purpose of this paper is to present an outline of research performed in Austria in 1975 and 1976 to test these hypotheses and to report preliminary findings from this work, particularly with regard to the first hypothesis.

Research Design

The goal of the research was to compare social life at three levels of urbanization, that is city, town, and village life. As a research site, Tirol (an alpine province in western Austria) has certain strategic advantages. Geographic factors and international borders make central place functions clear and constrain network options geographically, so that levels of urbanization and centralness are easier to define there than in more open areas. In addition, Tirol is relatively homogeneous ethnically, so that differences between groups are more likely to derive from rural-urban and class differences than in a more ethnically mixed area, where ethnic distribution would not be equal in different social and geographic categories. In addition, though small (Tirol is about 185 miles west-east and ranges from about 35 to 80 miles north-south), Tirol has a medium-size city (Innsbruck with a population of 115,000), lower-level central places in industrial towns and district capitals, and truly rural villages—all within fairly easy driving distance of each other. For the intermediate level of urbanness, the six district capitals (three to the east and three to the west of Innsbruck) were chosen; they range in population from 5,000 to 13,000 and serve equivalent central place functions. No villages were done in the district around Innsbruck, as many of the villages in this area are now half rural and half commuter communities, which would confuse the variables being measured. The villages were scattered throughout the other six districts and, with perhaps one exception, had populations under 2000 and often considerably lower.

The sample is composed of persons in five socially diverse occupations: doctors, who are high-status professionals; lumber businessmen, who are representative of small, traditional industry in Tirol; bank employees, who seem to be typical white-collar employees and are also widely distributed; skilled metal workers, who are the most widely distributed of blue-collar workers in Tirol; and farmers, who remain the typical rural workers, though at this point few of their households rely entirely on farming for their income. Very few farmers remain in Innsbruck and some of the district capitals, but some were found at each level of urbanization.

Ideally, one person in each occupation was to be interviewed in each district capital and in a village in each district; six were to be done in Innsbruck. The sample falls somewhat short of this ideal balance because persons were not always available at each level of urbanization in each occupation; nonetheless, the sample comes close to this ideal. The doctors, bank employees, and metal workers were approached by going to their places of business; lumber businessmen through an intermediary in the chamber of commerce (Handelskammer); and farmers from names provided by local agricultural extension service (Landwirtschaftskammer) personnel.

The data reported here is based on taped, structured interviews with persons in 100 households. The key occupation (with the exception of two doctors and some female bank employees) was that of the husband. Spouses of bank employees were not interviewed. About two-thirds of other wives were interviewed; in some farm families, only the wife was interviewed. Data on friendship and the quality of relationships is reported only for those persons actually interviewed, though spouses were considered accurate informants of less personal information such as family structure, education, and so on.

Findings

In general the hypotheses were supported, though not always linearly and not equally for different occupational groups or for men and women. Differences in friendship patterns, general social interactions, and attitudes toward friends, neighbors, acquaintances, and kin all reflect rural-urban differences. Friendship shows the most striking results, with urbanites and those raised in cities more often having friends than townspeople and villagers. Rural people are also less active socially than urbanites and much more often report the dangers of forming close relationships. While kin remain important at all levels of urbanization, the actual patterns of interaction vary somewhat.

Kinship relationships, however, reveal very few differences. Kin appear to be important at every level of urbanization. Most persons at each level prefer to solicit aid from kin than from nonkin. The large majority at each level have deliberate social contact with kin at least weekly. At each level, the parent-child tie dominates all other kin relationships in terms of mutual assistance and interaction rates; sibling ties follow at some distance; and relationships with other kin come in a very distant third. Few aunts, uncles, or cousins are seen except at certain family gatherings a few times a year, the most common of these being religious holidays, special birthdays, weddings, and funerals. There would usually be only a few such events for a given family in any given year. Persons in villages may see relatives more often, but they mean quite literally that: if you live near kin in a small place, you are more likely to run into them, but the interaction on these occasions if often limited virtually to greeting each other. Deliberate interaction with kin is not higher in villages and towns than Innsbruck. Indeed, persons who must go to some effort to socialize with kin, as is usually the case in Innsbruck, tend to plan a larger segment of the day for that interaction (an afternoon or an evening usually); whereas persons with nearby kin (the usual rural case) tend not to schedule such large portions of time for kin. As Pfeil (1972) notes, urban children remain longer in the parental house than do others, who must often go to boarding school for their educations.[4] In summary, the types of contact vary somewhat depending mainly on proximity of kin, but there is no evidence that kinship is significantly weakened or strengthened by rural-urban differences. Most of the variation that does exist falls within similar ranges of contact, usually high contact (weekly or more). Wherever they live, the very large majority maintain close and frequent contact with parents and children, rather less with siblings, and very little with more peripheral kin.

That contact with and emotional ties to kin are important and fairly intense in urban settings has often been noted, not only in Europe (Bott, 1971; Wilmott and Young, 1960; Rosenmayr and Kockeis, 1965; Simić, 1973; Pfeil, 1972) and the United States (Adams, 1968; Gans, 1962), but elsewhere around the world

(Aldous, 1962; Dore, 1958; Peattie, 1972). To the degree that the family has been weakened by urban life, it is probably in terms of social control functions, as urbanites are often less visible to kin and have greater opportunities for avoiding their relatives *if* they want to. Urbanites also devote more of their time and energies to friends and acquaintances than do nonurbanites. Urbanites, townspeople, and villagers exhibit quite different attitudes toward friends and acquaintances and have different incidences of friendship, although all define it similarly.

Persons in the sample were asked to define friendship and neighborliness and then to name any persons that they would consider friends in terms of their own definition.[5] There was consensus about the nature of friendship, which included basically two categories: friends and intimate friends. Some informants recognized only the latter as being real friends. Friendship is characterized by affection, mutual helpfulness, loyalty, and trust in such a degree that the person would be willing to make some sacrifice to help the other and to preserve the relationship. Intimate friendship includes, in addition, sufficient trust and affection to be willing to share family and personal secrets; intimate friends are confidants. As Paine (1969) notes, friendship in the intimate sense of the word is a personal, voluntary, and private relationship that requires protection from (isolation from) more social, public relationships, such as acquaintanceship and patron-client ties, which, though often congenial, may be institutionalized and routinized. McCall et al. (1970) also point out the very private nature of friendship, the development of rules particular to individual relationships, and the release from the restrictions of other roles. One of the tests of friendship is whether the participants trust each other enough to divulge the indecorous, asocial, or antisocial thoughts, feelings, and behavior that all normal people experience; one of the primary functions of friendship is just such release from the public, social demands made on the individual. Clearly, it will be more difficult to establish and maintain friendships where individuals are most easily and regularly scrutinized by the community at large (for example, in a village or small town), although these people would perhaps benefit from such role-release even more than those in more flexible environments (in cities).

In fact, urbanites are more likely than townspeople and villagers to have friends (table 5-1). We find that 35 percent of urbanites, 51 percent of

Table 5-1
Percentage of Respondents Reporting No Friends

	Living in			*Raised in*		
	City	Town	Village	City	Town	Village
Men	33	48	44	32	53	50
Women	47	54	50	33	39	69
All	39	51	47	33	47	59

townspeople, and 47 percent of villagers report no friends at all. In addition, rural-urban patterns of naming friends minimize differences to some degree. Informants were allowed to name kin as friends if they chose to do so. A few nonurbanites elected to name a favorite sibling or sibling-in-law or cousin as a friend, usually the only friend. On the other hand, this occasional naming of a favorite relative might be interpreted as supporting stronger rural ties with kin; however, if one looks at the relationships with siblings, siblings-in-law, and cousins described by urbanites, one finds that a few urbanites also have especially close relationships with some same-generation favorite relative. The difference is that they do not name them as friends, presumably because they more often have different persons to provide in answer to this question and because it would seem that urbanites less often consider the possibility of naming kin as friends.

For example, rural doctors and their wives tended to report friends from their university days as being their only real friends; urban doctors on the other hand reported friends made or developed subsequent to this period of their lives. Town doctors fell between village and urban doctors in this respect. When asked to describe their relationships to friends from their student days, however, urban doctors (and rural doctors reporting friends from a later period) described relationships identical to the ones commonly named by rural doctors as their only or closest friendships. Doctors and their wives usually retained one or more affectionate ties with persons met as students, whom they now saw an average of about once a year, but more urban persons had had the opportunity to make and develop other friendships which now transcended their student friendships in intimacy. Urbanites with friends usually (85 percent) have friends in their current place of residence; however, 34 percent of townspeople and 38 percent of villagers who have friends have them exclusively outside their own community (table 5-2). Their having friends thus depends much more on their ability to establish or maintain extralocal ties.

Level of urbanization of the place where one is raised also affects friendship patterns (table 5-1). Only 33 percent of those raised in a city report no friends, compared with 47 percent of those raised in towns and 59 percent of those raised in villages. Although more likely to possess friends, urbanites who do have

Table 5-2
Percentage of Respondents Reporting Friends Exclusively
Outside Their Place of Residence

	Living in		
	City	Town	Village
Men	12	37	44
Women	20	30	29
All	15	34	38

friends have slightly fewer on the average than friendly countrypeople. It would seem that some friendly adults manage to establish close ties wherever they live, while others depend much more on the environment. Urbanity facilitates friendship formation, so that persons who might remain friendless in a smaller community in fact make one or two friends; however, the average is somewhat lower, partly as a result of the increased incidence of friendship. Similarly, though urbanites more often have friends, they somewhat less often have more than weekly contact with them. Villagers who have friends in their own community are likely to see them at least accidentally and for short periods of time whenever they are out and about the community, whereas this is not true for urbanites. In general, however, urbanites are more active socially. In addition, urbanites and those raised in cities more often socialize with their spouses than countrypeople, that is they have more companionate marriages. As with kin, urbanites more often formally schedule and plan contacts with friends than do townspeople or villagers, who rely much more on informal encounters around their own community, to the degree that their friends are in their own community.

Village women much more often volunteered complaints about social restrictions on women than did other women. They felt that others monitored their behavior and affected it unpleasantly. No doubt they were correct. Village husbands were also more restrictive of their wives; some stated, for example, that they would not allow their wives to have friends, as it might affect the husband's relationships to other men adversely.

Avoidance of close contact with neighbors dominates every level of urbanization and also every occupational group. People repeat again and again that it is best to have pleasant relationships with neighbors but not to get involved or there will be trouble, usually squabbles developing from living close together. People say that they will help neighbors in an emergency, though often only if asked to do so, and that they expect this behavior to be reciprocated. A very few persons violated this rule and had friends who were neighbors, but it was rare. Nor do people generally seem to be behaviorally violating the ideal norm. When asked whether any neighbor had come to see them recently, most answered in accordance with their more general description of neighborly relations. To be sure, most could think of some single event when a neighbor had come to ask for something, but there was no frequent indwelling meeting of neighbors; neighbors meet on the street, in the corridor to apartments, or sometimes at the door if they have something important to say. Many persons said that they knew some people who had a morning coffee hour or whatever but that they had avoided it, as it only led to trouble and waste of time. Nonetheless, neighbors do rally around in sudden emergencies, such as sudden hospitalizations, and this is true in Innsbruck as well as in villages and towns. Though few such emergencies were reported, in those cases, class lines were crossed. That neighbors are of a different class (and therefore rather unlikely to socialize with each other under most circumstances) does not seem to matter as far as neighborly helpfulness is concerned, especially with regard to higher-class persons helping lower-class neighbors in need. Higher-class persons seem better able to provide for themselves without going to neighbors, but they nonetheless recognize neighbors as potential sources of aid and occasionally do turn to them. One of the reasons people avoid going to neighbors is fear of incurring obligations, and this may be a particular deterrent to higher-class neighbors turning to lower-class ones for help.

Persons without friends often expressed sentiments about people in general similar to those almost everyone expressed about neighbors, that is that close involvement is more trouble than it is worth. The ideal of friendship is fine, but usually the friend disappoints or betrays, and that is worse than having no friends. An often expressed fear was that the friend, having received confidences, would then repeat and perhaps even distort those confidences for his or others' benefit and to the detriment of the informant. A few persons said that this had happened to them and that they therefore intended to avoid such close relationships in the future. Another common comment among the friendless was the observation that friends might take advantage of one; these persons focused on need satisfaction and instrumental effectiveness rather than on the more pleasureful and purely emotional aspects of friendship. Nonurbanites were more likely than urbanites to point out the liabilities of close relationships.

Those inclined to dismiss these responses as individually neurotic (which the fear of intimacy and the inability to establish it expressed by many informants may well be), should remember that the sample was composed of quite ordinary persons, over 40 percent of whom found themselves friendless. Such a high figure is striking, as even the most intractable friendless valued the ideal of friendship, however much they thought this ideal impossible and disvalued the real opportunities they perceived in their social environment. In addition, many of those with friends had fewer friends than they desired or had less intimate relationships with them than they desired (friends as opposed to intimate friends), or had less contact than desired.[6] A number of persons, both those with and without friends, viewed lack of friends as a problem and had considered it a problem before the interview. As noted, urbanites seem to fare better than others in this regard.

People usually defined all nonintimates as strangers,[7] but villagers and townspeople talk much more about this sort of thing. Villagers may come into contact with fewer persons in single-stranded relationships, but they nonetheless tend to define all nonintimate relationships instrumentally. Perhaps they talk more about it because it requires greater effort and deliberateness to keep strangers in their place (not meddling in the private affairs of the informant) in small communities where people inevitably know more about each other than any person likes having known about himself, however much he may like to gossip about neighbors or consider it necessary for his best interests to do so.

Contrary to popular belief in Tirol, men are more likely to have friends than are women (urban 67 percent to 53 percent, town 52 percent to 46 percent, and village 56 percent to 50 percent), and they are more likely to see them oftener (high contact among the urban 45 percent to 27 percent, town 25 percent to 25 percent, and village 45 percent to 39 percent). Women working outside the home (though they have children) more often have friends than housewives. Contact with kin does not seem to suffer and may even be enhanced, as working mothers depend predominantly on their or their husband's mother for child care during work hours.

The sample is already approximately balanced for class because of the method of selection, so these findings relate primarily to rural-urban variation. If one were to project the qualities of a random population at each level of urbanization, these differences would be more pronounced, for higher-class persons tend to cluster at higher levels of urbanization than do lower-class persons. Higher-class persons also have more friends and more contact with them than do lower-class persons. Taking the sample as a whole and correlating for frequency of contact, one finds a direct relationship between class and contact. Median contact from high to low is exactly that of the occupational status from high to low: doctors, lumber businessmen, bank employees, metal workers, and farmers. The majority of farmers at each level of urbanization reported no friends. As most of these farmers have mixed household economies, they probably represent the typical village family, with metal workers coming next, then bank employees and just a smattering of the remaining two occupations. Occupation and education increase the likelihood of having friends significantly for both men and women; income does so for men. Class variables also significantly affect patterns of more general socializing with acquaintances.[8]

Discussion

The findings of this study contradict the negative stereotype of cities presented by the preponderance of urban theory and research studies, which implicitly or explicitly have conveyed the image of the city as intrinsically inimical to healthy individual social adjustment and positive affiliation. Rural and urban are not found to be polar opposites in terms of individual social networks. The differences that do exist, however, conflict with traditional notions of urban life. Urbanites have high contact with kin; they more often have friends; they spend more time with friends; and they are generally more active socially. They express fewer negative sentiments about forming close relationships and seem to be better at it.[9] Probably a variety of factors contribute to this pattern: greater social resources, greater privacy, greater control over information flow and personal contacts, the greater choice that results from these conditions, and decreased personal risk and cost consequently experienced in entering, maintaining, and, if need be, terminating intimate and personal relationships. It may also be that in having fewer ascribed interaction sets to contend with and fewer personal nonintimate ties, urbanites are impelled to more actively create their own personal interaction spheres (as well as being thus freed to do so), and prodded by this they may go on to have more contacts than others.

Looking at public opinion polls and surveys in the United States, Fischer concluded that urbanites are not unhappier than others (1973) and are somewhat more tolerant of deviant behaviors (1971) when other factors are controlled for. He subsequently (1975) went on to explain urban deviance in terms of urban facilitation of subcultures (ethnic and normative, especially the latter). While it is no doubt true that cities foster subcultural proliferation and development, these are not explained in terms of the choice-making individuals who compose the subcultures, and this subcultural theory contributes to but cannot explain the findings of the Tirolean research. The decreased interaction rates of rural doctors can no doubt be partially explained on this basis, for there are perhaps too few well-educated persons outside of Innsbruck to maintain a large, viable professional subculture. Towns do have more professionals than villages, but one could argue that professionals in towns never attain critical mass for the formation of a subculture. On the other hand, there are many farmers, blue-collar workers, and white-collar employees in villages and towns; yet they are less likely than doctors to have friends, and townspeople less likely than villagers. In other words, subcultures may facilitate network formation and influence attitudes toward personal relationships, but they cannot explain it. Rather, differential rural-urban and class dynamics seem to make network formation and maintenance more or less costly, threatening, and attractive to the individual. Viewed in terms of individual recruitment to deviant subcultures, however, the dynamics that appear to affect personal network structure, as postulated earlier, may also be the dynamics that facilitate subcultural formation.

Conclusion

The Tirolean research findings support the hypothesis that geographic and social centrality positively affects network structure and function. This suggests that geographic and social centrality equips the individual with greater social resources and freedom of choice in the construction of personal networks. Urbanites and higher-class persons have more opportunity for social contacts and in fact use those opportunities, probably because their greater resources and the greater flexibility of their positions make personal involvement less threatening. In short, urban life is not nearly so bleak nor rural life nearly so friendly as often believed (in Tirol as well as here), and the structure of urban life facilitates social contacts not only at the network periphery and midrange but also at the core.

The present study suggests a more personal definition of quality of life than social statistics such as crime rates or size of dwelling. It points toward investigation of personal motivation and of behavioral incentives and constraints as an explanation of rural-urban and class differences in behavior, for example, the importance of choice, privacy, and definitions of personal risk and their relationships to urban and class structure. In other words, ecological and class structures need to be related to individual constructs and behaviors, and these concerns need to be extended more widely to normal populations as well as to problem or deviant ones. Ordinary urbanites are more affected by the options presented in their immediate social environment than by the destructive behavior of a small segment of the population who may act antisocially. Further, it is unreasonable to assume that the negative deviance of cities (such as crime) has greater impact on the average urbanite than does its creative deviance (such as art). Urbanites in Tirol flourish in a way that country people do not, though Tiroleans regularly idealize rural life.[10]

Notes

1. This is used in the Durkheimian sense, meaning that persons are truly interdependent rather than belonging to small independent production units mechanically linked, as would be the case in subsistence agriculture.

2. *Central place* refers particularly to population aggregates differentiated from other levels of aggregation by economic and social functions, such as markets, governmental units, and transportation nexuses.

3. In the case of many special interests, there are more likely to be others who share those interests where one finds numerous diverse types (Fischer, 1975).

4. In Tirol, high schools are usually in towns, and students from remoter villages often board. Specialized schools for this age group, for example, home economics schools for girls, may require going to Innsbruck, so that even some town children must board in order to attend high-school-level classes.

5. There was general agreement as to what constitutes friendship. In those few cases where deviant definitions were given, the relationships to the informant's closest contacts were evaluated and coded according to the normal definition. Those persons reporting numerous friends were asked to name their closest friends and to answer various questions about them; they described more peripheral friends only in general terms. In reality, however, most persons who had friends had only a few. Informants also discussed acquaintances with whom they had regular contact, but these persons are not included here in discussions of friendship, as they are nonintimate contacts.

6. Very few persons were asked directly how they felt about the amount and intensity of their friendships, but most volunteered comments about this

either during the formal interview or afterwards. Persons reporting no friends were usually asked, however, whether this was deliberate or whether it was simply a matter of chance that they had not met anyone with whom such a relationship had developed.

7. Lesser acquaintances are of course talked about as such, when particular activities, such as sports or work, are discussed with them; but when it comes to talking about the private affairs of the informant, these persons are shoved over into the stranger category rather than being drawn into the intimate one.

8. The interviews were computer coded for up to 2,000 bits of information per household. Both urbanness and higher class affected networks in the same direction; however, class has a much more marked effect than does level of urbanization. Class variables considered were education, occupation, income, parental and grandparental education, and parental and grandparental occupation. Of the primary three, income was decidedly the least important but still significant. All the variables operate in the same direction. For more detailed discussion, see Crowe (1978).

9. The effects of geographic and social mobility are reported in Crowe (1978).

10. For reasons why they idealize rural life, see Crowe (1978).

References

Adams, B.N. 1968. *Kinship in an Urban Setting.* Chicago: Markham Publishing Co.
Aldous, J. 1962. "Urbanization, the Extended Family, and Kinship Ties in West Africa." *Social Forces* 41:6-12.
Barnes, J.A. 1968. "Networks and Political Process." In *Local-Level Politics: Social and Cultural Perspectives,* ed. M.J. Swartz, Chicago: Aldine-Atherton, pp. 107-130.
Boissevain, J., and Mitchell, J.C., eds. 1973. *Network Analysis: Studies in Human Interaction.* The Hague: Mouton and Co.
Bott, E. 1971. *Family and Social Networks: Roles, Norms, and External Relationships in Ordinary Urban Families.* New York: The Free Press.
Childe, V.G. 1969. "The Urban Revolution." In *Neighborhood, City, and Metropolis: An Integrated Reader in Urban Sociology,* ed. R. Gutman and D. Popenoe. New York: Random House, pp. 111-119.
Crowe, P.W. 1978. "Good Fences Make Good Neighbors: Social Networks at Three Levels of Urbanization in Tirol, Austria." Ph.D. dissertation, Stanford University.
Dore, R.P. 1958. *City Life in Japan: A Study of a Tokyo Ward.* Berkeley and Los Angeles: University of California Press.
Fischer, C.S. 1975. "Toward a Subcultural Theory of Urbanism." *American Journal of Sociology* 80:1319-1341.

_____. 1973. "Urban Malaise." *Social Forces* 52:221-235.
_____. 1971. "A Research Note on Urbanism and Tolerance." *American Journal of Sociology* 76:847-856.
Gans, H.J. 1962. *The Urban Villagers: Group and Class in the Life of Italian Americans.* New York: The Free Press.
Lloyd, P.D. 1959. "The Yoruba Town Today." *Sociological Review* 7:45-63.
McCall, G.J., McCall, M.M., Denzin, N.K., Suttles, G., and Kurth, S.B. 1970. *Social Relationships.* Chicago: Aldine Publishing Co.
Mitchell, J.C., ed. 1969. *Social Networks in Urban Situations: Analyses of Personal Relationships in Central African Towns.* Manchester: Manchester University Press.
Paine, R. 1969. "In Search of Friendship: An Exploratory Analysis in "Middle-Class" culture." *Man* 4:505-524.
Peattie, L.R. 1972. *The View from the Barrio.* Ann Arbor: University of Michigan Press.
Pfeil, E. 1972. *Gross stadtforschung: Entwicklung und gegenwartiger stand.* Hanover: Gerbruder Janecke, Verlag.
Redfield, R. 1947. "The Folk Society." *American Journal of Sociology* 52:293-308.
Rosenmayr, L., and Kockeis, E. 1965. *Umwelt und familie alter menschen.* Neuwald am Rhein: Hermann Luchterhand Verlag.
Simić, A. 1973. *The Peasant Urbanites: A Study of Rural-Urban Mobility in Serbia.* New York: Seminar Press.
Simmel, G. 1970. "The Metropolis and Mental Life." In *Neighborhood, City, and Metropolis: An Integrated Reader in Urban Sociology,* ed. R. Gutman and D. Popenoe. New York: Random House, pp. 777-888.
Spindler, G. 1973. *Burgbach: An Urbanizing German Village.* New York: Holt, Rinehart and Winston.
Wilmott, P., and Young, M. 1960. *Family and Class in a London Suburb.* London: Routledge and Keagan Paul.
Wirth, L. 1938. "Urbanism as a Way of Life." *American Journal of Sociology* 44:1-24.

**Part II
The Urban Challenge:
Controlling the Physical and
Man-Made Environment**

Interactions between Cities and Their Local and Regional Weather and Climate

William P. Lowry

Introduction: An Intentional Provocation

Recent history includes cases in which severe weather, in the form of lightning storms, has been cited as the first in a chain of events leading to the eventual cessation of all electrical service to major urban areas—the urban blackout. Although the best known of these cases took place in New York rather than in Western Europe, the questions and concepts related to the incident are valid for any modern urban society and ought to be raised whenever interdisciplinary urban studies are undertaken.

At the time of this writing, no one has challenged the claim that lightning caused the New York blackout of 13 July 1977.[1] Those who have proposed that causal chain refer to the storms as an act of God, for legalistic reasons of liability that need no elaboration. One can imagine the kind of reactions that would be generated by the provocative claim that the city itself caused the lightning storms and that God's role was somewhat less than paramount. Insurance claims and litigation would be so complex that the financial impact of the disaster would be immensely increased. It is not surprising, therefore, that no one has made such a claim in the case of New York in July 1977. Yet the claim that the ordinary operation of a city can produce modifications of local weather is a common one among climatologists (Landsberg, 1974). In particular it has been asserted that severe weather, including lightning storms, is sometimes enhanced by urban effects on local and regional atmospheric behavior.[2] It would be difficult to find a more revealing example of the interweavings of the physical environment and the social environment of urban man, with all its implications for the conduct of interdisciplinary inquiry, than the possibility that the people of a huge metropolis caused, or at least adversely influenced, the events triggering a power blackout, through a chain of causation so unsuspected and so obviously absent from the minds of those who developed the complex system of social arrangements of the metropolis.

This paper will present much of the conventional wisdom among climatologists regarding the inadvertent modifications of weather and climate caused by urban areas. The paper will also suggest something of the scope of problems related to the pollution of urban air and of problems connecting architecture and urban design to matters of environmental stress in the forms of extremes of air temperature, humidity, and wind.

This paper should be a reminder of the danger in the serious urban ecologist's forgetting or deemphasizing consideration of the physical environment, both built and uncontrolled, in his striving to enhance the quality of urban life.

Urban Effects on Local and Regional Weather and Climate

Weather and climate variables such as air temperature and humidity near the earth's surface have values determined largely by the way in which the surface accepts solar energy and then partitions it into the warming of soil, the warming of air, and the evaporation of surface water. Differences in this acceptance and partitioning across the earth's surface in turn determine the motions called wind and the patterns of cloud and rain. The amounts of solar radiation absorbed by the surface and the proportions into which it is then partitioned are determined, for a given amount of incident sunshine, by the nature of the surface itself: its color, roughness, wetness, and porosity (Lowry, 1969, especially chapter 8).

Among the many things that building and operating a city does is to change these same characteristics of the earth's surface. It should be no surprise, then, that the transformation from a rural landscape and surface to an urban one should result in detectable changes in the values of weather and climate variables. Though in the present state of knowledge some of the changes are better understood and more predictable than others, though the correct nature of the causal chains is sometimes in doubt, and though there is much room for disagreement about the extent of the impact of the changes on urban social systems, there is no doubt that cities change weather and climate.

Compared with the typical preurban surface, the city presents a much rougher face to the atmosphere. The *shape* of the surface is changed, often drastically. Then too, the *materials* of the urban surface are different: less soillike and more granitelike. Third, a city surface is engineered to be free of standing water, though there are many urban sources of vapor such as automobile exhausts and chimneys of several kinds; the *wetness* of the urban surface is changed in several respects. Fourth, the urban surface has many *sources of heat* not found elsewhere, or at least not in the spatial concentration of a city. Vehicles, furnaces, air conditioners, and industrial heat of all sorts are primarily urban sources of heat. Finally, the *sources of air pollution* in and surrounding a modern city change the local air quality, which in turn has effects on the behavior of the atmosphere.

The increased roughness of the city, with its vertical surfaces and air spaces contained between buildings, usually traps more sunlight than a typical rural surface because the sunlight can bounce around between buildings, thereby encountering more absorbing surfaces by internal reflection. Then, too, the rougher urban surface tends to retard windflow in the spaces where most human activities take place, though under some circumstances wind is channeled into long, straight urban canyons and speeds are increased. Whatever the speeds, the air in motion over a city is likely to tumble and be better mixed because it encounters the protruding elements of roughness.

The granitelike materials of streets and walls, and often of rooftops as well, not only conduct heat away from the surface more rapidly under a hot sun, but they also have a greater capacity than rural surfaces for the storage of heat. Likewise, once stored in urban materials by day, heat can later flow to the surface at night in greater amounts than if the surface were not urbanized.

The injection of moisture into urban air takes place from a relatively few, discrete sources—often highly patterned—rather than diffusely as from a more homogeneous rural surface. Moisture added by evaporation produces a local cooling (actually, more often it is a lessened warming) as part of the sun's energy is used to change liquid to vapor. Without water available there, the energy would have been used instead to warm surface materials and the passing air. It is often spatial contrasts in surface characteristics—in this case wetness and thus temperature—that produce weather events. Thus the urban moisture flow, if not reduced by a general waterproofing of the surface, is certainly rearranged spatially and temporally compared with the situation before the city was built.

The anthropogenic sources of heat in a city are also highly patterned in space and time, in addition to being added to that primary source of heat for any system, the sun.

Dirty air acts thermodynamically in two major ways. First, with respect to radiant energy, dirty air reduces the intensity of sunlight at the absorbing surface of a city, and it also retards the outward flow of infrared, or long-wave radiation, by which any surface disposes of excess heat as it cools. Second, dirty air changes the numbers and sizes of condensation nuclei on which water vapor molecules condense to form water droplets. In turn, these numbers and sizes play a major role in determining whether droplets, in the form of clouds, will grow or coalesce to form water drops large enough to fall out as rain. Clouds, like particles, also affect radiant heating and cooling of the surface.

Having suggested in a general way the physical principles and mechanisms by which changes in the urban surface produce change in the flow of heat and in the motion of the local atmosphere, the next section will outline the net results of these separate changes and effects as they occur together. Not all mechanisms are mutually reinforcing. Some tend to warm and some to cool. Some tend to moisten and some to dry. Some tend to mix the moving air, while some tend to retard motion. It is the net results, then, that are of interest. This paper cannot be definitive as to physical causes of observed effects, but it can leave the nonspecialist reader with the correct impression that there is no shortage of known mechanisms from which to construct explanations of the observations and even to predict atmospheric behavior not yet observed.

The net results of the various changes of surface on the temperature climate are twofold. First, the range of temperatures between day and night is reduced—a thermostatic effect. Second, there is a general warming, or increase in average temperature at any hour on any date. Thus, cities are predictably warmer than their environs, the more so on calm, cloudless nights. Even during midday, cities are slightly warmer than their surroundings. The extremes of observed contrast between midlatitude, industrial cities and their surroundings are likely to be around 10° to 12° Centigrade on selected nights, while an annual average in the difference is more likely 1° to 2° Centigrade. Incidentally, the impression that the city on a calm midday is much warmer than the countryside may only be an impression not supported by measurements of air temperature. The impression arises because people have a greater heat load placed on them in city canyons as the surrounding walls reflect and radiate energy to them and because the calmer air trapped between buildings reduces the amount of evaporative cooling from their moist body surfaces. Again, the physiological response of a pedestrian in the central city is not usually borne out by measurements of air temperature.

When air temperatures on calm, clear nights or annual averages at several locations are used to construct lines of equal temperature value, called isotherms, on a map of the city, the results look like topographic maps of an island with shorelines the shape of the urban boundary. Among the maps of such an urban heat island most familiar to climatologists is a series based on the observations of Chandler (1965) for London.[3] Two maps from the series appear in figure 6-1.

Although the isothermal contours of an urban heat island are closely packed near the urban-rural boundary, as would be the case when shorelines were cliffs on a topographic island, still there is usually a readily detectable area of highest temperatures within the city—a thermal peak. The difference between the temperatures found in peak areas and those representing the rural environs is a measure of the intensity of the urban heat island effect. Oke (1973) has shown that the maximum recorded difference—the height of the island—is clearly related to urban population for a collection of Western European cities, as shown in figure 6-2. Though not shown here, a relationship that Oke has constructed for North American observations extends downward in population to that of an individual modern shopping mall.[4] Presumably, similar results would be found if appropriate observations were to be made in Europe. Clearly, the presence of the urban surface changes the temperature climate. It is not so clear, however, either how much of the change is due to the passive reactions of the urban surface to the sun's heating (as opposed to anthropogenic heat from buildings and vehicles) or how important the changes are in the lives of urban dwellers.

The net results of the various surface changes on the climatic factors related to storms and precipitation are not so clearly delineated nor so readily agreed on

Cities, Weather, and Climate 87

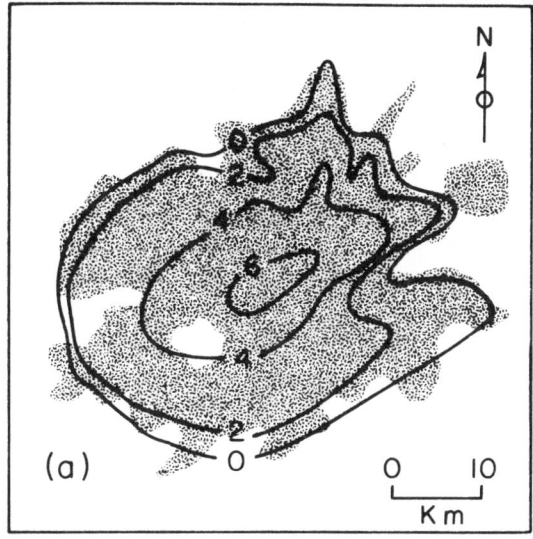

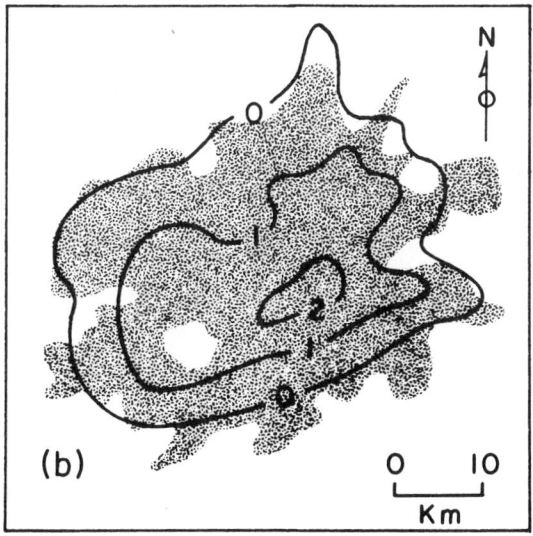

Source: After Chandler (1965).
Note: In degrees Centigrade relative to the temperature at the urban boundary.
Figure 6-1. Distribution of Minimum Temperatures in London: (a) 14 May 1959, Typical Intense and Well-Developed Heat Island; (b) 2 August 1959, Weak Heat Island.

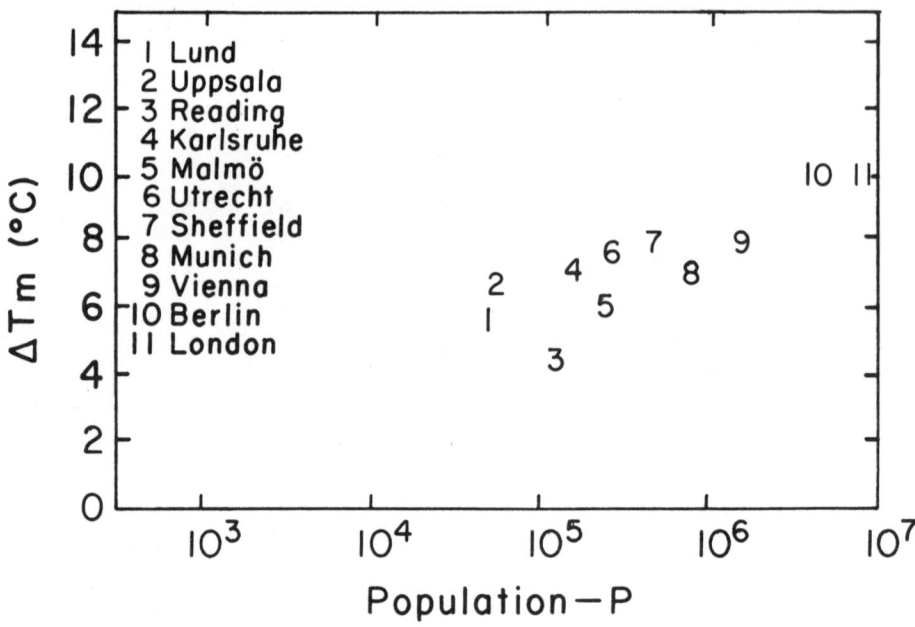

Source: T.R. Oke. 1973. "City Size and the Heat Island." In *Atmospheric Environment*, 7:777. Copyright 1973, Pergamon Press Ltd. Reprinted by permission.

Note: The center of the urban heat island may not always be in the same location (see figure 6-1) and the true maximum recorded temperature difference, ΔTm, may not have been observed.

Figure 6-2. Relation between Population, P, and the Maximum Temperature Difference between the Center and the Boundary of the Urban Heat Island, ΔTm.

by climatologists as the changes in temperature. The conventional wisdom about the basic mechanisms through which urban surfaces change precipitation processes is founded on the essentials for production of precipitation: a supply of condensation nuclei for formation of droplets and thence clouds, a supply of moisture to feed cloud growth, and a sustained updraft of air to hold growing drops aloft until they are large enough to fall unevaporated to earth. The alterations in the mix of nuclei and the sources of moisture have already been mentioned.

Updrafts are sustained by either mechanical mixing, as would be the case with a rough surface, or thermal mixing, as would be produced by a checkerboard surface of hot spots and cool spots. The updrafts would be enhanced over the hotspots (and probably compensated by downward motion over cooler areas). If, as may be the case in cities, the hot spots and the intense, local sources of water vapor occur in the same patterns, precipitation processes may well be altered significantly.

Early studies of rainfall in urban area (Schmauss, 1927; Kratzer, 1937) suggested local enhancement. More recent studies (Huff and Changnon, 1973; METROMEX Update, 1976)[5] suggested the same thing through much more elaborate observational techniques. Figure 6-3 presents results typical of those studies in which rain-gauge networks denser than most permit the mapping of lines of equal precipitation amounts, called isohyets. The believer can find ample evidence in such maps to support the hypothesis that cities enhance rainfall within their own boundaries. The skeptic maintains the hypothesis cannot be properly tested without some knowledge of what would have happened in the local area under similar weather conditions if the city had not been there (Lowry, 1977).

Three kinds of elaboration of the primary thesis that cities enhance precipitation will illustrate those developed in the literature of urban climatology. First is the scrutiny of the changes in the mix of condensation nuclei and the inferences about what ought to result, based on knowledge about the internal microphysics of clouds. The first studies established that nuclei became more numerous (no surprise to anyone who has seen dirty urban air) and in particular more numerous at smaller sizes (Braham, 1974). Cloud physics predicts, however, that such changes should *suppress* precipitation. More recently, it has been hypothesized and supported by rudimentary observational data, that enhancement really is possible by means of the injection by industrial cities of giant nuclei (Johnson, 1976), larger than previous detection methods could sense. Physical theory indeed predicts substantial enhancement in such a case, so the apparent earlier contradiction may have been resolved.

A second elaboration involves the emergence of the notion that the effects of cities on precipitation may be seen best not in the city itself but downwind of the city.[6] The conventional wisdom supporting this idea is that the initiation of enhancement begins within clouds as they pass over the urban landscape, but the culmination follows later in the life cycle of the clouds after time, and therefore distance, has seen the altered intracloud processes proceed to completion. Figure 6-4 suggests both the prediction and the observational confirmation of this downwind enhancement.

The third elaboration involves the separate examination of weekday records and weekend records of precipitation in order to detect differences that might be ascribed to urban processes operating during the work week but not on weekends. Early studies of this kind were tantalizingly supportive of the enhancement hypothesis (Ashworth, 1929, for example). The tempting notion is, of course, that a five-day, two-day cycle in precipitation amounts could not possibly be other than anthropogenic. Even those who would accept the conclusions as positive evidence for modification caused by urban areas agreed that such studies did little to elucidate causes. A skeptic would caution that without knowledge and records of times of operation of the true sources of modifying influences, the studies of weekday-weekend differences would be open to considerable doubts.

Description of these elaborations is meant to suggest the ends to which

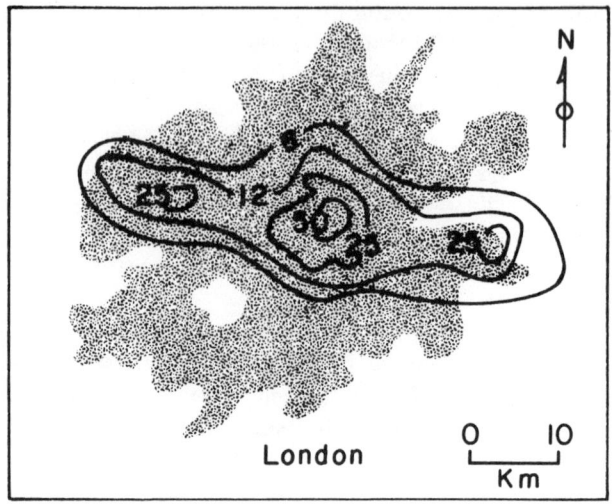

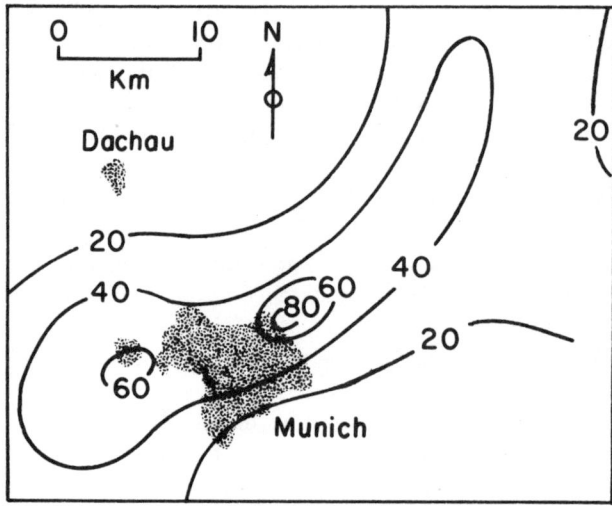

Source: (a) Atkinson (1970). (b) From Haeuser, after Geiger (1965). *The Climate Near the Ground*. Cambridge, Mass.: Harvard University Press. Reprinted by permission.

Figure 6-3. Examples of Precipitation Totals (in millimeters) from One Rainstorm Obtained with a Dense Network of Gauges: (a) London, 21 August 1959; (b) Munich, 25 July 1929.

Cities, Weather, and Climate

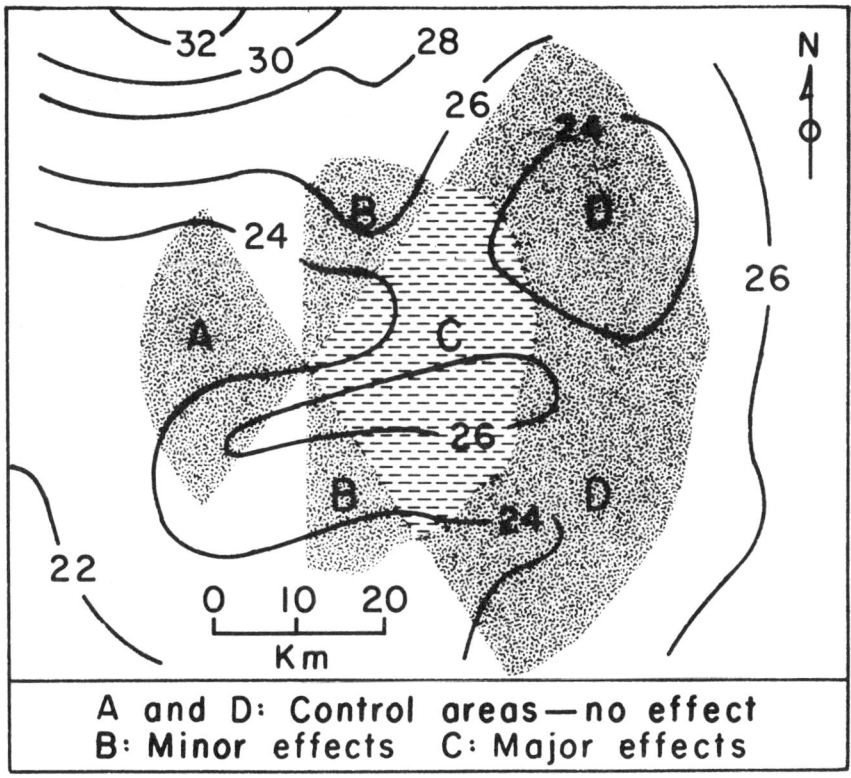

A and D: Control areas—no effect
B: Minor effects C: Major effects

Source: After F.A. Huff and S.A. Changnon, Jr. 1972, "Climatological Assessment of Urban Effects on Precipitation at St. Louis." *Journal of Applied Meteorology* 11:824, 827. Reprinted by permission of the American Meteorological Society.

Note: Centered on St. Louis, Missouri, a system of control and effect areas were described before analysis of rainfall records (prediction). Then various analyses were made, in this case the average summer rainfall totals (in millimeters for June-August) for the period 1959-68 (confirmation).

Figure 6-4. Control and Effect Areas in St. Louis.

scientists have gone to establish the existence, let alone the timing, location, and intensity of urban effects on precipitation amounts. Similar studies regarding severe storms and their attendant characteristics of wind, hail, lightning, and high-intensity downpours have been carried out. Despite all the effort, there is still a notable absence of accord regarding the existence, as well as causes, of urban effects on precipitation. The positive evidence is probably accepted by the majority of climatologists, enough so that assertions might easily be made in litigation, as suggested in the opening comments of this paper.

Observational results regarding hypothesized effects of cities on humidity and wind, and the occurrences of snow and ice, will be disregarded in this study. If the picture of research into the urban effects of weather and climate has not yet become convincing, the consideration of variables other than temperature and precipitation probably would not help.

Metropogenic Air Pollution: Scales of Social Impact

Ordinary operation of cities and their industrial areas not only concentrates the generation of common air pollutants within small volumes of the atmosphere but also adds exotic pollutants to the list of those injected into the air. The impacts of the resulting problems on the local scale are familiar in a personal way to the eye and nose of any resident who has ever experienced clean air for contrast. To the citizen who seldom ventures beyond the boundaries of his home neighborhood in a major urban area, the saying may not be entirely humorous that "clean air smells funny." The point here—and it is often overlooked in the search for public support of pollution control programs—is that in matters like these bad often exists only in contrast with good. When a whole generation of senior public officials has never personally known clean air, acceptance of air pollution as a problem comes less easily, as do solutions. When several such generations have lived, as in the British midlands and the Ruhr, the acceptance is even more difficult to achieve. Figure 6-5 suggests major features of a local air pollution problem.

To counter this difficulty of solving local problems is that, once clean air becomes a goal, at least the local sources and thus the means for control are well known. Perhaps the most vivid example of the chain leading from nonrecognition, through disaster and recognition, to goal setting and solution is the prolonged episode of filthy air in London in December 1952. The official estimate is that about four thousand people died during the three days of causes clearly attributable to the dirty air. The response of society was a Clean Air Act (see Stern et al., 1973, p. 60; Bach, 1972, p. 45),[7] which among other things brought replacement of soft coal in fireplaces by smokeless fuels in furnaces and electrical units for domestic space heating. A decade later, London's air was notably cleaner.

As the size and time scales increase, it becomes more difficult to identify sources of pollutants. Chemical and physical alteration of primary pollutants often takes place during transport through the atmosphere. Thus secondary pollutants may be the agents of damage in areas perhaps distant from the points of original injection. With time extended, the pollutants are more likely to meander across the countryside in shifting wind currents, thus covering their trail. Even if sources are identified, the spatial and often political separation of those near the sources from those near the points of damage makes for difficulty of control unless the two regions have a political base in common.

In illustration of this regional scale of the problem, figure 6-6 makes several points. First, the agent of damage (in this case to buildings and vegetation) is

Cities, Weather, and Climate 93

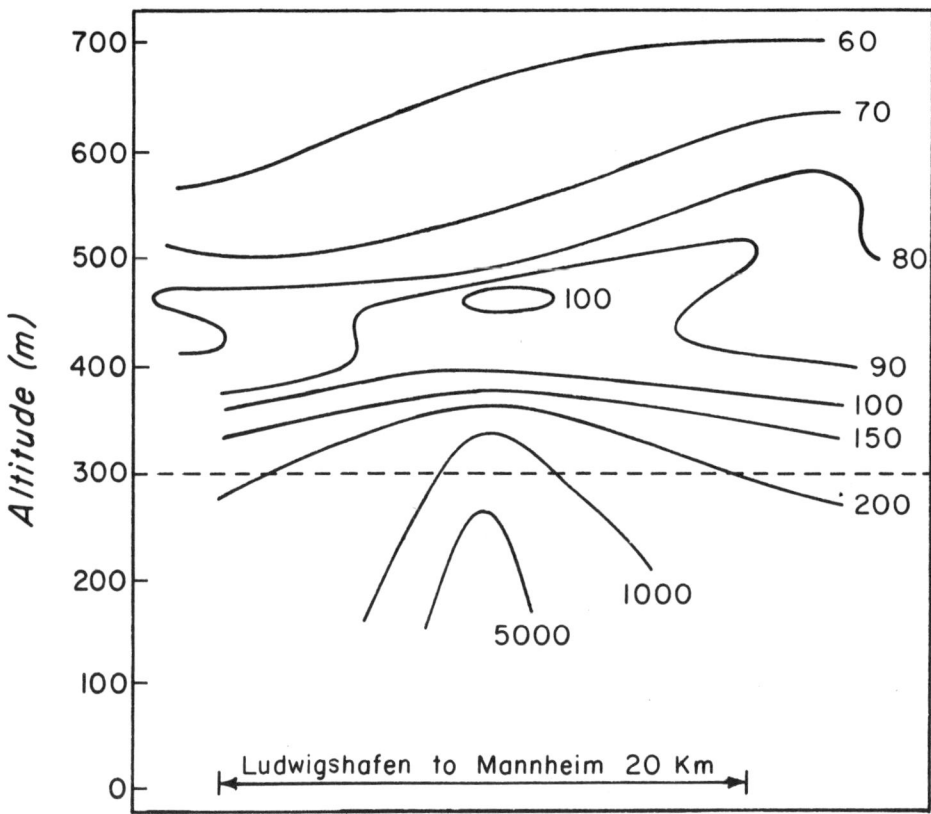

Source: After Georgii (1970).
Note: Measured by aircraft in micrograms per cubic meter. For reference, the national standard in the United States says that to safeguard human health, the concentration of sulfur dioxide should not exceed 80 micrograms per cubic meter as an annual average nor 365 as a twenty-four-hour average on more than one day per year. See Stern et al. (1973), table 13-1.

Figure 6-5. Concentration of Sulfur Dioxide Gas above Ludwigshafen-Mannheim, 3 April 1965: A Vertical Cross Section.

thought to be very dilute sulfuric acid rain, though the primary pollutant is sulfur dioxide. The chemistry of alteration in this case is almost trivially simple compared with many other cases, but the point about secondary pollutants is illustrated. Second, the area of greatest acidity in the Low Countries is very unlikely to be the source area of most of the primary pollutants. That is, mixing and transport of the pollutants, not to mention their transformation en route, is too complex to permit easy finger pointing as would be possible on the local scale. This does not imply that the Low Countries have no sources of sulfur-based pollutants but rather that they are probably not responsible for a

94   Western European Cities in Crisis

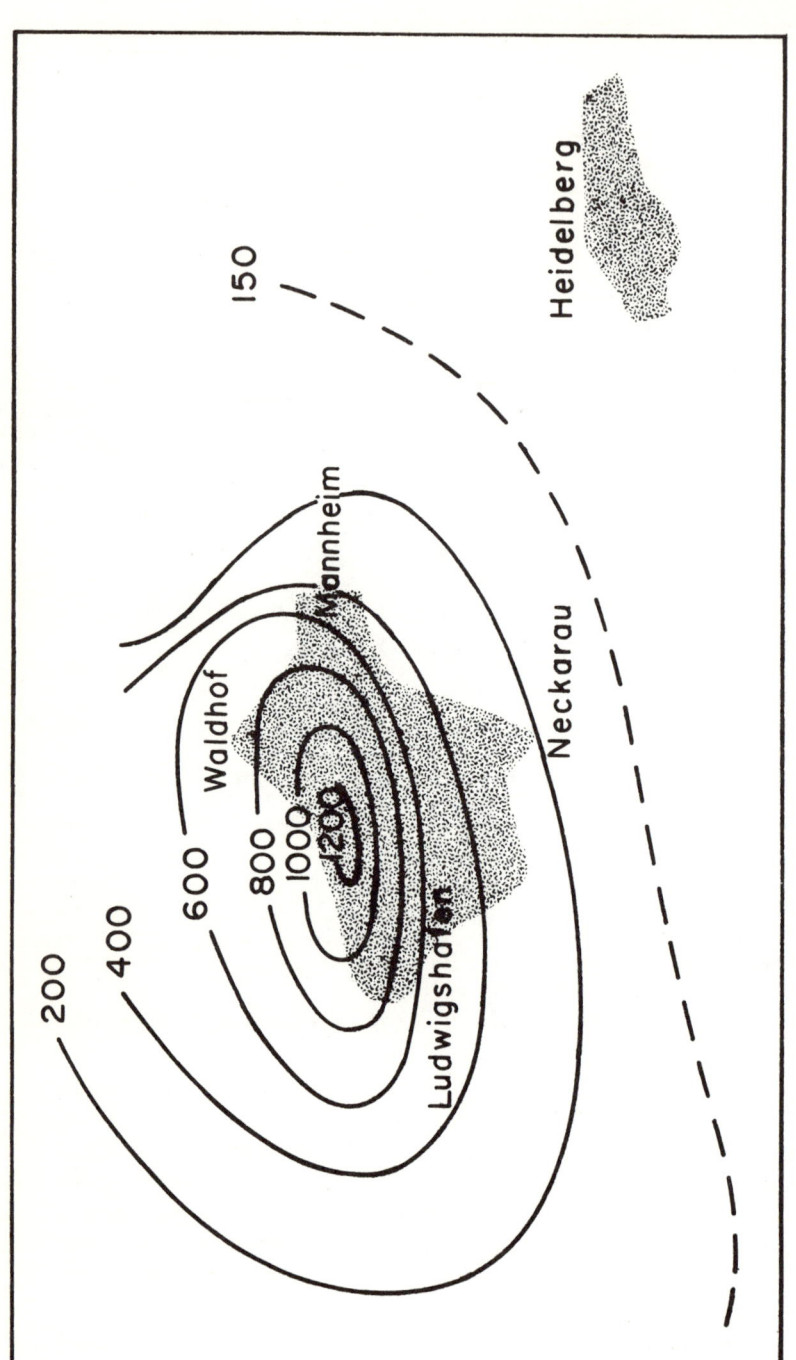

Source: After Georgii (1970).
Note: The concentrations were measured by aircraft in micrograms per cubic meter. This is a horizontal section at the height of 300 m above ground, indicated in figure 6-5 by the dotted line.

Figure 6-6. Concentration of Sulfur Dioxide Gas above Ludwigshafen-Mannheim, 3 April 1965: A Horizontal Section

very large fraction of the total represented in Western Europe, nor even in their own region. A third point is that political boundaries exist within the region even though the flow of the atmosphere does not recognize them. If covenants are made to remove international obstacles to control, so much the better, but one cannot always take workable covenants for granted.

As an aside, some notion of the relative contributions of various industrial regions to the outcome illustrated in figure 6-7 has been available by means of a mathematical model of the regional airflow (Reiquam, 1970). In the model, known sources were operated and typical windflow were simulated, producing a map similar to the one shown. Then sources in various subregions, such as the Midlands, were turned off, and the differences between results noted. Such a study would hardly be sufficiently definitive at present to form the basis for corrective action against one subregion rather than another, since the knowledge it represents is still thin. However, the time may not be too far off when similar methods may form the basis for regional social planning with respect to air quality.

The beginnings of such planning may already be appearing, as in the contents of table 6-1 from the Organization for Economic Cooperation and Development in Western Europe (SSM, 1977). The values in the table were most likely derived by means of mathematical models similar to the ones in Reiquam (1970). Although they are no doubt somewhat in error, they probably give the correct general state of affairs. Table 6-2 presents results obtained directly from the contents of table 6-1, in which the matter of pollution carried to a country from its neighbors is set forth. The United Kingdom is clearly upwind from nearly everyone, while Scandinavia is clearly downwind from nearly everyone. The correspondence between the variable representing national governments and the one representing pollutants and people is striking. From these same data in table 6-1 one may demonstrate intriguing results; for example, on the basis of the variable imported sulfur load per unit area, Scandinavia ranks lowest except for the United Kingdom (an artifact of the very nonuniform distribution of the small Scandinavian population over large areas). Another result illustrating the inherent complexity of dealing with transport of pollutants across international boundaries is that, while there is about a thirtyfold difference between the largest and smallest values in the last column of table 6-2, there is only about a threefold difference for the variable total sulfur load per capita. The irony, it seems, is that those who do not foul their own nests are fouled by others in an amount that reduces all to the same level of deterioration.

Atmospheric Interactions with Architecture and Urban Design

The familiar old city at the geographical heart of most European urban areas may have been planned in the sense that it contained a cultural center such as a

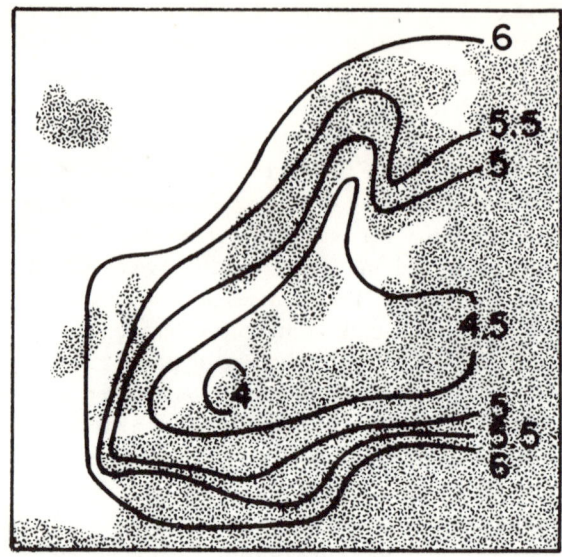

Source: After figure 4-4 of Stern et al. 1973. *Fundamentals of Air Pollution.* New York: Academic Press.

Note: Expressed as pH numbers in which 7.0 represents chemical neutrality and numbers less than 7.0 are increasingly acid.

Figure 6-7. Lines of Equal Average Acidity of Rainwater for 1965 in Northwestern Europe.

fort or a cathedral and that its site was selected for its commercial and military characteristics. But it was not planned in the modern sense in which a network of streets and other service arteries is designed all at once. As far as the impacts of weather and climate on the small-scale urban environments are concerned, the differences between old and new produce results worthy of comment. Likewise, these same differences may produce some notable results concerning the reverse: the effects of the city on the atmosphere.

One difference between old and new is in the general morphology of the street plans. The typical old city has narrow and winding streets that follow what were originally footpaths or animal trails, in turn probably dictated by topography. Furthermore, they often tend to have a concentric circular pattern, centered on the cultural hub. Such an urban area is unlikely to have windflow channeling in long, straight canyons, as newer parts of the city are. As a result of this more effective trapping of small pockets of airspace, humidity is usually higher among the buildings of an old city where vapor from fountains and kitchens enters the atmosphere. With narrow streets and only small courtyards, the extra trapping of sunlight mentioned earlier may not occur because these spaces, including the upper walls, are more often in shadow than if streets were

Table 6-1
Western European Countries as Emitters and Receivers of Airborne Sulfur Compounds

	Receivers									
	Austria	Belgium	Denmark	Federal Republic of Germany	Finland	France	The Netherlands	Norway	Sweden	Switzerland	United Kingdom
Austria	60	0	0	8	0	2	0	0	0	1	0
Belgium	6	100	1	60	2	40	10	4	7	2	8
Denmark	0	0	60	7	8	1	1	8	30	0	2
Federal Republic of Germany	40	20	6	700	10	50	10	10	30	7	10
Finland	0	0	0	0	100	0	0	1	10	0	0
France	20	30	3	100	4	600	10	9	10	20	20
The Netherlands	2	5	1	40	2	10	60	4	6	1	4
Norway	0	0	0	0	2	0	0	30	6	0	0
Sweden	0	0	2	2	30	0	0	9	100	0	0
Switzerland	5	0	0	7	0	6	0	0	0	30	0
United Kingdom	20	30	10	100	10	100	30	60	40	10	800
Area (10^4 km^2)	8.3	3.1	4.4	25.0	33.8	55.4	3.1	32.5	45.3	1.3	24.5
1977 population (millions)	7.5	9.9	5.1	61.6	4.8	53.3	13.8	4.0	8.3	6.3	56.0

Source: Pollution data are from the Organization for Economic Cooperation and Development for 1974 (SSM, 1977).
Note: Except for area and population, tabular values are in 10^3 tonnes of sulfur during 1974.

Table 6-2
Rank Orders for Two Variables Relating Air Pollution
Emitters and Receivers in Western Europe

Countries Adding More than 2 Percent of the Airborne Sulfur that the Country Emits to Itself		Imported Load of Airborne Sulfur per Population (10^3 tonnes/million)	
Rank	Country	Country	Load/Pop.
8a	Norway	Norway	26.3
8a	Sweden	Sweden	16.7
6	Switzerland	Finland	14.2
6	Austria	Austria	12.4
5	Finland	Belgium	8.6
4	Belgium	Switzerland	6.5
4	Federal Republic of Germany	Federal Republic of Germany	5.3
4	Denmark	Denmark	4.5
4	The Netherlands	The Netherlands	4.4
3	France	France	3.9
1b	United Kingdom	United Kingdom	0.8

Source: According to the Organization for Economic Cooperation and Development study in SSM, 1977.
aFor both Norway and Sweden, the exceptions are Austria and Switzerland.
bOnly France exports significant amounts of airborne sulfur to the United Kingdom.

wider and courtyards larger. The net results for temperature are a reduced range between day and night and between summer and winter. These results may be seen as advantages or disadvantages, depending on the overall climate. For example, maintenance of higher humidity and lower midday summer temperature would be a distinct advantage in a Mediterranean locality, but perhaps not so in a Scandinavian one.

Another difference between the older and the newer parts of cities is in the homogeneity of land use. Old cities are very limited in extent, as a rule, reflecting the compactness of the original urban settlements. With communication limited mainly to those within a short walking distance and with the need for proximity of the agricultural fields to the military defenses, land in the settlements was likely to be used exclusively for streets and roofed areas. Parks, ponds, and green areas were a waste of urban space. This is still evident in most old city sections. The point of this discussion is that there was a higher population density and a greater expanse of unrelieved urban surface, in the sense of the characteristics described earlier, such as granitelike materials and absence of water surfaces for evaporation.

The population was housed densely in buildings with thick walls, small windows, a small but usually uniform number of stories, and few large courtyards or wide streets. The relative absence of unroofed ground was probably due to the high premium placed on protected space in the city. The general morphology of the buildings was due to the limitations of technology. Walls were both membranes, as architects call the interface between interior and exterior spaces, and physical support for upper stories and roof. Modern buildings need not have these bearing walls but may have physical support by means of internal structural skeletons of beams and columns, with the membranes merely curtain walls made of various nonstructural materials. The skeletal materials and the means for hoisting them permit construction of large numbers of floors, whereas old buildings were usually limited to no more than half a dozen. Likewise, the need for a maximum amount of bearing capacity for each running foot of outer wall made small windows the rule.

Of course, there are many exceptions to these generalizations about unplanned old cities compared with planned new ones and about the land use patterns and architectural styles within each.

The concluding remarks connect the architectural descriptions of cities with the kinds of interactions between cities and the atmosphere discussed earlier. The air among closely packed buildings is likely to be more humid, less windy, and with less temperature variability than the air among more widely separated buildings. These are the same kinds of characteristics found in the air of a cave. The air inside these same thick-walled, small-windowed buildings is even more cavelike than outside. When walls are thick and windows small and tight, relatively small amounts of fuel are needed to maintain a comfortably constant temperature in cold weather. Finally, the volume contained per unit of surface area is largest in a cubical building (even larger in a sphere), where families share interior walls not exposed to heat gain and loss, and a single roof stands between the sky and several levels of occupants.

From the point of view of energy of operation, not to mention of construction, old buildings would seem to be preferable to tall, glass-walled skyscrapers with their huge dependence on heating and cooling technology. As the skylines of many Western European cities sprout isolated, multistoried cloud scratchers during times of increasing fuel shortages, questions must surely arise in the minds of urban planners about their products. Perhaps the older buildings are the better response to climate, even though for unrelated reasons.

Thermally, the large parks of European cities are truly rural. Chandler (1970)[8] has established that urban effects on temperature are essentially nil in the centers of vegetated areas approaching a kilometer in width or diameter. For both aesthetic and climatic reasons, then, large parks are a sensible design.

In the study by Oke (1973) Western European cities show an increase of about 2° Centigrade in the extreme of urban-rural temperature difference for every tenfold increase in population, beginning with a 4° Centigrade difference for a city of about 10,000. These extremes are found, as suggested, on calm, clear nights when the rural areas are cooling at a much more rapid rate than the urban areas. Extrapolation of Oke's data (figure 6-2) suggests that there would be no urban effect on temperature in a town of about 100. The same lower limit appears in Oke's data for North American cities, though the rate of increase in temperature with population is about half again as great. The reason for this greater rate is not clear. On three points, however, the difference between the two regions is what would be expected from these discussions. For one, the more compact architecture of European cities would permit the addition of many more people with less additional fuel consumption (which warms urban air). The smaller geographical extent of a city with high-density population would make the heat island smaller, and thus the center of the island would be nearer the upwind shoreline and exposed to winds that have been traveling over a shorter path of warming. The third reason for the result in Oke's data might be the greater use of vehicles with high rates of fuel consumption in American cities. Again, the goal of these discussions is not to make the reader an expert, but to demonstrate some of the dimensions of the complex interactions between urban areas and the atmosphere.

Very few urban residents have chosen to live in a city because of its more equable climate. Thus one may be tempted to ask, So what? about the foregoing discussion. Viewed from a larger, more continental perspective, however, these issues may be more clearly relevant to society. It has been suggested that an urban corridor, containing many cities strung out in a linear form, may be, for the atmosphere and its storms and motions, the thermodynamic equivalent of a low mountain range. Thus, as cities grow and merge, climatic features such as storm paths may be affected. The consequences may still be subtle for the distracted urban dweller, but even subtle interactions of cities and the atmosphere may have severe impacts yet unforeseen.

Notes

1. A widely and readily available discussion is in *Time*, 25 July 1977.

2. Early suggestions found in the European literature are in Schmauss (1927) and Berkes (1947). More extensive research on several North American cities suggests the same. See, for example, Huff and Changon (1973).

3. Perhaps it is fitting that mention of excess urban warmth makes many climatologists think of London, since the phenomenon was first described in detail by Howard (1818).

4. The thermal effect of a shopping mall was studied early by Landsberg (1970). The result was merged, as described in the text, by Oke in a review of urban climatology to be published as a Technical Note by the World Meteorological Organization, Geneva, probably in 1978. Thermal effects of another shopping mall are described in greater detail by Norwine (1973).

5. See also the many articles in *Journal of Applied Meteorology* 17 (May

1978) devoted to studies at St. Louis, Missouri-Illinois. In particular, Changnon (1978) restates the case for urban enhancement of thunder and lightning storms.

6. An early suggestion that effects may be found downwind was in Changnon (1963). As seen in Huff and Changnon (1973), urban effects on precipitation amounts are now generally thought of as being beyond, rather than in, the city.

7. The filth in the London air was soft coal dust in fireplace smoke combined with water droplets of fog, carried into human lungs. Called *pea soup* by Londoners, it became known later as *smog* (smoke and fog) for inexplicable reasons the term has been transferred to the mixture of products of sun-drenched automobile exhaust, which contains neither smoke nor fog.

8. Chandler (1970) makes a summary comment to this effect, based on his own research in England.

References

Ashworth, J.R. 1929. "The Influence of Smoke and Hot Gases from Factory Chimneys on Rainfall." *Quarterly Journal of the Royal Meteorological Society* 55:341-350.
Atkinson, B.W. 1970. "The Reality of the Urban Effect on Precipitation: A Case Study Approach." In *Urban Climates*. Geneva: World Meteorological Organization, Technical Note 108.
Bach, W. 1972. *Atmospheric Pollution*. New York: McGraw-Hill.
Berkes, Z. 1947. "A Csapadek Eloszlasa Budapest Teruleten." *Időjaras* 51:105-111.
Braham, R.R., Jr. 1974. "Cloud Physics of Urban Weather Modification." *Bulletin of the American Meteorological Society* 55:100-106.
Chandler, T.J. 1965. *The Climate of London*. Hutchinson.
_____. 1970. "Urban Climatology: Inventory and Prospect." In *Urban Climates*. Geneva: World Meteorological Organization, Technical Note 108.
Changnon, S.A., Jr. 1963. "A Climatological Evaluation of Precipitation Patterns over an Urban Area." In *Air over Cities*. Cincinnati, Ohio: U.S. Public Health Service, Publication SEC A62-5.
_____. 1978. Urban Effects on Severe Local Storms at St. Louis. *Journal of Applied Meteorology* 17:578-586.
Geiger, R. 1965. *The Climate Near the Ground*. 4th ed. Cambridge, Mass.: Harvard University Press.
Georgii, H.W. 1970. The Effects of Air Pollution on Urban Climates. In *Urban Climates*. Geneva: World Meteorological Organization, Technical Note 108.
Howard, L. 1818. *The Climate of London Deduced from Meteorological Observations Made in the Metropolis and at Various Places around It*. 2nd ed., 3 vols. Cornhill: Longman and Co.

Huff, F.A., and Changnon, S.A., Jr. 1972. "Climatological Assessment of Urban Effects on Precipitation at St. Louis." *Journal of Applied Meteorology* 11:823-842.

_____. 1973. "Precipitation Modification by Major Urban Areas." *Bulletin of the American Meteorological Society* 54:1220-1232.

Johnson, D.B. 1976. "Ultragiant Urban Aerosol Particles." *Science* 194:941-942.

Kratzer, A. 1937. *Das Stadtklima.* Braunschweig: Vieweg und Sohn.

Landsberg, H.E. 1970. "Micrometeorological Temperature Differentiation through Urbanization." In *Urban Climates.* Geneva: World Meteorological Organization, Technical Note 108.

_____. 1974. "Inadvertent Atmospheric Modification through Urbanization." In *Weather and Climate Modification,* New York: Wiley, pp. 726-763.

Lowry, W.P. 1969. *Weather and Life.* New York: Academic Press.

_____. 1977. "Empirical Estimation of Urban Effects on Climate: A Problem Analysis." *Journal of Applied Meteorology* 16:129-135.

METROMEX Update. 1976. *Bulletin of the American Meteorological Society* 57:304-308.

Norwine, J.R. 1973. "Heat Island Properties of an Enclosed Multi-level Suburban Shopping Center." *Bulletin of the American Meteorological Society* 54:637-641.

Oke, T.R. 1973. "City Size and the Urban Heat Island." *Atmospheric Environment* 7:769-779.

_____. 1974. *Review of Urban Climatology 1968-1973.* Geneva: World Meteorological Organization, Technical Note No. 134.

_____. n.d. *Review of Urban Climatology 1973-1976.* Department of Geography, University of British Columbia.

Reiquam, H. 1970. "Sulfur: Simulated Long-range Transport in the Atmosphere. *Science* 170:318-320.

SSM. 1977. "Exporting, Importing SO_2 Emissions." *Environmental Science and Technology* 11:1154.

Schmauss, A. 1927. Grosstädte und Niederschlag. *Meteor. Zeitschrift* 44:339-341.

Stern, A.C., Wohlers, H.C., Boubel, R.W., and Lowry, W.P. 1973. *Fundamentals of Air Pollution.* New York: Academic Press.

Time, 25 July 1977, p. 24.

7

The Quality of the Residential Environment: European Housing after World War II

Guido Francescato

To write of European housing is to a certain extent as rash and oversimplified as to write about any other historical, socioeconomic, or cultural phenomenon under the "European" label. The diversity and individuality of the people of Europe, so striking to an American observer, has not failed to be reflected in the man-made environment. In a more precise context one should perhaps speak of French housing or Swedish housing as having definitely different characteristics influenced by the particular conditions prevailing in each country. Indeed, even within the same country housing solutions in Europe have often responded to regional requirements and conditions to a greater extent than in other parts of the world.

Yet it is also undeniable that there are commonalities in the context of the European urban environment and of European housing. These commonalities have historical and cultural roots in various processes of human settlement and economic development (see for example, Braudel, 1976 for the preindustrial period, and Frampton, 1975 for an account of more recent conditions) and in the transformation, undergone by all West European countries between the eighteenth century and World War I, of the relationship between economic production and the city with the attendant rise of the capitalist-bourgeois state (for example, Sica, 1976).

On the foundation of these commonalities, tenuous as they may be in the case of some West European nations (Spain and Portugal, for instance, in Southern Europe or Finland in the North), World War II brought about a tragic sharing of destruction and, more importantly for my purposes, an upsurge of postwar investments in residential environments (and indeed in other domains of construction) that is quite certainly without precedent in recent history. Two phenomena are central to the understanding of this upsurge and of the housing situation that confronted most European countries at the end of World War II: the destruction of housing stock caused by the war (Pawley (1971) reports, for instance, that 2.5 million dwellings out of approximately 10 million were destroyed in Germany), and the urbanization pressures brought about by a great wave of rural migration to cities. The combined effect of these two phenomena resulted in a strong emphasis on the production of new houses. Housing needs were thought of mainly in quantitative terms, whatever qualitative considerations existed were either left to the esthetic preoccupations of architects or consisted in meeting basic, minimum standards of safety, health, and sanitation. In other words *the* problem of West European housing at the end of World War II was to build the greatest possible number of physical structures in the shortest possible time with limited resources. As a result of this emphasis on physical production, justified as it may have been under the circumstances, insufficient attention was paid to a most fundamental question: what kinds of residential environments were best suited for the postwar urban population of Europe? Three decades later the importance of this question concerning the *quality* of residential environments has emerged as a part of the more general debate on the quality of urban life in the industrialized world. On both sides of the Atlantic the social purposes of our interventions in the environment are being reassessed.

An intuitive understanding has emerged in all industrialized countries that not only the quantity but also the quality of housing is important to the well-being of the population. Recent research is beginning to provide empirical support for this intuitive notion. Campbell, Converse, and Rodgers (1976) found in a comprehensive study on the quality of American life that 88 percent of the respondents in a nationally representative sample considered housing to be either quite important, very important, or extremely important to their well-being. They also found that among twelve domains of life satisfaction housing ranked fourth in order of importance, being preceded only by family life, marriage, and financial situation.

Thus it appears legitimate to examine postwar European housing in regard to the question of the quality of residential environments. This housing is of interest because, as we shall see, it reflected the traditional predominance of a physical concept of urban planning and more specifically of an architectural concept of housing. The corollary of this architectural notion of housing (which was of course not entirely restricted to Europe) was that architects were qualified not only to design and build houses but also to formulate a theory of housing, or an intellectual framework in which the question of housing quality could be satisfactorily answered. In other words the assumption was that architects knew what the components of residential environmental quality were and they knew why a particular housing solution was appropriate in a particular situation. This was a rash assumption which has produced a great deal of confusion and has resulted in residential environments which often are not responsive to the quality criteria of the most interested party, namely the residents themselves.

This is obviously not the place to engage in a critique of architectural thought between the two World Wars. But it is worth noting that in the writing of the two best known propagandists of modern architecture, Le Corbusier and Walter Gropius, one finds constant references to buildings as objects possessed of intrinsic, absolute characteristics, which it was the task of modern architects to restore to the service of man by stripping away the overlays of ornament of "academic" or traditional architecture. "An object," Gropius wrote, "is defined by its nature." Translated into the housing that he advocated and designed, this meant that there were certain particular housing forms that by their own nature were appropriate to the life and activities of modern man. Hence, Gropius and his colleagues at the Bauhaus emphasized the problem of the *Existenz-minimum,* that is, the problem of designing rooms with the most concise spatial economy possible. As Argan (1951) has perceptively remarked, this search for a minimum standard was not aimed at responding to the users' requirements (which in themselves were thought to be only the product of traditional lifestyles, social conventions, and class prejudices), but rather was an attempt to impose an absolute and definitive rationality on the human environment where empirical utilitarianism and sensory gratification had prevailed. This approach represented a moral imperative, an ascetic view of man's needs in a world of bourgeois industrial capitalism. In this view, which paralleled Max Weber's and Ernst Troeltsch's ideas on the justification of capitalism, the bourgeois was seen as a believer in the limitlessness of the work ethic and in the principle that work is not directed at leisure and consumption but to continuous expansion of itself and of capital. It is worth keeping these views in mind when considering the architecture that emerged from them and comparing these visions of capitalist industrial society with the reality of the consumer ethic that has pervaded Europe and the rest of the industrialized world since the end of World War II.

The influence of Gropius and of the Bauhaus school of design on the architectural profession both in Germany and abroad was enormous. Although, as Pawley (1971) noted, the actual quantity of dwellings designed in Germany by these architects was a very small portion of the total housing effort of the Weimar republic, such *Siedlungen* (developments) as Siemensstadt in Berlin, begun in 1929 and designed by Gropius, Scharoun, Haring, Forbat, Bartning, and Hertlein, were widely admired by architects until well into the 1960s. The design of these developments was based on so called rational approaches which included uniform orientation (resulting in long lines of buildings bearing no relation to the street pattern), mass production and mass assembly (by crane, further emphasizing the linearity of building layout), the elimination of pitched roofs and of decorative features, and especially a startling sameness of form.

On the other side of the Rhine Le Corbusier (1921) was the architectural prophet who from the pages of *Esprit Nouveau* declared that "the home is a *machine for living:* baths, sun, warm water, cold water, temperature control, food refrigeration, hygiene, beauty of proportions." Unlike Gropius he had no opportunity to experiment on any large scale until after the end of World War II. So he drew up ambitious plans for entire cities in which, by taking advantage of modern construction techniques of steel and reinforced concrete, he proposed high-rise housing in long slabs, ribbons, or towers surrounded by parklike greenery and joined by elevated expressways. As Frampton (1975, p. 25) noted, "it was naively assumed ... that one simply could not suffer from a surfeit of the essential joys, namely sun, light, air, and green space." Le Corbusier was reacting in part to the overcrowding and lack of basic amenities that had often accompanied urban development in the industrial era. Nevertheless, as Banham (1960) has pointed out, Le Corbusier's visions, as well as those of other "functionalist" architects, were primarily aimed at generating an esthetic solution to the expression of the machine age. This purpose is also revealed by the direct translation of the esthetic vocabulary of such art movements as Futurism, De Stijl, and Cubism into architecture. That this esthetic vision was seen by the public as a private game played by architects for the benefit of other architects and art historians was ascribed by Le Corbusier (1930) merely to reactionary "academicism." It apparently never occurred to him that his esthetic vocabulary of flat roofs, buildings raised on *pilotis* (stilts), "streets in the sky," and exposed concrete sameness only relieved by an occasional splash of primary colors was simply too far removed from the forms traditionally associated in people's minds with the concept of home to be accepted as an appropriate residential environment. Nonetheless, like Gropius, Le Corbusier was enormously influential in the architectural world, as we shall see in some of the examples examined in this chapter.

Between the two World Wars and up to well into the 1960s the architectural profession was preoccupied with the notions of rationality and functionalism only to the extent that such notions could spark the generation of a new style. Moreover, architects did not seem to understand the implications of applying a new architectural style not only to churches, palaces, and other monuments, but also for the first time in history to the entire environment. In particular the new style was being applied to the one sector of the built environment, the homes of the populace, in which the pull of traditional forms, of the known, and of the experienced is the strongest. As a profession, architects did not explore the possibility that the function (the quality of "being used for certain purposes") of a building may not be a property of its form, but rather an attribute of the meaning read into that form by its user through a process of cultural coding tied both to experiences with other buildings and to expectations of what a building should be. Barthes (1970, p. 41) has pointed out that "as soon as there is a society, every usage is converted into a sign of itself." This statement calls attention to the notion that our ability to use an object repeatedly for a certain purpose (function) is tied to a communication process by which we recognize the meaning of that object in terms of the functions that it makes possible. As Eco (1968, p. 195) put it, "what permits us to use architecture ... is not only the functions that are actually possible in a building, but above all the meanings tied to those functions. These meanings predispose us to functional use."

The implications of a communication perspective of architecture for housing are important in conceptual and practical terms. From this perspective it is possible to hypothesize that the way people look upon housing, how they perceive housing, what kinds of associations they make with housing are important in defining the quality of the residential environment and their own satisfaction with it. Housing is thus not only shelter but also cultural artifacts by which "housing messages" (Becker, 1977) are exchanged.

It was not until the beginning of the 1960s that the architectural ideology of Gropius, Le Corbusier, and their followers started to be reappraised. As a result of many journalistic accounts of dissatisfaction in newly built housing developments, a number of research studies aimed at finding out the dimensions and criteria of housing quality *from the point of view of the residents,* were carried out initially in Sweden and in the United Kingdom and later in the other countries as well.

It is not the purpose of this chapter to review the literature dealing with these studies, many of which are individually not of a sufficient technical quality as to insure confidence in their findings. It is enough to note that, taken together, these studies suggest that residents' satisfaction with housing is a multidimensional concept that embraces both physical dimensions (such as the planning, design, and construction features of houses, open spaces, and roads) and nonphysical dimensions (such as personal characteristics of the residents, social patterns of associations and friendships, contacts with neighbors, and, where present, relations with management organizations).

Against this background it is of interest to examine a series of examples of housing built in several West European countries. In these examples some consequences of architectural ideologies in housing are apparent. Figure 7-1 shows a housing development built on the outskirts of Amsterdam, near Schiphol Airport, in the early 1970s. The buildings in this development are all exactly alike, constructed by assembly of prefabricated components in a repetitive manner based on the utilization of straightline traveling cranes. They are arranged in a green parklike setting in which pedestrian pathways are entirely separated from automobile traffic. Cars move on elevated roads that give direct access to parking garages connected to the apartment buildings by covered ramps (figure 7-2). The vertical circulation stacks of elevators and stairs are located at a considerable distance from each other (approximately 300 feet) and upon arriving to the appropriate floor, a tenant walks to his or her apartment along an outdoor walkway, a segment of which is visible in figure 7-3. These outdoor walkways are related both to Michael Brinkman's 1921 Spangen development in Rotterdam and to Le Corbusier's proposal for "streets in the sky," a device for vertical utilization of the space of the city. In Spangen, however, the buildings were only four stories in height and the walkways were wide enough to permit more functions than just circulation. Such activities as children's play, informal residents' encounters, and even door-to-door merchandising by produce and milk carts took place on those walkways (Grinberg, 1977). In the Schiphol development the streets in the sky are simply a narrow path between elevator and apartment door. Most other principles of Le Corbusier's ideology of housing

Figure 7-1. Le Corbusier's vision of high-rise buildings immersed in greenery is executed with monotonous grayness in this Dutch development.

Figure 7-2. Segregation of functions, one of the architectural tenets of the modern movement, is exemplified in the separation of parking and housing shown here. An elevated ramp connects the garage to the residential buildings.

Figure 7-3. The "street in the sky" reduced to a parody of the concept; a narrow corridor between elevator and apartment door.

(down to his preference for gray concrete) have been applied to the design and construction of this residential development, though not Gropius' insistence that long building slabs should be optimally oriented for maximum exposure to sunlight and therefore parallel to each other. The scale of this enormous complex, difficult though it is to appreciate it from the photographs, is also commensurate to that of Le Corbusier's plans for redesigning and rebuilding entire cities, as in his famous proposal for *La Ville Radieuse*.

Research has consistently shown that residents place great value on visual and auditory privacy, on the opportunities for personalization of the dwelling unit both inside and outside, on variety of shapes in buildings and landscape, on easy access to the ground and to their parked automobiles, on an enclosed piece of ground that one can call one's own, and on the small size of the development. But even a cursory look at the photographs shows that all these preferences have been violated in the Schiphol development. The amenities of open space, light, view, and modern conveniences are provided, but not a housing environment with which the residents can identify and which they can call home. There also is a definite lack of integration between homes and supporting service such as shops, schools, and recreation facilities: a sense of isolation pervades the entire site and the large empty spaces between buildings belong to no one and thus are likely to be not only useless for any particular purpose but also, as Newman (1975) suggested, dangerous from the point of view of crime occurrence. Even from a purely visual point of view it seems doubtful that the view of these open spaces from the apartment windows can be considered exciting since the landscaping appears to be quite unimaginative and there are no activities to watch as might occur in a more dense and varied environment. It can be said in summary that this development exhibits most of the dehumanizing characteristics that have been criticized in the architectural ideologies of Le Corbusier and Gropius without possessing the esthetic qualities that some housing proposed and built by these two architects did achieve.

Although the example examined above is perhaps more striking than others because of its sheer size, it is by no means unique in various European countries. More or less objectionable and more or less successful developments embodying these principles have been built everywhere. For instance, the well known Park Hill estate in Sheffield, which has received great acclaim (mostly by architects and art historians) as well as great criticism (mostly by sociologists and by residents) but which to my knowledge has not yet been subjected to any kind of rigorous research, is another example based on principles similar to those of the Dutch development just considered. Park Hill, however, is a more sophisticated attempt at responding to certain human needs. For instance, the streets in the sky are wider and are not interrupted at the end of each building but continue by means of bridges into the next building thus providing, in theory at least, a lesser need for persons visiting neighbors in the immediate community to use the vertical circulation systems.

Figure 7-4 shows a partial view of another large British development, the Aylesbury Road Estate in the London Borough of Southwark, which was built to replace part of an old working class neighborhood of row houses. Again, the architectural principles previously discussed were used as a basis for the design of this development, including the separation of vehicular and pedestrian circulation which resulted in parking garages and elevated walkways. Although the larger spaces between buildings free up more area than was available in the old neighborhood for the play of older children, Newman (1975, p. 66) points out that "the children still do most of their playing in the neighboring streets, and residents will not park their cars in the provided elevated garages because of vandalism and theft." The elevated walkways are so designed that they provide dark tunnels offering opportunities for assaults and muggings (figure 7-5). The contrast between the old neighborhood (in part still intact) and the new development is visible in figure 7-6. As Newman (1975) noted, not only is as much street parking provided in the old neighborhood as in the new estate, but both are actually built at the same density of thirty-six dwelling units per acre. Even a cursory visit to the site, moreover, points to other advantages of the old versus the new. For instance, the old row houses provide private backyards and a semiprivate "stoop area" in front of each house. Residents identify with their own house through the typical London device of painting doors, lintels, and window trim in a different color for each house. One would expect the plumbing and heating systems to be better in the new development than in the older neighborhood, but apart from this it seems apparent that the quality of the new environment is much less satisfactory overall.

In Antonioni's film *The Passenger* Maria Schneider, playing the part of an architectural student, appears briefly in the "courtyard" of the Lurnock Street Estate, a housing development also located in London (figure 7-7). The significance of her appearance to our discourse is that she is seen later in the film visiting other buildings of extraordinary architectural interest such as some of Gaudi's masterworks in Barcelona, thus establishing the claim to architectural fame of this development. The Lurnock Street Estate with its highly photogenic alternations of reinforced concrete rhythms and projecting glass enclosed balconies (figure 7-8) clearly represents an attempt at bringing a measure of visual excitement and interest to the design of a residential environment. In many other ways it seems to be an improvement over the two examples considered previously in this chapter. For instance, though still a rather large building (actually two parallel buildings approximately one block long enclosing a courtyard), it is not as overwhelming in size as the previous examples. Rather than respecting Le Corbusier's canons of splendid isolation in the midst of greenery or Gropius' insistence on optimal orientation, the buildings border on and parallel existing city streets, one of which is the site of a thriving open-air vegetable market. Continuity with the urban fabric of the surrounding neighborhood was obviously sought by the designers to the extent that space for a small

European Housing after World War II 113

Figure 7-4. The Aylesbury Road Estate in Southwark, England, was built to replace an old neighborhood of row houses. In this case, the new does not appear to have improved upon the old.

Figure 7-5. Not many would want to walk home after dark through this tunnel in the elevated walkway system of the Aylesbury Road Estate.

European Housing after World War II

Figure 7-6. In spite of the noticeable difference in scale, both the old and the new neighborhood are built at the same density.

Figure 7-7. The beginning of a reaction to functional segregation: a shopping center designed right into a British housing development.

European Housing after World War II 117

Figure 7-8. The architectural treatment of this development can be seen as an attempt to introduce variety and complexity in the building facade.

but diversified shopping center was provided at the courtyard level. This is not only a convenience for the residents of the development and the neighborhood but also tends in theory at least to break the sterility of a residential-only use in the middle of an urban area of mixed use. In practice, however, the effectiveness of this feature is lessened by the fact that the courtyard is elevated above street level and has to be reached by climbing a long flight of stairs (partially visible in figure 7-9). The monotony of the architectural solution (the same "greenhouse" feature is endlessly repeated along the building facades) underscores a basic difficulty in coming to grips with the tenants' desire for visual interest and variety that has often been brought out by research on residents' satisfaction. The monumentality of the design and the choice of exposed grey concrete as a surface material clearly do not convey a "home" message (see for example the stadiumlike structural members framing one entrance into the courtyard in figure 7-9). Further consideration of figure 7-8 reveals that visual privacy in the glass-enclosed balconies (which actually are not greenhouses but parts of the living rooms) is very difficult to achieve. Even the concrete fin separating two contiguous dwelling units between the open part of the balconies is not extended sufficiently far to the face of the building to constitute a privacy screen between apartments. The staggered back configuration of the building also militates against visual privacy between apartments located on different floors.

A recently built housing development in Stockholm seems to have been based on the same general concept of a central courtyard flanked by buildings parallel to the street but appears more successful in achieving a residential environment responsive to tenants' desires and expectations. Just about the only vestige of prewar architectural theories that can be identified in this development is the pedestrian bridge over a busy boulevard connecting the housing area with a parking garage (figure 7-10). The disadvantages of this arrangement, perhaps an inevitable one in the relatively high density situation of Stockholm's central city, are reduced by the fact that the development is located exactly over a station of Stockholm's efficient, clean, and rapid subway system, the entrance to which is visible in figure 7-11. The commercial signs visible in this illustration belong to various stores and services located this time on the ground floor of the building and easily accessible by both residents of the housing complex and other passersby. This ground floor shopping center is illuminated at a number of points by large skylights such as are shown in figure 7-12. The thoughtfulness of the designers is particularly apparent in this illustration, for the area shown is actually a noncommercial service, provided by the development management—a rest area in which both residents and shoppers can relax and read free newspapers. The roof of this shopping concourse is a semiprivate level, mostly devoted to playgrounds and tot-lots (figure 7-13). From the provision of deeply recessed, more private balconies and the partial use of brick of the same color as that used in surrounding buildings, to the attempts at introducing visual variety

European Housing after World War II 119

Figure 7-9. In spite of the designers' intentions, it is doubtful that this type of architectural treatment conveys a "home" message.

Figure 7-10. In reaction against another tenet of the modern movement, this Swedish development reinstates the continuity of the street by bringing the new buildings up to the plane of the older building facades.

Figure 7-11. Shopping center and subway stop are integrated into this housing development.

Figure 7-12. A pleasant rest area for shoppers and residents alike.

European Housing after World War II

Figure 7-13. As shown by this Swedish example, it is possible to provide open space and play areas without creating expanses of landscaped emptiness.

by means of different surface material, fenestration, and different building height, this development shows great concern for the residents and great disregard of the architectural dogma criticized earlier in this paper.

Much the same characteristics can be found in the Lillington Street Estate, another development located in Westminster, London, shown in figures 7-14 and 7-15. In this housing scheme there is an even greater variety of apartment types, some of which are basically row houses, and some the more typical London "flat." Cars for the rowhouse residents are actually parked in carports by the door (figure 7-16), a clear anathema in Le Corbusier's thinking; the rest are parked in an underground garage (a solution which is both expensive and disliked by residents). A sympathetic attempt was even made to relate the development visually to an interesting church building that existed on the site by "wrapping" the housing around the church (figure 7-17), while more mundane needs were catered to by designing two pubs right into the development (figure 7-18).

These few examples cannot be considered representative in a statistical sense of the housing built in Europe after World War II. Nevertheless, all but the last two seem to be typical of a response to housing needs that naively assumed a particular architectural ideology embodied the solution to the housing requirements of the postindustrial world. These examples reveal that a discrepancy exists between the orderly architectural visions of the 1920s and 1930s and the realities of a world that is much more complex (and more puzzling) than those visions had led us to believe. In such a world, ideological approaches (whether architecturally based or otherwise) are losing ground to more pragmatic and responsive solutions.

There seem to be two avenues, neither exempt from potential pitfalls, through which higher quality can be achieved in urban residential environments. The first involves a greater participation of the residents themselves (or at least of the future residents) in the process by which decisions about housing are made. Becker (1977) has discussed some of the advantages and disadvantages inherent in this approach. Although it is probable that some of the worst mistakes made in housing might have been avoided with greater residents' participation in decision making, it is nevertheless clear that participation is at best a long and difficult process that is not too well suited to the kind of complex political organizations that West European nations have evolved. Even in countries with a long tradition of participatory democracy (such as Switzerland) it may be too cumbersome in practical terms to approach problems of environmental quality on the basis of citizen participation.

The second avenue through which higher housing quality may be achieved is based on a much more widespread use of scientific research into residents' perceptions and particularly into residents' satisfaction with a variety of residential options. Whereas research studies of this kind have not yet become commonplace, results from these investigations have shown that many of the

Figure 7-14. A concern for variety and relatively intimate scale is evident in the Lillington Street Estate, a development located in Westminster, England.

Figure 7-15. Pleasant and easily supervised open spaces are created in the open courts of the Lillington Street Estate.

Figure 7-16. A solution to the parking problem which permits easy access to one's dwelling and offers security from vandalism and theft.

features commonly found in urban residential environments are not liked by the residents. People tend to prefer a housing environment that is not overwhelming in scale, is designed with a certain amount of respect for local traditional forms (including, in some areas, the pitched roof so hated by the "functionalist" ideologues), permits a certain amount of privacy and control over one's immediate environment, affords some appropriate place for the play of children and the recreation of adults, and allows the use of an automobile up to one's door. Figures 7-19 and 7-20 showing a housing development near Amsterdam demonstrate that these qualities can be achieved by very simple means, and that where the size of the development is relatively small, even sameness of design does not seem to be particularly objectionable.

Because of the focus of this paper, the nonphysical aspects of housing have been mentioned only in connection with particular planning or design features. However, as noted earlier, research in residential satisfaction suggests that the social and managerial (or organizational) aspects of residential environments are also importantly associated with environmental quality.

The challenge that now faces European societies (and those of other industrialized nations) is to respond to the popular expectation for environmental quality in the face of escalating land and construction costs and diminishing economic strength. Surely, one answer lies in a new attitude that is emerging in various parts of the industrialized world: that of conserving and

Figure 7-17. An old church is visually related to the new development by using similar materials and by orienting the housing so that it wraps around the older building.

Figure 7-18. Pubs are an integral part of the Lillington Street Estate.

Figure 7-19. Small scale, simple means, and respect for traditional forms are in evidence in this successful Dutch development.

European Housing after World War II 131

Figure 7-20. Repetition is not objectionable if the size of the development is small.

Figure 7-21. A restored warehouse in Amsterdam captures some of the qualities people value, albeit at a price not all can afford.

Figure 7-22. A permanently moored boat converted into a house represents another way in which enterprising Amsterdam dwellers have achieved some of the amenities offered by restoration without incurring its high cost.

rehabilitating existing housing stock rather than levelling to the ground the old "decrepit" neighborhoods. Some of the environmental attributes people are looking for can be found in rehabilitated old structures, such as the restored Amsterdam warehouse (now an apartment building) shown in figure 7-21 or even in the gaily painted, permanently moored "houseboat" found in one of Amsterdam's canals (figure 7-22).

But, beyond conservation and restoration, whatever new housing is built should be designed on the basis of empirically derived understanding of the residents' likes and dislikes rather than on the basis of ideologies and abstract visions. This should not be interpreted as a plea for the introduction of mediocrity and mass taste in the architectural design of housing. On the contrary, it should be understood as an opportunity for designers to participate in the generation of social order in an area—that of housing—which really matters.

References

Argan, G.C. 1951. *Walter Gropius e la Bauhaus.* Turin: Einaudi.
Banham, R. 1960. *Theory and Design in the First Machine Age.* New York: Praeger.
Barthes, R. 1970. *Writing Degree Zero and Elements of Semiology.* Boston: Beacon Press.
Becker, F.D. 1977. *Housing Messages.* Stroudsburg, Pa.: Dowden, Hutchinson & Ross.
Braudel, F. 1976. *The Mediterranean and the Mediterranean World in the Age of Philip II.* New York: Harper & Row.
Campbell, A., Converse, P.E., and Rodgers, W.L. 1976. *The Quality of American Life.* New York: Russell Sage Foundation.
Eco, U. 1968. *La Struttura Assente.* Milan: Bompiani.
Frampton, K. 1975. "The Evolution of Housing Concepts 1870-1970." *Lotus International 10,* vol. 2.
Grinberg, D.I. 1977. *Housing in the Netherlands 1900-1940.* Delft: Delft University Press.
Le Corbusier (Jeanneret, C.E.). 1921. "Des Yeux qui ne Voyent pas." *Esprit Nouveau 8.*
_____. 1930. *Précisions.* Paris: Crès & Cie.
Newman, O. 1975. *Design Guidelines for Creating Defensible Space.* Washington, D.C.: U.S. Government Printing Office.
Pawley, M. 1971. *Architecture versus Housing.* New York: Praeger.
Sica, P. 1976. *Storia dell' Urbanistica.* Rome: Laterza.

8 Milan and Public Housing Policy: A Case of Municipal Initiative

Alberta Mary Sbragia

Political scientists have often assumed in discussing Western European political systems that municipal governments act as agents of central government. Even the governments of major cities have not usually been thought to exercise much discretion or initiative in matters of public policy. Their policies, when cities are recognized as having any policies at all, are assumed to reflect the preferences of national government. But is this assumption valid? This chapter argues on the basis of a case study of Italian public housing policy that it may not always be so—that under certain conditions cities can exercise a considerable, though not complete, autonomy in policymaking, even in nominally centralized political systems. The study draws this conclusion from a comparison of, on the one hand, public housing programs formulated and implemented by the Italian national government between 1949 and 1971 and, on the other, municipal public housing programs and objectives in the city of Milan during that same period.[1]

First, this chapter will consider how the changing Italian political environment has historically been related to the evolution of Italian public housing policy. Second, the chapter will compare public housing policy at the national level with that in Milan for the period 1949-71. Third, the limits on municipal autonomy and the limits that are likely to exist in the future will be considered.

Public housing policy in Italy has been strongly influenced by the changes which the Italian political system has undergone since the establishment of the Italian state.[2] The principles behind the first national housing law passed in 1903 were accepted by all governments under the parliamentary system which perished with the seizure of power by Mussolini. That law, known as the Luzzati Law after its sponsor, was the first to provide for the investment of private capital in public housing. It authorized banks to invest their deposits in the public housing sector (Conosciani et al., 1969, pp. 30-31). Crudely stated, investing in public housing was promoted as good business for institutions such as banks.

Further, the Luzzati Law authorized the establishment of local agencies to build and administer housing for low-income groups. Reflecting the political preferences of the tiny oligarchy represented by the national government,[3] the

---

I wish to thank Mary Lenn Miller and Martin Staniland for their thoughtful comments on an earlier draft of this paper. I am also grateful to Michael Romanos and to the reviewers for their helpful suggestions.

law did not delegate the responsibility for public housing to municipal governments, as the Socialists, notably, wished. Rather, the law called for the establishment of autonomous local agencies, which would be more insulated than municipal governments from popular demands, to build and administer housing for low-income groups. Such housing was only to be rented and would not be sold, even to sitting tenants. In accordance with their function as agencies of investment the Autonomous Institutes for Public Housing (or IACPs, as the agencies were called) depended on bank loans to finance construction. The institutes were in fact designed to reconcile and integrate public and private initiatives in the public housing arena, thereby hopefully destroying the idea that public housing should be the concern solely of public authorities (Istituto Autonomo per le Case Popolari, 1972, pp. 99-113).

In addition to authorizing the use of bank loans by the Institutes, the Luzzati Law offered the IACPs national government financing in the form of interest subsidies. That is, national government funds were only to be used to help pay the interest on bank loans taken out by the Institutes. A major modification to the law was introduced by the Unified Text passed in 1919. The Unified Text authorized the allocation of capital grants to various builders of publicly financed housing, the IACPs among them. After 1919 both capital grants and interest subsidies were available to the IACPs; a framework for public housing policy in Italy had been established which still influences government action in many respects.

In the case of Milan the Autonomous Institute for Public Housing in Milan (IACPM) was officially established in May, 1908. It was an autonomous body to which the city contributed funds and the housing which it had already built. In addition, banks contributed to the Institute's endowment.

At the end of World War I a critical housing shortage developed in the city. Demobilization and increased migration from the countryside led to greater pressure on the housing stock along with demands for new construction. In order to provide a remedy the city in 1919 decided to fund four public housing projects to provide 615 units. The IACPM built them, but the expenses were completely paid by the city. The city administration at this time was controlled by the Socialists, and they provided funds for these projects despite the fact that the city budget showed a deficit due to the amount of public assistance the city had provided for its residents during the war. The deficit was larger than it needed to have been, however, because the central government frequently excluded Socialist-controlled cities from receipt of various types of aid and subsidies. The financial situation became even more difficult when in the period immediately before the establishment of Fascist control the local banks stopped lending to the city the money it required (whether out of prudence or out of a wish to help the Fascists). The provision of public housing in the face of a budgetary deficit and the concern for low-income groups which it reflected were not long-lived, for the new Fascist city government had ideas very different from those of its predecessor about the role of public housing (Chiumeo, 1972, p. 151).

In this respect and in many others the Fascist government set up in 1922 represented a radical change in Italian politics. Fascist policy towards publicly financed housing in general, and low-cost housing in particular, was linked to the regime's strategy for building up political support from the middle and lower middle classes. In spite of antimigration laws aimed at stopping further urbanization, migrants kept flocking to cities in an effort to escape from worsening rural conditions and the demands for housing increased accordingly. Under the Fascists, however, the beneficiaries of publicly financed housing were not those who most needed it: migrants, in fact, were often forcibly returned to their hometowns, while public funds were used to build housing for the middle class.

Fascist legislation made the public housing sector serve a predominantly middle class clientele, and the needs of lower-income groups were increasingly ignored.[4] It emphasized the sale (rather than the renting) of publicly financed housing; it provided for the building of luxury rental units; and it created in 1924 a housing program called INCIS for predominantly middle class state employees. To provide housing for the middle class the Fascist government gradually transformed the IACPs from organizations primarily responsible for providing low-cost housing into agencies concerned with constructing high-quality publicly financed housing.

First, legislation passed in 1923 authorized the IACPs to set up another, legally separate body (the Institute for Economic Housing) to build high-quality housing which would be sold rather than rented (Chiumeo, 1972, p. 161). "Economic housing," as this higher-quality accommodation was called, was more expensive than "popular housing," the term for low-cost accommodation. Secondly, in 1926, Law Number 386 authorized the IACPs themselves to build "economic housing." Thus the IACPs were empowered to build lodging of a higher quality than was considered suitable for working-class families. The same law also appropriated funds for the construction by the IACPs and INCIS of housing for sale. Significantly, the funding provided was in the form of a capital grant which would pay for 20 percent of construction costs. By contrast, lodgings built by the IACPs for renting and intended for lower-income groups received only interest subsidies.

Thus both INCIS and the "commercial" program of the institutes used two kinds of approved financing. They could raise loans and they could exploit government capital grants to pay for some of the costs of construction. The latter means was obviously preferable from their point of view, since less money would have to be borrowed (and therefore less interest would be paid). *Rental* housing built by the institutes, however, could be paid for only by borrowing, and the greater costs involved in this method of financing were only partially offset by government interest subsidies. The remainder, made up of repayment of the principal plus interest charges not covered by subsidies, were passed on to the tenants in the form of higher rents. In sum, under Fascist housing policy, those in the market for high-quality housing benefited from the provision of government capital grants, while the building of low-cost housing remained dependent on costly bank loans. High-quality housing was therefore subsidized more generously than low-cost housing (Conosciani et al., 1969, p. 46).

In Milan the city's housing policy during the Fascist period reflected the attitudes of the national government. Of the twenty-two schemes built between 1926 and 1931, thirteen consisted of housing for sale and in the rest the rental units were generally too expensive for low-income families.[5] Using the provision for government capital grants under Law Number 386, the IACPM, with the cooperation of local banks and the city administration, was able to build eight estates of "economic housing," as well as several estates of somewhat more modest housing. The latter were part of the government's effort to encourage homeownership by the lower middle class. The only accommodation built for low-income families was that provided as temporary quarters for those previously inhabiting the shantytowns around Milan. Since their residents were officially expected, somehow, to move into regular institute housing (housing which, of course, they could not afford), these low-cost houses were built very cheaply and in fact came to be known as "minimal houses" (Ufficio Statistica, 1971, pp. 5-7).

In addition, the IACPM built "economic housing" for various categories of salaried workers such as city employees. The general policy was not one of adding to the institute's own rental housing stock but rather one of constructing homes which could be sold. In fact, it was feared that if the institute became too important a property owner, it would play too large a role in the housing market and thereby pose a threat to the development of private housing (Chiumeo, 1972, pp. 165-66).

The Fascist regime, then, used publicly financed housing to bolster its support among those classes which were potentially or actually friendly to the regime. The needs of low-income families were downgraded in favor of serving the more affluent. It was not until the end of World War II that the assumptions and objectives of public housing policy were at least partially changed.

However, Italian housing policy after the war did keep many of the features of Fascist legislation, though it also embodied major innovations. The postwar period thus saw the creation of a partly old, partly new housing policy system.

Public Housing Policy after World War II

Government in Italy since World War II has been conducted under a liberal democratic regime, generally dominated by the Christian Democratic party. The country has experienced an economic boom which has transformed an agrarian nation into an industrial power. High rates of economic growth, coupled with continuous rural-urban migration, characterized the 1950s and 1960s. Urban population increased dramatically, due particularly to the migration of peasants from Southern Italy into northern, industrialized cities, where they encountered unfamiliar life-styles and values.

The Christian Democrats maintained and consolidated their power during this period through the creation of an extensive system of patronage and clientelism. They saw the Italian Communist party both as their major political rival and as a threat to the liberal democratic regime established after World War II.

Until 1963, when the Socialist party entered the governing coalition (the so-called "opening to the left"), public housing policy naturally reflected the preferences of the Christian Democratic party. After 1963 the center-left coalition, when discussing public housing, used different symbols and rhetoric from those deployed by the centrist coalitions. In practice, however, the system of patronage and the bureaucratic inefficiency to which patronage contributed generally prevented significant changes in the character and impact of policy. Public housing was not a major priority for either the various centrist coalitions in the 1950s or the center-left coalitions in the 1960s, and the deficiencies of policy in that area reflected this lack of priority and political commitment.

During the immediate postwar period the concern for reconstruction after the damages of war dominated the political agenda. Legislation was passed to meet specific problems falling under the rubric of reconstruction, but no coherent public housing policy was forthcoming. By 1949 the concern with reconstruction had declined, and the government began to formulate the housing policy which was to last nearly thirty years.

Two types of legislation set up the basic outlines of public housing policy: (1) legislation following the principles of the Fascist regime as codified in the Unified Text of 1938—that is, the use of capital grants was limited to housing intended either for the relatively privileged or for the destitute victims of natural disasters (Conosciani et al., 1969, p. 56); and (2) legislation which departed significantly from these principles.

In the first category the principal law passed was the Tupini Plan approved in 1949. The Tupini Plan appropriated interest subsidies for low-cost housing; these subsidies were placed under the jurisdiction of the Ministry of Public Works which allocated them to each individual IACP. In the same category is the Romita Law (passed in 1954) which dealt with housing for the destitute. This law, however, was somewhat innovative in that it provided capital grants not only for the rehousing of victims of natural disasters but also for the rehousing of destitute families living in shacks, caves, and other unhealthy places. Romita thus enlarged the definition of destitute; nonetheless, housing for nondestitute low-income families was to receive interest subsidies only. The Tupini Plan and the Romita Law were the two major pieces of postwar legislation which incorporated the idea that low-income families should be assisted primarily by interest subsidies rather than capital grants.

In the second category the major departure from the Unified Text of 1938 was the establishment of the INA-Casa program in 1949. INA-Casa became the single most important public housing program. Between 1951 and 1961 it accounted for approximately 42 percent of all the funds spent on publicly financed housing (Conosciani et al., 1969, p. 115). Ironically, however, its primary concern was to increase employment rather than to fulfill housing needs.[6] Established not because national policymakers were primarily concerned about the severe national housing shortage but rather because housing was a sector in which it was thought unskilled and semiskilled labor could be readily employed, INA-Casa was nevertheless given control over most of the funds designated by the national government for publicly built housing. Other housing programs, while expressly concerned with housing (and administered by the Ministry of Public Works), were smaller in scope and the size of their respective budgets never approached that of INA-Casa's budget. For example, in the years 1951-65, the Ministry of Public Works allocated roughly 30 billion lira to the IACPs in the form of interest subsidies (Conosciani et al., 1969, p. 126). During that period INA-Casa and its successor Gescal spent roughly 800 billion lira (Conosciani et al., 1969, p. 115). The INA-Casa program therefore dominated the field of low-cost housing in the 1950s.

INA-Casa differed significantly from the Ministry of Public Works in the way it spent its funds. INA-Casa's large budget, the size of which was due to the earmarked taxes that supported the program, allowed the agency to use capital grants to fund its low-cost housing. The use of such grants was an important departure from previous as well as from other ongoing low-cost housing programs.

Since INA-Casa housing was funded by capital grants, it was much cheaper for tenants or buyers than public housing built under other national programs such as the Tupini Plan. Rent monies for INA-Casa needed only to cover administrative and operating costs, while other programs had to levy rents high enough to permit repayment of the principal that had been borrowed as well as the portion of the interest charges not covered by the ministry's interest subsidy. Thus INA-Casa housing was cheaper to occupy than low-cost housing built under other programs. The use of capital grants in the INA-Casa program could have had significant implications for low-cost housing generally—INA-Casa could have become an important source of housing for families with very low incomes.

INA-Casa's potential, however, was not to be fully realized. The program, as established by statute, was not intended for the unemployed poor, and this restriction limited the program's potential for improving the housing situation of lower-income families as a whole. Nonetheless, in the early years of the program emphasis was given to providing housing for those who, while employed, received such modest incomes that they could not find adequate housing in the private housing market (Parenti, 1967, pp. 41, 45).

However, two elements gradually limited the access of the neediest, badly housed wage earners to INA-Casa housing: legislative provisions limiting the proportion of INA-Casa housing units that were to be rented rather than sold, and resentment on the part of natives within various cities (especially cities in Northern Italy) against the allocation of housing to recently arrived migrants (who were usually from Southern Italy).

First, statutory provisions, by specifying the maximum proportion of INA-Casa units which could be rented, limited the availability of INA-Casa housing for lower-income families. The legislation establishing INA-Casa stipulated that in the first seven-year period of the program half the lodgings were to be sold and half were to be rented. In the second seven-year period ownership was emphasized even more: two-thirds of the constructed lodgings were to be sold. In addition, one-fourth of the funds were to be used to construct housing sold to those who could afford a down payment to buy their home in a shorter time span. In 1958 the proportion of funds to be spent on houses requiring a down payment was increased from one-fourth to one-third (Parenti, 1967, pp. 41-43). Thus low-income families were hurt by the weight given to homeownership in the INA-Casa program.

The emphasis on ownership made less housing available for lower-income families who either could not meet the higher payment levels usually involved or could not afford to be burdened by the maintenance problems of property. INA-Casa's increasingly strong orientation toward ownership was an important deviation from the spirit that had animated INA-Casa in its first years, a spirit which had sought to give housing to those among the employed who most needed it.

The increased emphasis on ownership reflected the Christian Democrats' concern about the challenge from the Communist party. It was believed that homeowners would be less susceptible than tenants to the electoral appeal of the Communists. Thus, public housing policy gradually began to concentrate on assisting potential homeowners rather than dealing directly with the needs of low-income families. Along these lines in 1959 Togni, a right wing Christian Democratic minister of public works, sponsored legislation which authorized public housing tenants to buy their dwellings at prices far below market value (Associazione Nazionale, 1971). This one-time subsidy to tenants was an attack on the idea of a public housing stock owned and administered by a public body. Some cities indeed saw their public housing stock badly depleted; Messina, for example, had so much housing bought that Parliament later had to appropriate funds so that Messina could "reconstruct" (Conosciani et al., 1969, p. 75). In general, then, the Christian Democrats saw public housing policy as an opportunity to mobilize political support and to weaken (or at least to stabilize) support for the Communist party—they thus encouraged homeownership.

The lowest-income families among the employed gradually found access to even the INA-Casa rental housing that was available more and more restricted. At first INA-Casa gave priority to those who were living in the most precarious housing conditions—these often being migrants recently come to the city. Such migrants usually had the lowest incomes and lived in the worst private housing. However, those families who had lived in a certain area longer than recently arrived migrant families had much less chance of being assigned a lodging even if they too lived in bad conditions, since usually their incomes would be higher than those of recent migrants and their housing conditions would be somewhat better.

Protests were made regarding this type of unintentional discrimination against long-term residents. By 1957 the criteria used in assigning INA-Casa housing had evolved so that three factors were weighted most heavily: the applicant's need for lodging, the length of time he had worked in the area in which lodging was being sought (the longer the better), and his family size (Parenti, 1967, p. 46). In this way the poorest, who usually had only recently arrived in the city, were often denied INA-Casa housing, which instead was allocated to families that, while also of modest means, were not as far down the income scale but were long-term residents. Thus, both the emphasis on ownership and on length of residence tended to exclude families with very low incomes from INA-Casa housing.

Since housing rather than unemployment began to be seen as a problem, the INA-Casa program's organizational structure was modified and the program in 1963 was renamed Gescal. Housing and not employment was designated as the new program's chief concern. Gescal thus was the major national housing program for the 1960s. Its activities, however, came under severe criticism. Its procedures were incredibly long and bureaucratic and it invested its funds rather than using them to build public housing.

The problem was that Gescal did not build much public housing. It was true that INA-Casa had been irregular in its construction activity; for example, it built only 7,200 dwellings in 1957 but 48,700 in 1960 (Conosciani et al., 1969, p. 105). It was also true that the percentage of total housing starts represented by INA-Casa had steadily declined due to the boom of private housing construction in the 1950s and the 1960s. (In 1951, INA-Casa housing represented 18 percent of all new housing, but this figure had fallen to 5 percent by 1962 (Conosciani et al., 1969, p. 126). Nonetheless, as an agency INA-Casa had at least been visible: between 1951 and 1960 it constructed an average of 23,000 lodgings annually. Gescal, however, built so little housing that it might almost be seen as moribund. For example, in 1963 Gescal constructed 9,000 dwellings, in 1964 the number fell to 5,000, and in 1965 the number rose slightly to 6,900 (Conosciani et al., 1969, p. 105). Whereas INA-Casa built a total of about 300,000 housing units, Gescal by 1972 had built roughly 60,000 units. As a national housing program, Gescal was a disastrous failure.

While Gescal did not build, it did invest. The importance of Gescal funds (estimated at almost $1.5 billion deposited in various banks and other investment institutions) was dramatized when Parliament began considering various proposals to reform Gescal. The minister of the Treasury, stating that to subtract present and future Gescal monies from the banking and investment cycle would have the effect of a deflationary economic policy, threatened to resign. The Bank of Italy insisted on its prerogative of controlling the financial maneuvers of Gescal (De Lucia, 1971, pp. 10-11). Gescal in fact was more important in the arena of macroeconomic management than in that of public housing.

Thus, Gescal funds were used for investments rather than for building public housing. Gescal was more important to the housing policy system for what it did not do than for what it did do; it came to be a symbol of central government inefficiency and the distorted use of public funds. In fact it came to symbolize a certain manner of administering public monies, a manner which benefited the private sector and excluded the supposed beneficiaries.

In sum, neither INA-Casa nor Gescal made much headway in resolving the chronic Italian housing shortage. Both programs were plagued by inefficiency, corruption, and long bureaucratic procedures that kept the programs from accomplishing what they might have. Perhaps even more importantly, the national political agenda simply never gave public housing high priority as an issue area. The result has been that Italy, since World War II, has had an extremely ineffective national public housing policy.

Milan

Against this background of an essentially inactive public housing program, Milan's public housing policy stood out by 1971 as quite different. More concerned with lower-income groups than was the national government, policy-makers in Milan were also more active in building public housing and in introducing technological innovations to the public housing sector. In the period after World War II Milan essentially gave public housing higher priority than did the central government.

Milanese policymakers who wished to be dynamic and innovative benefited from an affluent environment in whatever policy sector they operated. Milan is the "economic capital" of Italy: it is the country's leading financial, commercial, and industrial center.[7] The local government's financial policies have reflected this rich economic base. Milan historically has spent more than any other local government in Italy. Comparing the per capita expenditures of the national government, all communes, and Milan, one finds that Milan in 1912 and 1928 spent more on a per capita basis than did the central government as well as far more than did all communes; in 1956 Milan's per capita expenditures were 70 percent as much as those of the central government. Milan spent 43,500 lira per person in 1956, the national government spent 60,400, and the per capita expenditure for all communes was 14,511 (Volpi, 1960, p. 43).

In the 1950s and 1960s Milan's finances were very sound and provided a solid foundation for policy initiative. Not only was there a wealthy base to tax, but Milan's tax rates were also higher than those in other large Italian cities (Fried, 1973, p. 125). In addition, the health of its revenue sources was complemented by the city's judicious debt management policy. While many other cities borrowed to pay for operating expenditures, Milan borrowed primarily to carry out capital investments (Casalengo, 1971, p. 180).

The confidence granted by wealth was buttressed by a municipal tradition of local initiative mixed with contempt for the national government's deficiencies. The national government was traditionally viewed by Milan's officials as reflecting the worst in Italian culture, while Milan's norms and traditions were viewed as the vanguard, as representing the best in Italy's modern sector.

Supported by this general environment of wealth, competence, and confidence, policymakers in the public housing field were able to initiate programs that were technologically innovative, as well as (especially in the 1960s) concerned with the needs of lower-income families. Officials did not see their duty as that of implementing national government policy preferences. On the contrary, they saw themselves as having an obligation to make up for the national government's errors when possible and, most importantly, to avoid the national government's lethargy and pattern of inactivity.[8]

Thus even in the early 1950s Milan's public housing policy was marked by a concern with innovation and initiative. Social work centers and day-care centers, among the first in postwar Italy, were established in Milan's public housing projects. A research institute was established to study various technical aspects of housing, and sociological problems were also studied. Further, technological innovations that would make public housing projects more convenient and economical were numerous during the 1950s. For example, the heating plant designed for the project Comasina provided not only heat for the neighborhood but also electricity. As such, it was an important innovation in that field in Italy (Lodola, 1962, p. 140; Istituto Autonomo, 1958, p. 41). Public housing policy in Milan, was characterized by an unusually high degree of concern for research, social work activity, and technological innovations.

Such initiatives carried out by the IACPM were made possible largely because Milan's elected officials were willing to allocate municipal tax revenues for public housing (in the form of interest subsidies) rather than relying solely on national housing programs to meet their housing needs. In 1954 the Milan city council appropriated funds from the city treasury and promised long-term support to the IACPM. Such an appropriation from a municipal budget was unusual, for most municipalities did not allocate city funds for public housing. For example between 1951 and 1965 the IACPs in the aggregate received 10 billion lira from local governments. However, roughly 6 billion of those 10 were given by Milan's local government to the IACPM (Conosciani et al., 1969, p. 126). The IACPs typically had to rely on fairly small allocations from the Ministry of Public Works or on funds from INA-Casa/Gescal. Consequently the scope of activity for the IACPs was generally narrow. In Milan, however, the high priority given to public housing was reflected in the city's allocation, from its tax revenues, of interest subsidies; such allocations in turn allowed the IACPM to be innovative and to show initiative.

The city administration was indeed a significant contributor. Between 1951 and 1965, the city government contributed approximately 5.5 billion lira, while the Ministry of Public Works contributed only about 3 billion. Between 1964 and 1968 the city contributed at least three times as much as the ministry.[9] The allocation of these city funds allowed the IACPM not only to be active in research and social work but also to begin its own building programs. Using the interest subsidies allocated by the city, the IACPM was able to build public housing on a large scale. By 1972 the IACPM administered the largest public housing stock in Italy. Fourteen percent of all the IACP housing in Italy was in Milan in 1972.[10]

A considerable portion of that housing stock was built in the 1960s. In 1962 the IACPM was able to propose to the city administration a large new construction program based on the use of prefabrication, which would permit the building of public housing units more rapidly and (it was thought) more cheaply than would traditional construction methods (see Istituto Autonomo, 1962, 1964). Since prefabrication had never before been used in a public housing project in Italy, such a proposal was a good illustration of the IACPM's capacity to be both innovative and technically advanced.

The proposal for a large construction program was agreeable to the city administration, which had recently been taken over by a coalition composed of the Socialist party and of "left" factions of the Christian Democratic party. The city administration agreed to help substantially in the financing of the program—indeed, Milan was to pay for much more of the program's costs than was the Ministry of Public Works. Further, the city administration took the significant step of designating all the housing constructed under the program as housing for rent. None was to be sold into ownership. Both the Socialists and the left wing of the Christian Democratic party had a political commitment to providing public housing for lower-income groups and felt that rentals were the best way to provide such housing.

Generally speaking the city's policies stood in sharp contrast to those of INA-Casa-Gescal. The city was more ambitious than the national agencies, and the beneficiaries of its policies were not the same groups which benefited from the national programs. In fact the city financed the building of 23,000 housing units (120,000 rooms) between 1965 and 1969—a number higher than the *total* number of units financed by Gescal *nationwide* in the three-year period between 1963 and 1965 (see Conosciani et al., 1969, p. 105; Ufficio Studi, 1967). Further, whereas INA-Casa-Gescal favored those able to buy, Milan's housing policy in the 1960s favored those who wished to rent. Thus by 1970, of the roughly 20,000 lodgings built by INA-Casa-Gescal in the Milan province since

1949, only 4,000 were for rent;[11] by comparison, all the 23,000 lodgings constructed by the city in the 1960s were for rent. The number of units built and their designation as rentals reflected the high priority Milan's policymakers gave to the problem of housing for low-income families, a commitment which stood in sharp contrast to that of INA-Casa-Gescal.

Perhaps the single most important difference, between Milan's policy and that of the national government was that public housing was treated as a high priority issue in Milan and it was not so treated at the national level. Policymakers concerned with public housing in Milan were exceptionally competent, innovative, and active—they *wanted* to build housing. They were able to mobilize support from the city administration, which in turn felt that public housing should receive priority. In contrast, national policymakers involved with public housing were not anxious to build and in fact seemed to be more concerned with questions of political patronage than of shelter. Further, ownership was stressed in such a way that preference was given to the relatively affluent sector of the eligible population. By contrast, Milan's officials put a high priority on building homes for low-income families while policymakers in the capital did not.

Limitations on Municipal Initiative

In spite of the high priority given to public housing by Milanese officials, their ability to assist low-income groups was limited by the amount of money they had at their disposal. Whereas INA-Casa-Gescal had large budgets and could afford to finance housing by using capital grants, the city of Milan had a much smaller amount that it could allocate to housing. It could not therefore realistically use capital grants.

Milan's officials could assist public housing construction only by allocating city funds in the form of interest subsidies to the IACPM. Municipal funds would stretch much further if used in conjunction with bank loans than they would if allocated in the form of capital grants and many more housing units could be built. It must be remembered, however, that the use of bank loans rather than capital grants involves higher rent levels for tenants.[12] Thus if a tenant living in a Gescal house paid 210,000 lira a year in rent, he would have had to pay 360,000 lira a year for the same house if it had been built under the municipal program (Cavalera, Intini, and Tortoreto, 1970, p. 21).

Ironically, then, Milanese policymakers could provide housing more cheaply than the private market but not as cheaply as INA-Casa-Gescal. They could indeed, by building rental units, make public housing *available* for low-income families, *but* in order to do so, relatively high public sector rents had to be levied. Such rents would still be lower than those charged in the private housing market for equivalent housing; in that important way, municipal policy assisted lower-income families. But rents in municipally financed housing schemes could not be as low as those charged by INA-Casa-Gescal.

Municipal policy, then, could only be paradoxical: it could make housing available to the poor only by charging them relatively high public-sector rents. That paradox begins to reveal the limits structurally imposed on municipal attempts to build housing for the elderly, the unemployed, and others at the bottom of the income scale when national subsidies are not available for both the repayment of loans and payment of interest charges.[13] Municipal budgets cannot provide capital grants on a large scale, and municipal housing programs must therefore rely on loans (whether from public or private credit institutions). That reliance places a limit on how cheaply public housing can be offered, since it cannot be made available on a large scale so cheaply that debt service requirements cannot be met.

In Italy, since national policy generally favored giving cheap housing to families who were not at the bottom of the income ladder, the option open to municipalities was either to ignore low-income families' need for public housing or to make such housing available by using bank loans and municipal interest subsidies. Milan chose the latter option, which is certainly more favorable to lower-income families than the first. While it is important to note that municipal policy could not benefit people to the degree the INA-Casa-Gescal program benefited its clients, it is also important to emphasize that the Milanese program *did* make housing available more cheaply than could the private market.

The Milanese case illustrates both the benefits and constraints of a municipally financed housing program relying on loans. It cannot benefit tenants as much as can a program with a budget large enough to be able to afford capital grants rather than having to rely on loans. It can, however, provide adequate housing to a larger number of lower-income families than can the private market, and it can do it more cheaply.

A municipally financed housing program such as Milan's requires that a city have the tax revenues necessary to finance it. Milan had both a rich economic base and relatively high tax rates. If, however, the city's discretion in taxing were to be reduced, initiatives such as the public housing programs discussed would be seriously threatened. In fact, such a centralization of the tax system is currently occurring in Italy (see Martinotti, 1978, pp. 34-36); Milan's discretion in tax matters has been reduced, as have its tax revenues. Such centralization is likely to have serious implications for local initiative, for it will be difficult for a city to exercise initiative in any field. For example, Bologna's innovative land-use planning is likely to be threatened (Erba, 1970, pp. 46-53; Angotti, 1977, pp. 73-84), for such planning, if it is actively to direct rather than simply react, usually requires a degree of local government intervention difficult to achieve without discretionary tax revenues. The ongoing centralization of the tax system makes local government initiative less and less likely.

Undoubtedly the various political groups that were so successful in mobilizing mass support for the passage of the Housing Reform Law of 1971[14] (which was supposed to restructure the housing policy system) will organize mass protests in an attempt to force local governments to continue their respective initiatives in spite of fiscal scarcity. However, just as such groups have failed to force the implementation of that housing reform in the face of entrenched interests, they may find that their political pressure on local governments will be neutralized by those governments' lack of revenue. It is indeed possible that the centralization of taxation may eliminate the possibility that the type of policy initiative discussed in this chapter will recur.

The case of Milan in the public housing sector in the period 1949-71 represents perhaps an extreme example of the opportunities and constraints faced by a city administration more dynamic than the national political system of which it is formally a part, for the Italian system has been notoriously ineffective in the provision of low-cost housing. Exceptionally dynamic municipal administrations in, for example, Great Britain or France would be acting within the parameters of a national housing policy more effective than the Italian policy. Nonetheless, the major constraint faced by Milan, the inadequacy of municipal nonborrowed funds, would also be faced by dynamic British and French city governments.

No matter how affluent a city may be, it does not have the taxing powers available to its central government. Its residents will pay more taxes to the center than to the local administration. If the city administration decides to provide large-scale, capital-intensive services, the city's tax revenues will not be great enough to fund them. The city government will need to borrow the necessary funds. But when it engages in that very process of borrowing, the city will find itself constrained in ways that would not occur if it had its own funds sufficient to pay for the desired services.[15]

Thus in Milan, rent levels were higher for municipally sponsored houses financed by loans than for nationally sponsored houses funded by INA-Casa-Gescal capital grants; municipal public housing could not be as cheap as it would have been if the city had not had to borrow its funds and incur debt charges. The ability of city governments to be more active than the national government in the provision of capital-intensive services, therefore, almost inevitably will be limited along some dimension by the lack of large sums of municipal funds available for capital investment.

The case of Milan, then, suggests that municipal governments are limited in the extent to which they can compensate for the weaknesses, deficiencies, and biases of the national system to which they belong. It also suggests that in spite of such limits, municipal governments can, through their initiative and competence, have a significant impact on the way their residents live. Given a certain level of economic affluence and discretion in taxation, city governments are not forced merely to reflect the deficiencies of their national system. While they cannot compensate for those deficiencies entirely, they can make them considerably less sharp.

Notes

1. The research on which this chapter is based was carried out in 1972 and 1973. Local policymakers in Milan and central government officials in Rome were interviewed, and documents, journals, and books were examined. For the larger study from which this chapter is taken, see Sbragia (1974) and Sbragia (1979b).
2. In this study "public housing" is defined as publicly financed housing built by a public agency and intended for lower-income groups. Other types of publicly financed housing such as that built for state employees are not included in this definition.
3. For a brief discussion of the Italian political environment in the period before Fascism, see Allum (1973, pp. 3-11); Adams and Barile (1972, pp. 33-39).
4. My discussion of public housing policy during the Fascist period relies heavily on Rosa Chiumeo's superb study (1972), especially pp. 139-233. See also Conosciani et al. (1969, p. 46).
5. In 1924 the IACPM established its Institute for Economic Housing (ICE) and gave it a considerable sum of money as well as 82,000 square meters of land. Though the ICE claimed to be constructing housing for sale to the lower middle class, its first scheme was built for the Milanese upper middle class (Chiumeo, 1972, p. 161).
6. For a general discussion of INA-Casa, see Parenti (1967).
7. For an excellent study of Milan, see Dalmasso (1971).
8. For a more extended discussion of those factors which allow Milan to exercise policy independence, see Sbragia (1979b).
9. Calculated from Conosciani et al. (1969, p. 126) and from data presented in the Budget Reports of the Istituto Autonomo per le Case Popolari della Provincia di Milano from 1951-52 through 1968.
10. By comparison, 5.6 percent of all IACP housing was found in Naples, 4.75 percent in Rome, 4 percent in Turin, and 3 percent in Bologna. Data provided by the Associazione Nazionale fra gli Istituti Autonomi per le Case Popolari.
11. Data received in interview.
12. Of course rent levels could have been lowered to some extent by relying still more heavily on local tax revenue to subsidize loan charges. As it was, local tax revenue was used to subsidize loan charges to the point that rent levels, while relatively high, were still low enough to be acceptable. Higher levels of subsidy were not chosen, perhaps because of the relatively high taxation levels in Milan and the feeling that the city administration was already making a special and unusual effort by appropriating substantial amounts of local monies while other city governments were often allocating nothing at all.
13. In Britain, for example, debt charges incurred by local authorities for

public housing construction are heavily subsidized by the national government. Even then, such loan charges are a heavy burden on local authority budgets.

14. For a discussion of the mass political movements that were mobilized over the issue of public housing reform, see Achilli (1972); Angotti (1977, pp. 24-63).

15. Many economists argue that financing a long-lived capital project by a loan is more equitable than financing it out of revenue, for the repayment of the loan spreads out the costs of the project so that those generations that will benefit will also help pay. Further, in inflationary times borrowing means repaying in "cheap" money. However correct such logic may be in the abstract, debt charges incurred by heavy borrowing have become an extremely heavy burden to Italian local governments and to many British local authorities as well. For a discussion of the impact of such debt charges on public housing politics in Milan, see Sbragia (1979b).

References

Achilli, M. 1972. *Casa: Vertenza di Massa-Storia di una Riforma Constrastata.* Padova: Marsilio.

Adams, J.C., and Barile, P. 1972. *The Government of Republican Italy.* 3rd ed. New York: Houghton Mifflin.

Allum, P.A. 1973. *Italy: Republic without Government?* New York: Norton.

Angotti, T. 1977. *Housing in Italy: Urban Development and Political Change.* New York: Praeger.

Associazione Nazionale fra gli Istituti Autonomi per le Case Popolari. 1971. *Cessione degli Alloggi in Base al D.P.R. 17 Gennaio 1959, n.2 e Successive Modificazioni.* Rome.

Casalengo, F. 1971. "Situazione Finanziaria degli Enti Locali: Interventi Finanziari e Questioni Relative con Carattere di Priorità." In *Atti del Convegno Nazionale su Partecipazione ed Efficienza nella Costruzione delle Strutture Politico-Amministrative Regionali e Locali.* Pavia: Camera di Commercio, Industria, Artigianato e Agricoltura di Pavia.

Cavalera, G., Intini, U., and Tortoreto, E. 1970. *Italiani Senza Casa.* Milan: Nuova Mercurio.

Chiumeo, R. 1972. "Edilizia Popolare a Milano tra le Due Guerre: 1919-1940." In *Urbanistica a Milano in Regime Fascista,* ed. D. Franchi and R. Chiumeo. Florence: La Nuova Italia.

Conosciani, L., D'Albergo, S., Mattioni, E., and Tortoreto, E. 1969. *L'Organizzazione Pubblica dell'Edilizia.* Milan: Franco Angeli.

Dalmasso, E. 1971. *Milan: Capitale Economique de l'Italie.* Paris: Editions Ophrys.

De Lucia, V. 1971. "La Questione della Gescal." *Alternativa,* n. 13, May 20.

Erba, V. 1970. Alcuni Esempi di Applicazione e Attuazione della Legge 167. *Città e Società*, January-February, pp. 46-53.

Fried, R.C. 1973. *Planning the Eternal City: Roman Politics and Planning since World War II*. New Haven: Yale University Press.

Istituto Autonomo per le Case Popolari della Provincia de Milano. 1958. *Quartiere Autosufficiente Comasina: Milano 1955-1958*. Milan.

———. 1962. *Per una Industrializzazione dell'Edilizia*. Milan.

———. 1964. *Aspetti dell'Industrializzazione dell'Edilizia in U.R.S.S.* Milan.

———. 1972. *Case Popolari: Origini dell'Istituto Case Popolari a Milano*. Milan.

Lodola, A. 1962. L'Istituto dal 1909 at 1960. In *Cinquant'anni di Storia e di Attivita dell'Edilizia Popolare in Milano, 1909-1960*. Milan: Ufficio Stampa dell'Istituto Autonomo per le Case Popolari della Provincia di Milano.

Martinotti, G. 1978. "Local Financial Problems in Italy." Paper presented to the Ninth World Congress of the International Sociological Association, in Uppsala, Sweden, August 14-19.

Parenti, G. 1967. *Una Esperienza di Programmazione Settoriale nell'Edilizia: L'INA-Casa*. Rome: Giuffrè.

Sbragia, A.M. 1974. *Urban Autonomy within the Unitary State: A Case Study of Public Housing Politics in Milan, Italy*. Unpublished dissertation, University of Wisconsin.

———. 1979a. "Borrowing to Build: Private Money and Public Welfare." *International Journal of Health Services* 9, No. 2, May.

———. 1979b. "Not All Roads Lead to Rome: Local Housing Policy in the Unitary Italian State." *British Journal of Political Science*. July.

Ufficio Statistica dell'Istituto Autonomo per le Case Popolari della Provincia di Milano. 1971. *Le "Case Minime" a Milano: Esiti di una Indagine Socioeconomica*. Milan.

Ufficio Studi e Statistica dello Istituto Autonomo per le Case Popolari della Provincia di Milano. 1967. *Prefabbricazione Anno Uno*. Milan.

Volpi, F. 1960. *Le Finanze Comunale di un Grande Centro Urbano: Spese, Entrate, Disavanzi del Comune di Milano dal 1938 al 1958, nel Quadro della Situazione e delle Prospettive della Finanza Locale in Italia*. Milan: Feltrinelli.

Reorienting Urban Transportation Policy in Social-Democratic Stockholm and Hamburg

Frank C. Colcord, Jr.

The key issues in urban transportation in recent years in both North American and West European cities have been to make transportation policy more consistent with newly defined social and environmental goals and to achieve greater public and political access to the decision-making process.

While considerable progress toward these objectives has been made in the United States, it has been slow and difficult. Semiautonomous metropolitan transit authorities and state highway commissions have been relatively impermeable to political and grass-roots demands. Recent years have seen the development of new federal, state, and metropolitan institutions for planning and policymaking, but there continues to be only a limited relationship between transportation policy and the social, economic, and environmental goals of the impacted cities (Lupo, Colcord, and Fowler, 1971, pp. 186-87). Freeway revolts have often succeeded in stopping construction, but it has typically taken a long time to achieve acceptance of new transportation priorities and meaningful participation.

Stockholm and Hamburg are examples of Western European cities that have achieved both policy change and greater accessibility relatively quickly. It is suggested here that the explanation for this more rapid response lies in a combination of factors. First, the two cities (and their national governments) have political institutions which facilitate rather than resist change. Second, the dominant ideology of the two cities, represented by the largest party, the socialists, is consistent with the policy changes being demanded by the citizenry.

As in North American cities, grass-roots citizen groups that articulated the demands for changes in policy and process arose in the early 1970s. These groups found allies for their causes within the bureaucracy and among the elected politicians and parties.

Hamburg and Stockholm: Institutional Differences

There are several major institutional differences that require description before programs and politics can be discussed. Stockholm is the national capital, but despite this has long had significant autonomy (Hancock, 1972, pp. 93-94). This is greatly enhanced by the Swedish tax structure, which allows cities to determine their own revenue needs and collect that amount by "riding on" the national income tax (Robson and Regan, 1972, p. 879). Stockholm was independent of any county until 1971, when it became a part of a new Stockholm County, enlarged to be able to deal with metropolitan problems (Colcord and Lewis, 1974, pp. 63-64). The county has transit and regional planning responsibilities among others, but the city's planning functions remain paramount ("planning monopoly" is an oft-cited phrase), and these include roads, parking, and traffic planning. The city and county are both governed by elected multiparty councils, the functions of which are conducted by committees. There is no mayor, and thus coordination is collegial.

Hamburg, West Germany's largest city, its commercial capital, and a prominent cultural center, is a city-state (one of the few remaining of the Hanseatic cities) with a long tradition of strong autonomy on civic matters. Though part of a federal system, Hamburg has no superior state to contend with, as do other German cities (except Bremen) (Leonhardt, 1964). Under the federal constitution states have major powers in domestic affairs, and thus Hamburg has such powers itself, including strong taxing authority.

The city is governed by an elected parliament (*Bürgershaft*) of 120 members. The *Bürgershaft* performs its work through substantive committees, generally corresponding with the departments of government (Vogel, 1972, pp. 21-22). The executive branch is headed by the *Senat*, a body of 10 to 15 members elected by the *Bürgershaft*. The Senators serve as ministers heading up the departments of government; together they compose the equivalent of a cabinet and choose the chief executive, the *Bürgermeister* (Vogel, 1972, pp. 21-22). There is no strong metropolitan or regional political body in the Hamburg area, as exists in Stockholm, although about 40 percent of the area's population lives in the suburbs. It should be emphasized, however, that this is a large city both in population and in territory (228 square miles).

Stockholm

Stockholm has been a socialist city since 1919 except for two brief interludes of "bourgeois" government. Planning ahead is inherent in socialism and this was evidenced in the postwar decades by the extensive land banking program carried out by the city. Stockholm emerged from the war with a comprehensive plan for new housing in satellite cities (made possible by the land bank) connected to the center by an ambitious new rail transit system and a more modest new system of highways (Ödmann and Dahlberg, 1970, pp. 83-84). A very strong and highly respected planning organization developed in the city in the postwar years and was responsible for all aspects of land-use planning, including transportation. In

1971 a regional planning body was created in the reconstituted county of Stockholm, which contains the entire urbanized area.

Throughout the postwar period transit has been emphasized over the private automobile, although the latter had a brief day in the sun in the early 1960s. Work began immediately after the war on the city's new rail transit system, with the first line completed and operating in 1952. A total of three lines extending over sixty miles has been built with the final link completed in 1977 (Berglund, 1972, p. 13). In 1965 the national parliament approved diversion of highway funds to transit infrastructure expenditures, with the decision as to distribution between the two modes essentially the city's (Ödmann and Dahlberg, 1970, p. 199). Between 26 percent and 38 percent was being used for transit in the early 1970s. As a part of the restructuring of Stockholm County, that regional body assumed control of planning and operating public transportation (including rail transit, buses, commuter rail, and so forth) in 1971.

The original postwar highway plan was rather modest but was significantly enlarged in the revised 1960 city plan in response to an unexpected growth in the use of automobiles and the consequent congestion. Critics of this plan called it "car-friendly" and a major departure from the city's previous primarily social orientation. After parliamentary approval of the diversion of highway funds to transit, the highway program was substantially reduced in scale in a 1970 plan to fit the available funds. Environmental considerations also entered into the plan modification (Colcord and Lewis, 1974, pp. 84-85).

This reduction in highway emphasis was also expressed in new planning for the pedestrian and in the development of auto restricted zones (ARZs). In the 1960s the city removed most motor vehicle traffic from the old city (*Gamla Stan*) and in the later 1960s began redevelopment of the central business district with extensive pedestrian streets. In the early 1970s a major residential area adjacent to the central business district, *Ostermalm*, became an ARZ, in which a hierarchy of streets was created, largely eliminating cars from all but the commercial thoroughfares. A second major traffic restraint scheme was instituted on Sodermalm island in 1974 and others were being planned. Thus traffic was being controlled and discouraged on a wide variety of fronts (Colcord and Lewis, 1974, pp. 85-88).

The 1960s saw the development of a new phenomenon for Stockholm, namely citizens' groups concerned with the quality of life in the city. Two significant ones were evident at the time of our interviews in 1973, the *Stads Miljo Gruppen* (City Milieu Group, founded about 1963) and "Alternative City" (begun in 1969). The former group worked within the system, pressing for an opening up of planning to the citizen. The latter, a more radical body, used more demonstrative means to make their point. Their victorious mass confrontation with the police in 1971 over the proposed removal of some trees from the King's Park (a small but heavily used and handsome downtown facility) for a new transit station was called the "Battle of the Elms" and seems to have directly resulted in a requirement for consultation by the city council with citizens' groups on all new plans (Colcord and Lewis, 1974, pp. 138-144).

Unlike the typical U.S. experience, Stockholm's experience was not a freeway revolt. Citizens' groups did indeed object to freeways and made their views known, but one cannot argue that the changed policy reflected in the 1970 plan was a result of citizen activism. Instead, it was a practical, political decision made at the highest levels of city, county, and national governments, after lengthy negotiation, and based on perceived priorities. New funding was not provided in the 1965 act, only the opportunity to use existing highway funds. Their use for transit necessarily reduced the availability of funds for roads. The major single citizens' action was directed at a transit decision (the station location in the park) and at what was perceived to be a bureaucratic planning and decision-making process.

The Swedes have a strong tradition of consultation on important issues before decisions are made, both among government agencies and with important private interest groups. While such processes were typically employed with respect to major urban planning decisions, the citizens' groups had not been taken as seriously as economic interest groups. However, after the Battle of the Elms the city of Stockholm required consultation with citizens and neighborhood groups and took the unusual step of actually providing a subsidy for Alternative City.

In the 1973 election the question of popular participation in planning and decision-making was an important plank in the platform of the Center party, the party which gained the most seats in that election. Although this was a national campaign issue, its impact was obviously felt at the local levels as well. The strengthening of this party seemed to confirm the need to open up the planning process in Stockholm. Despite resistance in the bureaucracy, the political leadership accepted the new approach.

Hamburg

Like Stockholm, Hamburg has a long socialist tradition, which has naturally led to an acceptance of planning and government involvement in land-use decisions. Hamburg was devastated in World War II and had a giant rebuilding job to accomplish after 1945. Housing and industry were first priorities, and the city did not significantly replan in the manner of Rotterdam; it rebuilt much as before, including the old street pattern, and even similar architecture. Unlike Stockholm, Hamburg did not emphasize comprehensive planning until recently; thus housing plans were not closely coordinated with transportation plans, despite the fact that both responsibilities were contained within the same agency, the *Baubehörde*. Communication between the two types of planners was not close until quite recently.

Hamburg has one of the oldest and best developed rapid transit systems in Europe; until the 1960s it was the only one in West Germany (except Berlin). The *U-Bahn* system is run by the *Hamburger Hochmahn Aktiengesellshaft* (HHA) and comprises both rail transit and buses. The German National Railways operate the commuter lines, called the *S-Bahn.* The prewar system was begun in 1906 and was completed in 1934. Work began on the first postwar extensions in 1955, and both systems have ambitious future plans (Freie and Hansestadt Hamburg-Baubehörde, 1968, pp. 12-15).

The combined system is extraordinarily efficient. Much of this is attributable to a major managerial innovation known as the *Hamburger Verkehrsverbund* (HVV), an umbrella organization established in 1965. It includes the two major providers plus five additional ones, encompassing nearly all the transportation services. Its functions include research, timetables, and allocation of services, joint fare systems, distribution of revenues, and public relations and advertising. With the beginning of joint fares and coordinated timetables and services, patronage has increased substantially. More than 70 percent of the city's downtown workers use public transit. The system has been so effective that the federal government has successfully encouraged its use in other German cities (Pampel, 1969).

Federal matching assistance for rail transit and urban streets and highways became available in 1967. In the next six years this aid was increasingly liberalized and directed toward transit. The total funds available tripled, the share covered by the federal government grew from 50 to 60 percent, and the share of the total fund designated for transit was raised from 40 to 60 percent (Colcord and Lewis, 1974, p. 59).

In the 1960s Hamburg developed a freeway plan with the cooperation of the federal government which included two north-south tangents, on either side of the core city and an east-west connector through the core. Only the west tangent has been built, having been completed in 1974. Otherwise there are no freeways within the city, and by 1973 it did not appear that there would be any more in the near future. In 1970 a directive issued by the *Senat* placed greater emphasis on transit and required a reduction in the freeway plan. In 1973, against the advice of staff, business interests, and the automobile club, the *Burgershaft* deleted the east tangent and crosstown roads, thus emasculating the freeway plan. All three political parties supported the general antihighway policy, although the Christian Democrats opposed the deletion of the east tangent (Colcord and Lewis, 1974, pp. 72-73).

In the late 1960s and early 1970s Hamburg witnessed the growth of a major citizens' movement known as *Burgerinitiativen* (citizen initiatives). These groups have sprung up in response to what they view as threats to the environment of their neighborhoods, and they have been strongly opposed to highway construction. There were no dramatic confrontations by radicals as in Stockholm; in Hamburg it has been more a matter of continued citizen pressure. Demonstrations have been staged but no violence has ensued. The groups used their middle-class expertise to investigate and question the decisions of the bureaucrats and thus caused the politicians to raise questions not previously considered (Colcord and Lewis, 1974, pp. 69-71).

As in Stockholm, the style of planning and decision making was as much at issue as were the policies and programs themselves. The German tradition had clearly been to view such decisions about highway locations as technical ones to be made by the bureaucracy. The early efforts of the *Burgerinitiativen* found both the party leaders and the bureaucracy immovable. But ultimately all three parties adopted an antihighway position.

Another important effect of citizen activism has been that the highway planners for the first time began to seek the help of the land-use planners in the initial stages of their work, thus causing a higher degree of comprehensiveness of planning. This has been demonstrated in two major projects (one commercial, one residential). Public involvement in the early stages of planning has also recently evolved; at the time of my visit a new city plan was in the works, and citizen group comment was being built into the second version of that plan.

Conclusions

By 1973 Stockholm and Hamburg had arrived at very similar urban transportation policies. In both instances, the development of popular participation had been instrumental in significantly modifying previous policies and bringing about these changes. The citizens' groups, as well as nontransport agencies and political leaders, succeeded in bringing environmental and social considerations to bear on transportation planning and policy. They had succeeded in subjecting transportation policy to the role of servant to other policy goals perceived to be more important.

Three key factors have made this more feasible in these two cities. The first and second are institutional, the third is ideological.

First, Stockholm and Hamburg have an unusual amount of local autonomy, both with respect to their ability to determine their own policies and their ability to finance their programs from locally generated revenues. Neither city has suffered from the phenomenon common in the United States and some other countries of "antiurban" legislatures imposing transportation solutions that are not suitable to cities' needs. In both cases they and other cities were successful in persuading their national governments to provide funds for transit as well as highways, thus allowing flexibility in local decisions.

The second factor, also institutional, is that all planning in both cities took place in the same organization through most of the postwar period. This led to more positive results in Stockholm than Hamburg, since in the latter the land-use planners and transport planners were in different divisions of the Baubehörde, and the custom had developed, thanks to engineering-oriented top management, of allowing autonomous transport planning. In Stockholm the land-use planners were given stronger powers, but this study found that the problem of conflict between engineers and land-use planners really did not exist, in part because engineering and architectural education are closely associated in Sweden and have a common urban planning curriculum. While it is true that in 1971 regional and transit planning were transferred from the city to the newly constituted county, thus creating a split of function, as of 1973 this seemed not to be creating any serious difficulties because of the strong Swedish traditions of consultation and overlapping political offices.

The ideological factor is interesting but somewhat ambiguous. The two cities have long socialist traditions, and they clearly embrace the socialist ideal of setting goals and devising plans and strategies to meet those goals. A rationalistic decision-making system, rooted in what the political leaders saw to be a confluence of popular support for emphasizing working-class needs and a respect for technocratic expertise prevailed in both cities before the rise of citizens' organizations. The freeway plans and other services for automobiles were not in fact seen to be inconsistent with working-class interests, since in these two prosperous countries increasing numbers of workers owned cars and were thus part of the demand for improved facilities.

The popular uprising was aimed at both the bureaucratic style of decision-making and its programmatic output. The citizens' organizations demanding grass-roots participation ranged from the extreme left to bourgeois in their ideological orientations, but all shared a common distaste for the prevailing style of policymaking and program development.

There seems little question that the policy changes in the two cities were largely responses to citizen group demands. Yet, it seems to have been too easy, given the apparent very limited power of these groups. They appeared to be considerably less potent and broadly based than their counterparts in many American cities.

One explanation for their success is that the policies demanded by these groups were recognizably consistent with socialist ideals and thus relatively easy to accept. A second explanation, distinguishing these cities from their American counterparts, is that the interest groups supporting freeway programs are not closely linked to the governing parties, but rather to the bourgeois parties, thus limiting their capacity to influence decisions. In these cases they were unable to prevent changes in policy.

In a liberal-capitalist democracy the ideal remains freedom from overarching governmental control, leaving the maximum possible number of decisions to the operations of the private market place. An emphasis on automobile transportation reflects this kind of consumer orientation and is inconsistent with socialist goals and socialist decision-making processes. As is illustrated by the Hamburg and Stockholm experience, social democracies do not always maintain this consistency, but that is the ideal. Since both West Germany and Sweden are political systems which harbor a mixture of competing ideologies, it is not surprising that the liberal-capitalist perspective is also evident in their politics, such as in the roads program.

It should be emphasized, however, that this brief change in priorities toward the automobile did not at all result in downgrading the importance of public transportation. Both cities continued to invest major resources in that activity, and in both instances there was a conscious effort to reduce automobile usage and to provide quality transportation to those who did not have access to an automobile. This is in sharp contrast with the American experience, where public transport was allowed to deteriorate in the face of growing competition with cars and declining patronage. Only after the point of desperation had been reached in a number of cities did states and the federal government assume any financial responsibility for this function, and thus a major rebuilding process has been required. Consumer demand was the prevailing ethic until almost too late.

While it is true that a number of nonsocialist cities have experienced much the same policy reorientation (for example, Paris, Boston, San Francisco, Vancouver, Toronto), the argument that the socialist ideology facilitated the change in Stockholm and Hamburg is persuasive. In the North American cases, the development of a new comprehensive policy involved great and lengthy controversy; the absence of the socialist ideological framework weakened the case for greater emphasis on public transit.

In both Stockholm and Hamburg the demand from the citizens' groups for greater participation met with considerable resistance within the system. Although in both cases the demand was accepted at the political level rather quickly, it was resisted by the bureaucrats because it was perceived to be inconsistent with the accepted goal of rationality in planning. This stronger resistance in Europe than in the United States to grass-roots participation is a reflection of a more powerful tradition of bureaucratic decision-making, long accepted by socialists but by no means invented by them. Despite their misgivings, however, it was evident that popular participation in the planning process significantly increased in the two cities studied in the early 1970s.

Many European cities, with Stockholm and Hamburg in the vanguard, have completed their brief romance with the automobile, and turned their attention to finding ways of making their central and adjacent areas more attractive to the pedestrian and resident. Unquestionably, the fuel crisis of late 1973 (which did not strike until after our Stockholm and Hamburg interviews) further encouraged this development in European cities. Restraints have been placed on the automobile, and the provision of quality public transportation has been greatly emphasized. The experience of Stockholm and Hamburg suggests that a combination of active citizen participation, responsive politicians, flexible and comprehensive public institutions, local autonomy, the socialist ideology, and national financial assistance within the context of a political system that accepts planning as an appropriate governmental function can provide the framework for rapid policy change.

References

Berglund, H. 1972. *Greater Stockholm.* Stockholm: Stockholm Lokaltrafiks.
Colcord, F.C., Jr., and Lewis, R.S. 1974. *Urban Transportation Decision Making; Hamburg: A Case Study.* Washington: U.S. Department of Transportation.
Freie and Hansestadt Hamburg-Baubehörde. 1968. *Schnellbahnbau in Hamburg.* Hamburg: Baubehörde.
Hancock, M.D. 1972. *Sweden: The Politics of Postindustrial Change.* Hinsdale, Ill.: Dryden Press.
Leonhardt, R.W. 1964. *This Germany: The Story Since the Third Reich.* Middlesex, England: Penguin Books, Ltd.
Lupo, A., Colcord, F.C., Jr., and Fowler, E.V. 1971. *Rites of Way: The Politics of Transportation in Boston and the U.S. City.* Boston: Little, Brown.
Ödmann, E., and Dahlberg, G.-B. 1970. *Urbanization in Sweden: Means and Methods for the Planning.* Stockholm: Allmanna Forlaget.
Pampel, I.F. 1969. "The Hamburg Transport Community, an Example of Coordination and Integration in Public Transport." Paper prepared for the UITP Conference in London.
Robson, W.A., and Regan, D.E., eds. 1972. *Great Cities of the World: Their Government, Politics, and Planning.* London: George Allen and Unwin, Ltd.
Vogel, P.O., ed. 1972. *Hamburg: Die Freie und Hansestadt.* Hamburg: Hans Christian Verlag.

Part III
National Politics and the Emergence of Regional Institutions

10 Territory and Social Conflict in Belfast

John V. O'Loughlin

Since 1968 Northern Ireland has occupied a prominent place in the forefront of world news. To many outsiders the situation in that small country (total population 1.5 million) appears confusing. Social, political, nationalistic, religious, and economic conflicts are evidenced by a bewildering array of organizations and splinter groups. Between 1969 and December 1977 the conflict took 1837 lives in Northern Ireland, 73 in the Republic of Ireland, and 65 in Great Britain. The British government has paid $570 million in property, life, and damage claims during these years and the costs of the police and security emergency are now about $1 million each day (Whalen and Ryder, 1978a). Belfast, by far the largest agglomeration with 360,000 people in the city and 600,000 in the urbanized area, has become a battleground in the struggle between opposing forces. This chapter attempts to outline the scope and nature of the present conflict in Belfast by focusing on its social, economic, religious, and nationalistic dimensions within the context of the political setting encompassing the rest of Northern Ireland, and to a lesser extent, Great Britain and the Republic of Ireland.

It is impossible to attribute the cause of the conflict to any one set of factors. Various commentators have tried to isolate the causes, but much depends on the perspective of the observer (Whyte, 1976). Nationalism and religion are closely intertwined. In answer to the question "Which of these terms best describes the way you usually think of yourself?" 76 percent of Catholics in Northern Ireland answered Irish, but 71 percent of Protestants said either British or Ulster (Rose, 1971, p. 485). Controlling for religion, Rose found no significant difference in attitudes toward the link with Britain between respondents with different levels of education, travel experience, and social class. "Within the middle class, Protestants and Catholics differ by 36 percentage points in their readiness to support the [Northern Ireland] Constitution and manual workers by 30 percentage points" (Rose, 1971, p. 281). But to view the conflict in Protestant-Catholic terms is as unrealistic as viewing it as a conflict between the working class and the middle classes. A brief review of the development of neighborhoods in Belfast in the context of the political setting is necessary before an analysis of present strife. As Boal (1978, p. 77) claims, the strife in Belfast "is *part* of the Irish conflict. It is a particular example of general human territorial behavior in an urban context, and it stands as a warning of what is possible in cities elsewhere" [his italics] .

The Historical and Geographical Setting

The roots of the present conflict are in the seventeenth-century Ulster Plantation. Large numbers of Scottish and English colonists arrived in Northern Ireland after the subjugation of that area by the English Crown and the subsequent flight of the native Irish aristocracy. Unlike previous Crown plantations in southern Ireland, the settlement of the North was permanent despite the efforts of the native Irish to uproot the newcomers. Little contact occurred between the two groups; and compared with their previous situation in Britain, the life of the new settlers in Ulster was to their liking. The lowlands and river valleys were most densely colonized, especially in the eastern part of the province. The native Irish were forced to move to the mountains in the west and south. This settlement pattern is still evident, as a map of the distribution of religious groups in Northern Ireland shows (figure 10-1).

Belfast remained a small port until the latter part of the eighteenth century.

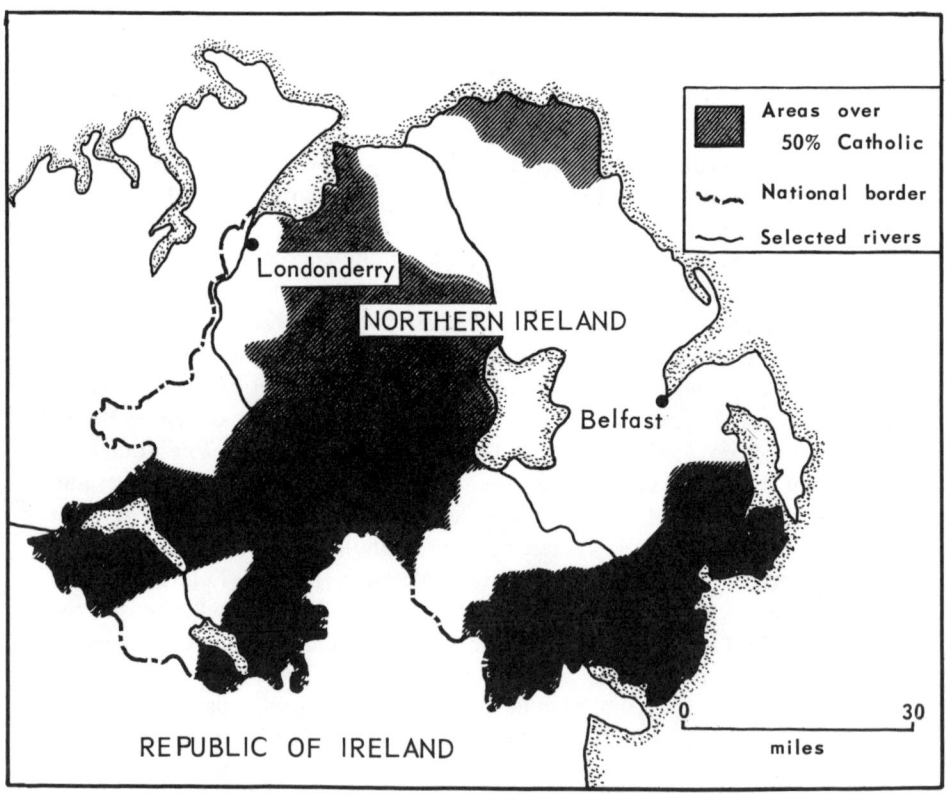

Figure 10-1. Northern Ireland.

With the growth of its textile and shipbuilding industries it quickly became the only city in Ireland to experience the full effect of the Industrial Revolution and a primate city within Northern Ireland. The physical landscape of Belfast is similar to those of Glasgow, Manchester, Leeds, and Birmingham, other cities which grew rapidly in the early nineteenth century. The population of Belfast increased from 50,000 in 1830 to 100,000 in 1850 and to 350,000 in 1900. The population within the city limits peaked at 444,000 in 1951.

A predictable product of the growth of employment opportunities in the new industries of Belfast was the in-migration from rural areas. The earliest Catholic settlements were west of the central city and as the Catholic population grew, their territory expanded westward along the Falls Road sector (figure 10-2). Four smaller Catholic enclaves (Ardoyne, Short Strand, Markets, and along York Street) were also established. In each case the availability of employment in nearby industrial estates explains the neighborhood's origin and location (Busteed, 1972). From the beginning working-class Protestants, descendants of the Scottish and English settlers, lived separately from Catholics. In some instances, especially in West Belfast, a line of factories, warehouses, transport facilities, and other industrial artifacts separated the two types of neighborhoods.

Twentieth-century neighborhood growth saw a continuation of this religious segregation as the two groups extended their territories outward along sectors towards the edge of the city (figure 10-2). The majority of Belfast's Catholics today live in the western and southwestern sectors. This segregation was reinforced by the practice of local housing authorities in granting houses to Catholics in Catholic wards and to Protestants in Protestant areas. Thus, the large housing estates in Ballymurphy and Andersontown in the southwest sector are predominantly Catholic (Cameron Report, 1972). The basic demographic and socioeconomic structure of Belfast today is a series of alternating high- and low-status sectors. In general, social status also increases towards the periphery (Boal, 1975).

Sectarian riots in Belfast first occurred in 1835 and reoccurred in 1843, 1857, 1864, 1872, 1880, 1884, 1886, 1898, 1920-22, 1935, and 1964 before the present strife began in 1969 (Boyd, 1969). Boal and Murray (1977) attribute these conflicts to two sets of circumstances, economic and nationalistic. The vast influx of rural poor into Belfast placed large numbers of Catholics and Protestants in close urban contact for the first time. Competition for jobs and housing increased friction. In addition, Protestant interests were irrevocably linked to Britain as a result of Belfast's economic importance in the British economy, while Catholics were supporting the nationalist demands of a growing activist group based in southern Ireland.

The locations of the riots during the nineteenth century were similar to those in 1920-22 and in 1969. The border zone between the Protestant Shankhill Road and Catholic Falls Road was a focus of disturbances in all three

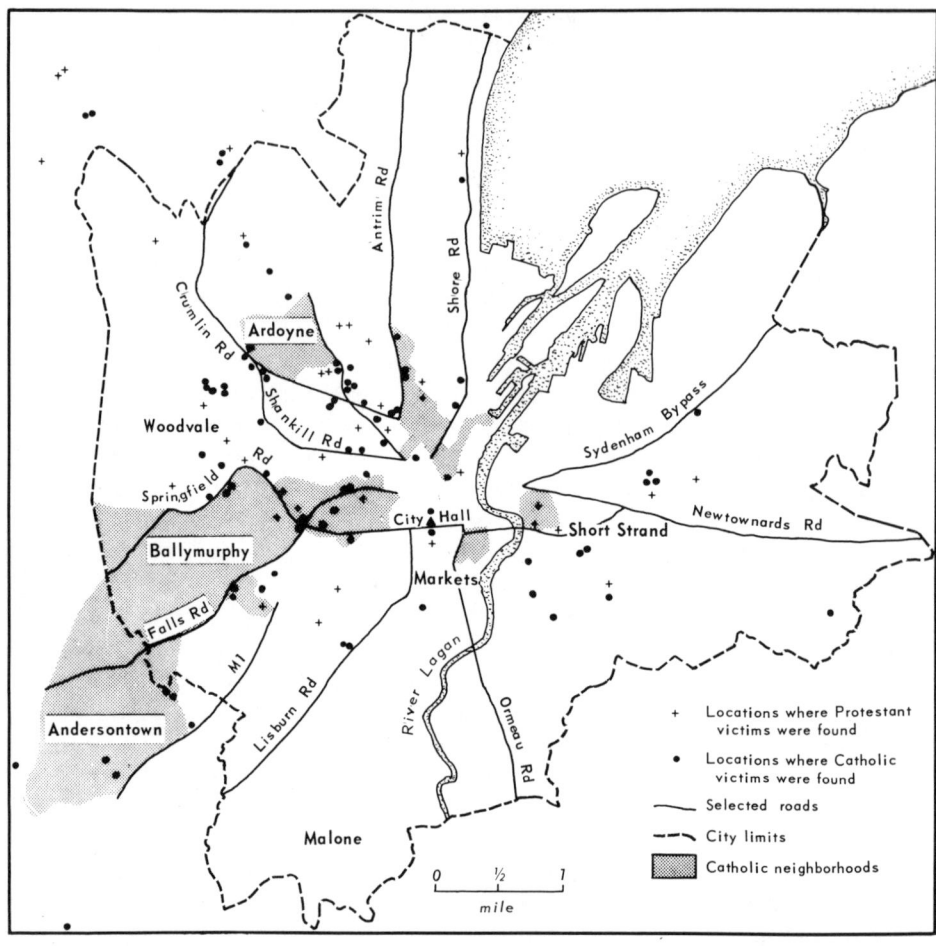

Figure 10-2. Sectarian Murders in Belfast, January 1972 to June 1973.

time periods. From a survey of the reports of government commissions of inquiry completed after each outbreak of strife, Boal (1978) concluded that sharp boundaries existed between Protestant and Catholic areas from early in the nineteenth century and that the degree of segregation between the two groups tended to increase as a direct consequence of outbursts of open conflict. To prevent a reoccurrence of the intrusions by each group into the other's territory, the British army built a barricade, termed the "peace line." This 1969 division is a de facto recognition of the permanence of the territories and the forces operating for their preservation and defense.

The sectarian conflict in Belfast during the nineteenth and early twentieth centuries must be placed in the context of the struggle for Irish independence. The Home Rule movement, 1870-1914, designed to achieve a parliament for Ireland but still maintain the tie to Britain, led to a fear among Ulster Protestants that they would be dominated by the Catholic south. Protestants made up about one-quarter of the population in a united Ireland while Catholics were outnumbered two to one in Northern Ireland. This anti-Home Rule sentiment in Ulster was fostered by the British Conservative party, which needed the parliamentary votes represented by Protestants. By 1890 religious differences were fully equated with different political aspirations; Protestants, termed Unionists, wished to maintain the link with Britain, and Catholics began to agitate for some degree of independence.

The Home Rule struggle was replaced at the end of the nineteenth century by a desire for total independence. Sinn Fein (Ourselves Alone) and its military wing, the Irish Republican Army (IRA), organized and staged the Easter Rebellion of 1916 in Dublin. Although the uprising failed, public sentiment in most of the country, except for the northeastern corner, switched to the republican movement, a shift reflected in the 1918 elections when Sinn Fein won more than two-thirds of the parliamentary seats in the whole island. Only in Protestant northeast Ireland was Unionist sentiment evident. The strength of this Unionist sentiment led the British government to partition the country in 1920, with Northern Ireland remaining a part of the United Kingdom but gaining a parliament in Belfast with local powers. In the rest of Ireland, the guerrilla war of the IRA against the British continued until 1921 when a treaty gave independence to the South, which later became a republic.

The border was intended only as a temporary solution, following county lines but leaving large numbers of Catholics in Northern Ireland (Douglas, 1976). But the planned readjustment to its line never occurred. Consequently, one of the biggest problems for the British army is Catholic areas close to the border that harbor IRA guerrillas who can slip across the boundary to sanctuary in the south. Elections to the fifty-two-seat Northern Ireland parliament between 1921 and 1969 never produced less than forty seats for the continuation of the partition of the island and no more than twelve seats for the Nationalists. Every election was a referendum on the border, with the Unionist forces in favor of its continuation firmly in power.

Strife was renewed in 1969 with the demands of Catholics for equal rights. Well-documented abuses in housing allocation, electoral gerrymandering, and job discrimination gave rise to the civil rights movement demanding an end to these inequities. A Protestant backlash to the granting of the demands led to bitter sectarian riots in 1969 and the revival of the IRA in Catholic neighborhoods. British troops were sent to Northern Ireland in August 1969 to maintain peace. The political situation changed in 1970-71 with a renaissance of Irish republicanism and the beginning of an open war between the IRA and the British army. The Northern Ireland parliament was suspended in 1972 and direct rule from

London instituted (Sunday Times "Insight" Team, 1972; Rose, 1972; Winchester, 1975; Deutch and Magowan, 1974).

The combatants in Northern Ireland may be divided into three main groups. The British army has between 15,000 and 20,000 men in the province. The republican IRA, comprising the activist Provisionals and the Marxist-oriented Officials, number about 2,500 men. The Loyalists or extreme Unionists, splintered into various groups, number about 6,000 men (Institute for the Study of Conflict, 1974). The escalating violence since 1969 is visible in the number of convictions for violent crimes (figure 10-3). A lag is present between occurrence and conviction, but it is obvious that present violence is three times higher than pre-1970 levels and murder rates have skyrocketed. The drain on the British exchequer is substantial as compensation claims for personal injury and property damage continue to pour into claim centers and a growing demand for British troop withdrawal is now evident in Britain itself (Whalen and Ryder, 1978a).

These were the major political events of the past century and documented the shifts in sentiment which led to the installation of a provincial government in Northern Ireland while the south broke the political link with Britain. We now turn to a consideration of present sectarian conflict in Belfast. It is in this agglomeration that violence is intensified, fears are greatest, danger to life and property magnified, and the security problem most difficult because of the density of people, the juxtaposition of rival territories adjoining each other, and the presence of poverty and extreme political viewpoints.

Social Spaces in Belfast

Since the classic work by Emrys Jones (1960) on the social geography of Belfast, other authors have pointed to the segregation of the two major religious groups as the dominant feature of the social landscape. A recent comparison of integration levels at the census tract and ward levels in nine cities indicated that segregation between Catholics and Protestants in Belfast (0.585, where perfect integration is 1.0) fell between the very high segregation levels between blacks and whites in American cities (0.329 in Atlanta, 0.369 in Detroit) and the lower segregation of other bicultural Western cities (0.649 in Montreal, 0.792 in Brussels) (Kenyon, 1976). The levels of segregation in Belfast would be even higher if the index was computed street by street, since many large wards contain both Catholic and Protestant neighborhoods.

Within Belfast the highest levels of segregation are found in the area west of the central city. Here along the Falls, Shankhill, and Crumlin Road working-class Catholics and working-class Protestants live in streets where over 90 percent of residents are of the same religion. (See figure 10-2 for street locations.) Lower levels of segregation are found in east Belfast with the exception of the Catholic enclave of Short Strand. The lowest segregation indices are found in the middle-class southern sector along the Lisburn, Malone, and Ormeau Roads (Poole and Boal, 1973). Conflict between the two working-class groups is

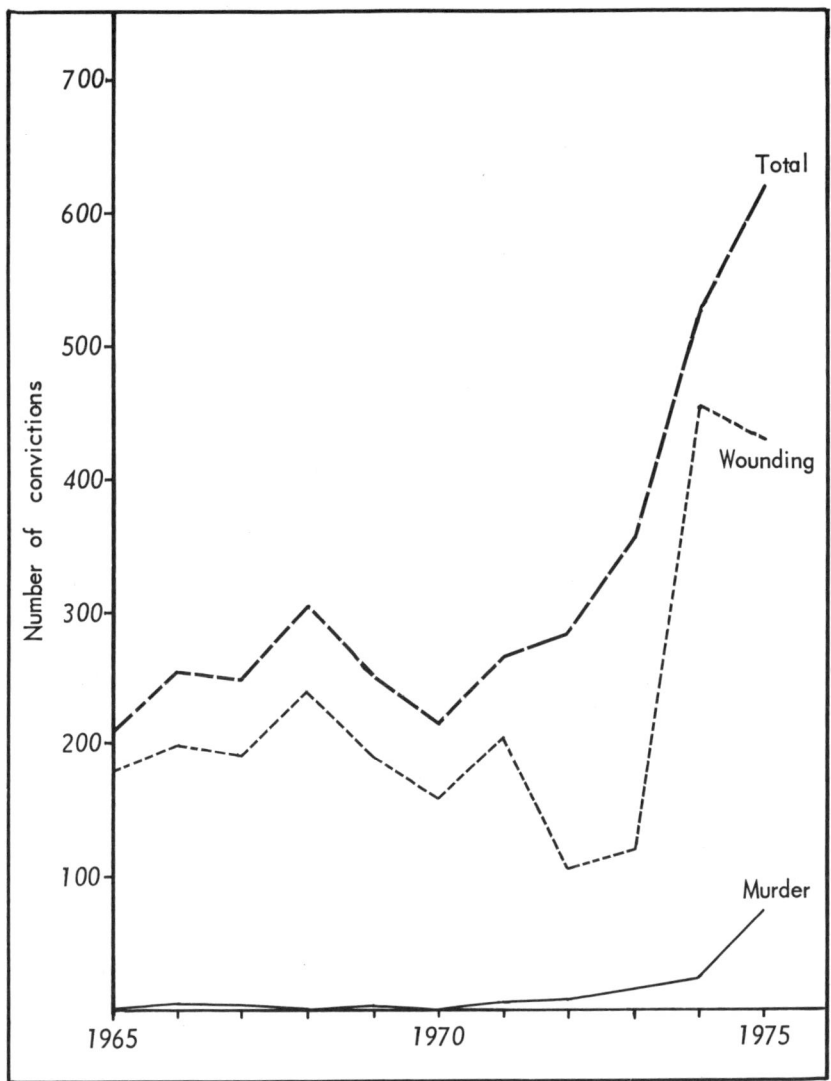

Source: Annual Abstract of Statistics. London: HMSO, 1976.
Figure 10-3. Number of Persons Found Guilty of Offences against the Person in Northern Ireland, 1965-75.

evidenced by the graffiti, wall slogans, banners, bunting, decorations, marches, and celebrations in west Belfast. The middle-class neighborhoods, although close to the conflict zone in physical space, are very far removed from it in social space.

Since 1969 the segregation of Catholics and Protestants has increased in Belfast. As a result of assaults, beatings, and in some cases murder, a large resettlement has occurred. Over ten thousand families have been forced to move since 1969; more than half of them moved in 1973. Catholics have been especially affected by this forced migration. Eighty percent of the movers were Catholics moving to the large Catholic ghetto in west Belfast from smaller, isolated Catholic enclaves or from previously mixed streets. (See Boal [1978] for a detailed examination of flight in the Cupar Street areas between Catholic and Protestant areas in west Belfast during the 1969 riots.) In 1971 about one-quarter of the people living in local authority (public) housing resided in mixed areas. Now that number has been reduced to near zero (*Time*, 1971). In the large Rathcoole estate just north of the city fewer than twenty Catholic families remained in 1973 from the eight hundred Catholic families that lived there in 1969 (Northern Ireland Community Relations Research Unit, 1971; Fenton and Hitchens, 1973).

The sense of territory is solidified by the nature of the daily activities undertaken by residents. There is little overlap in the activity spaces (that area of the city that an urban dweller uses habitually on a daily or weekly basis) of residents from the Shankhill and residents of the Falls. For example, to avoid crossing through a Catholic area, Protestants will travel a longer distance to the Shankhill Road to board a bus and shop rather than go via the Falls Road. Boal (1969) has shown how friendship ties are completely segregated, with Catholics traveling to see friends in Catholic areas and Protestants to visit friends in Protestant wards. Little opporunity exists for intimate contact between the two groups since the schools are also segregated. Catholics attend parochial schools while Protestants attend state schools. Naturally the curricula are biased, with a heavy emphasis on Irish history and culture in parochial schools and a more British orientation in state schools.

The segregation of everyday life is reinforced by the sources of information regarding local events. In Clonard, a neighborhood that was 98 percent Catholic in 1968, the *Irish News* was read by 83 percent of the population. The same newspaper, however, was read by only 3 percent of the adjoining, totally Protestant area, Shankhill (Boal, 1969). The *Irish News* takes an anti-Unionist line in politics, publishes IRA obituaries and press releases, and gives a large amount of coverage to Gaelic games and Roman Catholic church news. The divided loyalties even extend to sports teams, with Catholics supporting the Glasgow Celtic soccer team and Protestants supporting Linfield, a local soccer club that had no supporters in the Catholic areas (Boal, 1975). The media sources shared equally by both groups are television and the *Belfast Telegraph*, an evening newspaper, which was read by two-thirds of the respondents in both Catholic and Protestant neighborhoods. Residents in each area are segregated from each other physically and the lines are drawn along social, psychological, media-support, and nationalistic bases.

Personal Safety and the Religious Geography of Belfast

Although the well-defined sectarian territories of Belfast are very interesting from an abstract and detached viewpoint, they are quite literally a life-and-death matter for Belfast residents. As Boal (1978, p. 58) has explained, "territoriality" is an interesting academic concept only to those who do not live in the Belfast environment in which daily violence, beatings, and murders occur along the territorial boundary. For persons who have grown up in an area in which neighborhoods are continually at war, personal safety depends on a correct understanding of territory.

Since the outbreak of political violence on a large scale in 1971, an intimate knowledge of the sectarian line between the two camps in the city has become essential for Belfast's residents. Protestant areas became off limits to Catholics and vice versa. A stranger apprehended by neighborhood vigilantes is questioned and often killed. At the least, the intruder will get off with a stern warning or a beating. With the breakdown of civil authority in the cores of extremist sentiments, local organizations have filled the void. In west Belfast the Provisional IRA runs mail and taxi services, allocates public housing and charges for it, runs lucrative drinking clubs, and collects protection money which helps to finance their military operations. Similar activities are present in strongholds of the Ulster Defense Association (UDA), a militant Protestant group (Whalen and Ryder, 1978b).

In 1972 sectarian murders began in earnest and continued at a high rate for three years in an eye-for-an-eye pattern. The shocking brutality of some of the murders appalled even the battle-hardened residents of Northern Ireland, but the killings went on despite ceasefires between the main combatants. It is known that most of the killers are young (many in their teens), unemployed, and operate in gangs. Few have been brought to trial and only a handful convicted (Dillon and Lehane, 1973). More than two-thirds of the victims are Catholics. The decline in assassinations after 1975 is attributed by Whalen and Ryder (1978b) to the secret agreement between the Provisional IRA and the UDA to control their forces, which began the talks that still exist between the groups at the opposite ends of the political spectrum.

The locations where the bodies of sectarian assassinations were found in 1972 and the first half of 1973 are plotted in figure 10-2. These data were compiled from the daily reports in the *Belfast Telegraph* and cross-checked against the information in Dillon and Lehane (1973). The data do not include the victims of bombings or those who died as a result of battles between the British army, the IRA, and the extremist Protestants. By overlaying the body locations on a religious map of Belfast, a clearcut pattern emerges (figure 10-2). The victims can be classified into two categories—those killed by hit-and-run attacks through their neighborhoods by outside assassins and those dumped deep within the killers' territory or in an isolated spot. Not all Catholics were killed by Protestants or vice versa. Some were murdered by members of the same group for fraternizing with the enemy or by mistake.

An analysis of the map indicates some obvious spatial patterns. The western sector of Belfast is very dangerous, particularly along the Crumlin Road where Catholic ghettoes adjoin Protestant areas. It is in the border zones that most victims are apprehended or shot on the street. A Protestant assassination squad was based in Woodvale and another one in East Belfast, as indicated by the clustering of the bodies of Catholics. Catholic squads were centered in the Falls Road area, the core of the pro-IRA sentiment. On the other hand, large areas of the city are free of sectarian murders especially in the middle-class areas of south and east Belfast. In addition, the absence of Catholic victims in the Catholic area of southwest Belfast is noteworthy and points to the importance of a safe territory far from sectarian borders.

Most of the victims, like their killers, were working-class youths. This fact points to the strong and causal links between poverty, social malaise, and violence. Many of the youths convicted of murder were unemployed and lived in houses classified as substandard. The divisions in Northern Ireland are not along class lines, and efforts of working-class politicians in both Protestant and Catholic camps are to find a common ground in the poverty they both experience. Instead, the sectarian conflict is between two lower-class groups along nationalistic lines and is quite divorced from class issues.

Voting Patterns in Belfast

Since the suspension of the Northern Ireland parliament in March 1972 the province has been ruled directly from London. Because a return to complete Unionist domination was unacceptable, the British government attempted to derive "power-sharing" compromises which would give Catholics some influence in decisions and end discrimination in jobs, housing, and politics. A new Assembly for Northern Ireland was proposed in 1973. To ensure minority (Catholic) representation, a proportional representation system of voting was used rather than the single-seat system used previously for parliamentary elections. Voting in Northern Ireland is characterized by a rigid split along religious and nationalist lines. Using Alford's index of religious voting (the percentage of Protestants supporting one party, Unionists, minus the percentage of Catholics supporting the same party), Lijhart (1975) computed the score of +81. (The index has a maximum value of 100.) This compares with a figure of +16 for the United States, +7 for Great Britain, +29 for West Germany, and +14 for Australia. Northern Ireland is exceptional among Western democracies in that its political cleavages are based almost totally on religious lines whereas in most other countries, class and regional alignments explain voters' choices.

Territory and Social Conflict in Belfast

The 1973 Assembly elections in Belfast produced ten seats for the Unionists, four for the Alliance party (nonsectarian), three for the Social Democratic and Labor party (SDLP—a moderate, predominantly Catholic but nonsectarian party), one for the Northern Ireland Labor party, and six for a splinter group of Unionists opposed to any power sharing with Catholics. Republican parties received little support, and the Provisional Sinn Fein boycotted the elections. The 1973 election showed that little had changed in the political patterns of support and Unionists of one shade or another were numerically dominant. The power-sharing attempt failed in 1974 after a nationwide strike by militant Protestants.

The pre-1973 election trends in Belfast are portrayed in figure 10-4. Up to 1973 the central city and southwestern sector along the Falls Road elected antipartition Catholics, and the Crumlin Road sector returned labor members, elected with some Protestant support. But since 1969 right-wing Unionists,

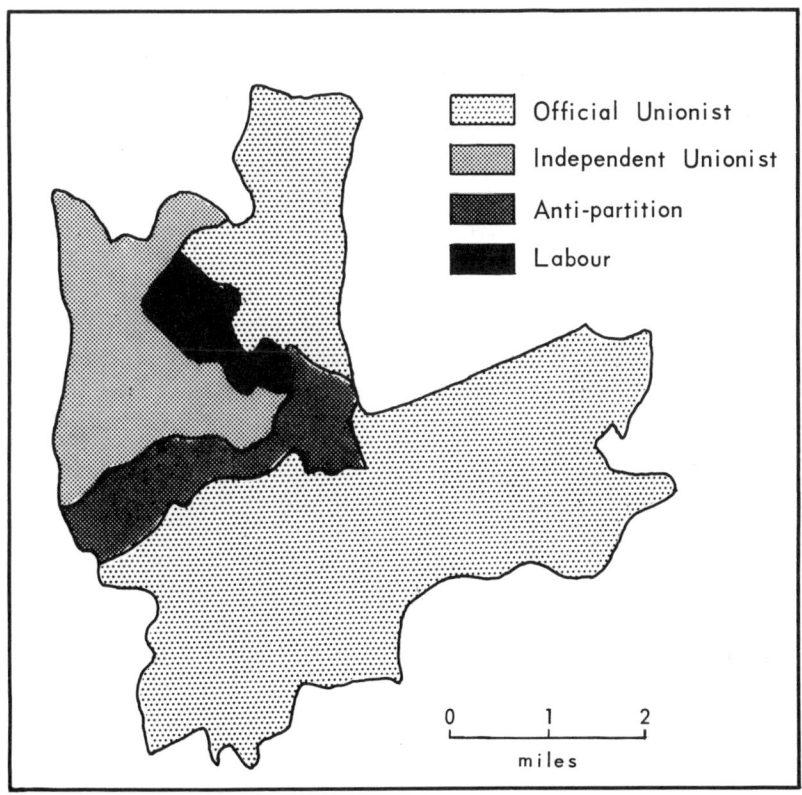

Figure 10-4. Pre-1973 Election Trends in Belfast.

opposed to the moderate policies of the government, were elected in West Belfast (figure 10-4). Both in Belfast and in the rural areas independent Unionists had their greatest successes in Protestant constituencies with large numbers of Catholics and in areas close to predominantly Catholic wards (Boal and Buchanan, 1969; Busteed, 1972). The Protestant fear of Catholic successes is greatest in these wards: consequently the backlash vote reaches its greatest extent here. This phenomenon is not peculiar to Belfast but can be seen in the United States in support for racist candidates in white areas close to ghettoes or in votes for right-wing candidates in British cities with large numbers of colored immigrants.

In May 1975 elections to the Assembly were held again on the issue of power sharing with Catholics. In Northern Ireland as a whole anti-power sharing groups (UUUC) won forty-seven of the seventy-eight Assembly seats with 54 percent of the first preference votes. Only five official Unionists, dedicated to power sharing, were elected. The Unionist front, which had ruled since 1922 and which had cracked in 1969 over the issue of civil rights, was finally splintered.

The Provisional IRA had urged a boycott of all elections. In the 1973 referendum on the border between Northern Ireland and the Republic of Ireland, although 90 percent of the Unionist electorate voted, only 1 percent of Catholics did so (*Times*, May 10, 1973). The maintenance of the border was approved with 99 percent of the vote. For the 1975 elections only 58 percent voted in West Belfast, a lower figure than in the other three city districts. The Official Unionists won only two seats, while the Alliance Party won four and the SDLP only three. The UUUC won four seats in both North and South Belfast and showed strength throughout the city (figure 10-5). Despite the efforts of the center parties to build a nonsectarian coalition, Northern Ireland remains as polarized as ever. The political stalemate continues with anti-power-sharing Unionists numerically dominant and the British government unwilling to allow them to form a government. The only possible breakthrough is a cross-sectarian coalition, but such cooperation is unlikely in the present atmosphere of fear and conflict.

Social Deprivation in Belfast

Northern Ireland's economy lags behind that of the rest of the United Kingdom. The British government has added to pre-1969 incentives for industry to locate in the depressed province. Between 1978 and 1983 it will spend $2 billion in this effort (Moore and Rhodes, 1977). The unemployment rate in the province was 4½ times the rate for the rest of the United Kingdom during the 1950s and 3½ times the United Kingdom rate in the 1960s and had fallen to twice the rate by 1970. At present because of economic recession and political strife the Northern Ireland unemployment rate hovers around a postwar peak of 13 percent.

Territory and Social Conflict in Belfast 177

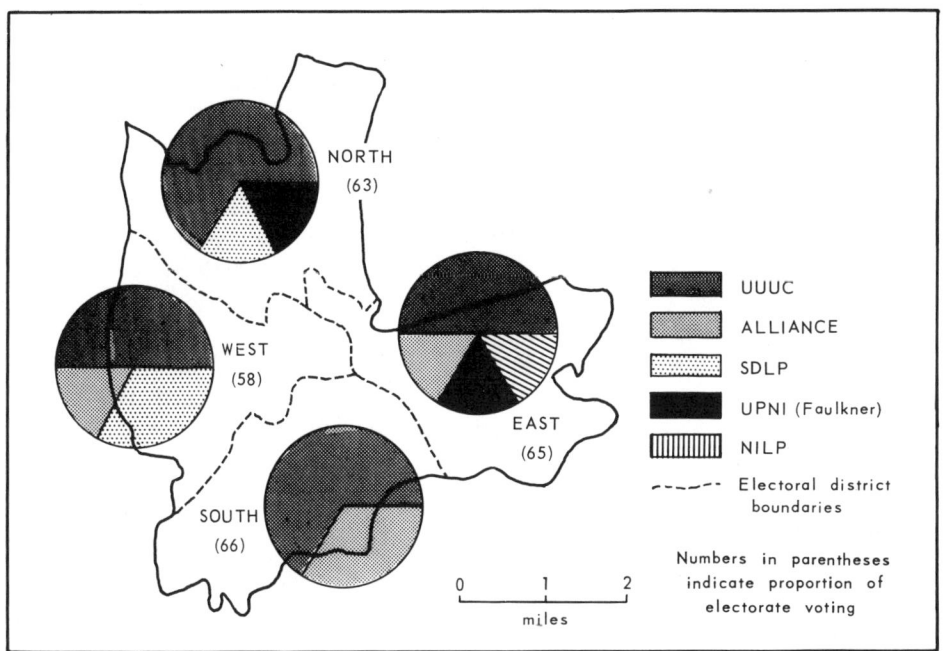

Note: Each district elected six members. Numbers in parentheses indicate proportion of electorate voting.

Figure 10-5. Distribution of Belfast's Seats in the Northern Ireland Assembly Election, May 1975.

The overall employment figure hides some large variations both within the province and within Belfast. Poverty and unemployment have been greater in the western part of the province, especially in Londonderry where one-fifth of workers are idle. Catholics claim that this fact reflects the provincial government's orientation of new industries to the area around Belfast. The regional employment incentives created new manufacturing jobs in Northern Ireland at the rate of thirty-five hundred per year between 1960 and 1970 with three-quarters of these jobs in firms diverted from outside Northern Ireland. Since 1970 the situation has been radically different. Moore and Rhodes (1977) estimate that fifteen thousand manufacturing jobs have been lost because of the political instability, with only two foreign firms attracted each year to the province.

Belfast's industry, based on heavy manufacturing, textiles, and shipbuilding, is increasingly outmoded and needs large government subsidies to survive. In the city the unemployment rate of Catholics is much higher than for Protestants, up to three times as high in west Belfast (*Graticule*, 1969). But as a Protestant stated, poverty is well known in Protestant areas. "One has only to look at the Shankhill Road.... We have known squalor. I was born and reared in it.... We have suffered every bit as much as the people of the Falls Road or any other underprivileged quarter—in many cases, more so" (quoted in Dillon and Lehane, 1973, pp. 170-171). Although the dangerously narrow dependence on shipbuilding and textiles in Belfast (and, consequently, in Northern Ireland) has been reduced from 55 percent of the manufacturing work force in 1949 to less than 25 percent today, further contraction and readjustments are needed in these industries and a continued expansion of electronics, synthetic fiber, food-processing, and light engineering industries is necessary.

Another important aspect of social deprivation is the acute housing crisis in Belfast. Much of the housing in the inner city dates from before 1900. The terraced, two-story homes with backyard toilet facilities dominated by huge mills and clouded over with a pall of industrial pollutants is reminiscent of many other industrial landscapes in northern Britain. The typical inner-city street in Belfast was built after local authority bylaws set minimum standards for size and amenity in the 1870s. But by modern standards these houses are grossly inadequate. As late as the mid-1960s virtually every house built to the 1857 bylaw standards was still occupied (Busteed, 1972, p. 40). Forty-one percent of all households in Belfast have no hot water tap and 40 percent have no fixed bath. In the development areas (figure 10-6) over 90 percent of the houses have no fixed bath, inside toilet, or hot water system (Litchfield and Associates, 1967). To meet this housing crisis, it was estimated that 74,500 new homes would have to be built between 1966 and 1981, but the actual number completed up to 1969 fell far short of this pace. Only 300 new houses per year were built by the local housing authority in the late 1950s when it was estimated that 2,000 per year should be built (Ministry for Health and Local Government, 1963).

Since 1945 public housing has been provided for thirty-five thousand families in housing estates in the outer parts of the city. Most of this housing is short-terrace, semidetached buildings with some maisonettes and flats. High-rise projects were also built in the inner city. This housing was deliberately segregated, and these huge estates now provide large areas of support for terrorists. Since "mixed areas" are points of tension and conflict, the public housing authority allocated estates to residents of one outlook. Consequently, this pattern confirmed and consolidated voting patterns and perpetuated large sectarian ghettoes. When the Belfast Corporation assigned Ballymurphy estate in southwest Belfast to Catholics, they reinforced the overwhelmingly Republican vote in local and national elections and left undisturbed equally strong Unionist majorities in neighboring seats (Busteed, 1972).

The area of the worst slumlike housing has been designated a redevelopment zone (figure 10-6). This zone rings the central city commercial district corresponding to a belt of nineteenth-century housing and including factory and

Territory and Social Conflict in Belfast

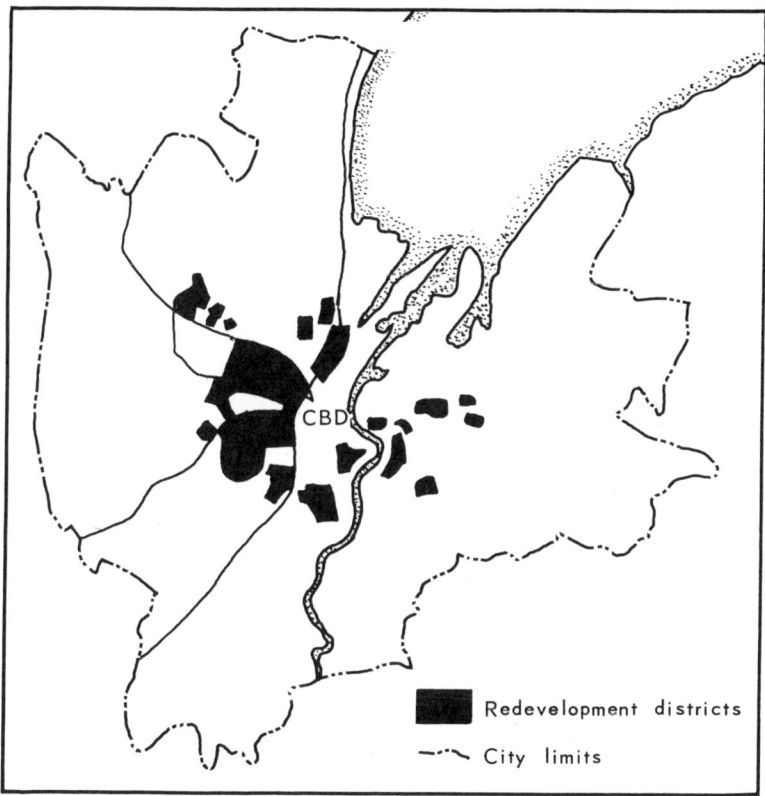

Source: Belfast Design Partnership, *Belfast Urban Area Plan: Main Report.* vol. 1, p. 29. Belfast, May 1969. Reprinted with permission.

Figure 10-6. Location of Redevelopment Districts in Belfast.

warehouse districts. The zone extends into the Falls and Shankhill neighborhoods and is less widespread in the wealthier east and south Belfast. Over sixty thousand houses are located here, thirty thousand of which are seriously defective in structure. A decade ago one house in four was overcrowded; up to half were underoccupied, mostly by old people (Litchfield and Associates, 1967). A severe lack of open space for recreation compounds the congestion problem. But like many similar situations in American cities, the residents retain a strong attachment to their homes and neighborhood and wish to remain, although in better houses.

A concentric belt around the redevelopment zone was designated a "twilight zone" by the 1969 Belfast Urban Area Plan. Here, two of three houses lack standard amenities. Over half the householders in this twilight area are still living in the same house to which they went after marriage more than twenty years before. Selective rehabilitation would appear to be the best approach in this transitional area.

Another important factor in social deprivation is social malaise. Social malaise is an index comprising variables such as unemployment, juvenile offenses, infant mortality, and crowding. A recent examination of social malaise in Belfast found a close correspondence between its incidence and the distribution of the lower classes in the city. Using squares 200 meters by 200 meters, the Queen's University (Belfast) team found two basic spatial patterns of social malaise in the city. The first shows the patterns for male, female, and juvenile unemployment, and male juvenile crime. The western sector of the city along the Crumlin, Shankhill, and Falls Roads ranks highest in these problems; these are areas in which families are larger than average, birth rates higher, the proportion of males in semiskilled and unskilled occupations higher, and the proportion of households living in public housing greater than elsewhere in the city. These areas are also the core of sectarian conflict and personal safety fears are highest there. The second spatial pattern of high social malaise reflects the distribution of illegitimate birth rates, of high proportions of children in day care, and of high death rates for those aged twenty-five to sixty-five, including deaths from bronchitis. It is most marked in inner-city areas where most of the housing is rented from private landlords, population densities are highest, and the average age of the population is relatively high for the city. As can be seen from figure 10-6, the zone roughly corresponds to the ring of redevelopment districts around the center of the city (Boal, Doherty and Pringle, 1974).

The solution of social problems in employment, housing, and crime is severely hampered by the political impasse. Some families have abandoned the province as evidenced by a fivefold increase in the number filling out emigration papers in 1971-72 over the 1966-67 period. More Protestants than Catholics have been leaving and a significant shift in population sizes is happening. Because of higher birth and lower emigration rates, Catholics will outnumber Protestants by the end of the century if present trends continue. At present, Catholic school-age children outnumber Protestant ones and the gap is continuing to widen (Whalen and Ryder, 1978b). Industrialists are reluctant to locate in Northern Ireland, thereby reducing the attractiveness of the province as a supplier of cheap labor. The IRA policy of attempting to wreck the economy by bombing commercial establishments has caused many potential industrialists to look to other development areas in Britain where they can get similar incentives to locate. Despite government efforts to attract industry, little change has occurred in the past five years and the unemployment lines are as long as ever on the Shankhill and Falls Roads.

Conclusions

Since political, social, and economic issues are intertwined, the solution of one set of problems is partly dependent on the related issues. If a resolution to the seemingly hopeless and unending conflict is to appear, it must go a long way toward meeting both nationalist and unionist demands. What appears as a possible solution to an academic observer is violently opposed by some segment of the Northern Ireland community. Indeed, as Russell (1975, 1977) has recently shown, the socialization of children into the opposing camps continues as it has for a century.

Lijhart (1975) has suggested five possible solutions. They are (1) economic—improve the situation of the poor; (2) decolonization—Britain withdraws from the province; (3) democratization—political reforms have already been implemented; (4) power sharing—this device has already been defeated by extremist unionists; and (5) further partition—adjust the border to maximize the number of Catholics to be shifted to the Republic of Ireland. However, solving the economic problem does little to end the political crisis, and a withdrawal of British troops may lead to a bloody civil war. An adjustment of the border, while helping the military situation from the British army standpoint, does not get to the core of the problem, the very existence of Northern Ireland separate from the Republic of Ireland. Reducing the size of the Northern Ireland state would not appease the IRA demands and might lead to a backlash as the Unionists see their country being whittled away.

Other observers have also suggested the border realignment with incentives for Catholics to move south and Protestants to move inside the shrunken Northern Ireland (Wilson, 1972; Kingston, 1972). This proposed migration is unlikely to occur given the attachment of both groups to their homes and the disparities between Northern Ireland, part of the British welfare state, and the Republic. In 1970-71, the public expenditure (pounds per capita) for education was 47 in the North compared to 28 in the Republic. Similar differences were visible in housing (36 in the North, 14 in the Republic) and social services (118 in the North, 65 in the Republic) (Buchanan, 1977).

In recent years, a much discussed solution has come into the limelight. It would be a "federal" solution, with an independent Northern Ireland loosely federated with the Republic. As part of the plan, Britain would support Northern Ireland economically for fifteen years after British troops withdraw. Such a plan is not feasible unless it is accepted by the extremists on both sides who retain the power to wreck any solution. Whalen and Ryder (1978b) claim that leaders of both extremist camps have begun to talk on the future of Northern Ireland, now that the British government is committed to eventual withdrawal.

Perhaps the best hope for a solution to the myriad of problems facing Northern Ireland lies in the context of an expanded Europe. Already suggestions have been made for joint Irish-British political jurisdiction, United Nations peacekeeping forces, and a massive reorganization of the local government system to guarantee more local autonomy. However, the problem created by a hundred thousand Catholics in Belfast makes such solutions difficult, isolated as they are from their coreligionists in the rural areas.

The bitter hatreds aroused by the violence of the past eight years are not likely to disappear (Lyons, 1975). Indeed, as White (1977) has pointed out, the deepest troubles may lie in the hearts of children who are now inured to violence. Eighty percent of boys interviewed in Belfast now approve of violence as an acceptable means to political ends, up from 60 percent in 1971. When ten-year-olds were asked their reactions to finding a cigarette pack, letter, or parcel in the street, 75 percent identified the object as a bomb. The interviewers found that children who had friends of another religion were less accepting of violence than other children, but few people in Belfast have a chance to form friendships across the religious divide. Other researchers measured attitudes toward strangers in a sample of boys aged six and ten in schools in troubled areas of Belfast. They found that the child's awareness of his "tribal affiliation" was high from an early age, that hostility to strangers appeared when the child was young, and that this increased with age (White, 1977). With a strong awareness of territoriality and hostility to outsiders inculcated at the earliest age, any solution which requires contact between the antagonists of the past eight years is probably doomed to failure.

Belfast is unusual among European cities in that political violence on its streets is an everyday occurrence. Separatist groups in other European nations tend to be confined to remote rural peripheries. Political violence in cities in Italy, West Germany, Spain, the Netherlands, and Portugal are usually hit-and-run guerrilla tactics. The core of support available to the IRA or UDA in Belfast is not available to radicals in other nations. Urban terrorism is difficult to combat successfully and there are signs of growing conflict in industrial nations (Burton, 1976; Glass and Obler, 1977). The experience of Belfast may enable us to understand the causes and consequences of urban warfare. One hopes that the future in Belfast will point the way to its peaceful resolution.

References

Boal, F.W. 1969. "Territoriality on the Shankhill-Falls Divide, Belfast." *Irish Geography* 6:30-50.

———. 1975. "Social Space in the Belfast Built-up Area." In *Readings in Social Geography*, ed. E. Jones. London: Oxford University Press, pp. 149-68.

———. 1978. "Territoriality on the Shankhill-Falls Divide: The Perspective from 1976." In *Invitation to Geography*, 2nd ed., ed. D.A. Lanegran and R. Palm. New York: McGraw-Hill, pp. 58-78.

Boal, F.W., and Buchanan, R.H. 1969. "The 1969 Northern Ireland Election." *Irish Geography* 6:78-84.

Boal, F.W., Doherty, P., and Pringle, D.G. 1974. *The Spatial Distribution of Some Social Problems in the Belfast Urban Area*. Belfast: Northern Ireland Community Relations Commission.

Boal, F.W., and Murray, R.C. 1977. "A City in Conflict." *Geographical Magazine* 49:364-71.
Boyd, A. 1969. *Holy War in Belfast*. Tralee, Ireland: Anvil Books.
Buchanan, R.H. 1977. "A Land in Need of Industry." *Geographical Magazine* 49:237-42.
Burton, A.M. 1976. *Urban Terrorism: Theory, Practice and Response*. Riverside, N.J.: Free Press.
Busteed, M.A. 1972. "Northern Ireland: Geographical Aspects of a Crisis." Research Paper No. 3, School of Geography, University of Oxford.
Cameron Report. 1971. *Disturbances in Northern Ireland*. Belfast: Her Majesty's Stationary Office.
Dillon, M., and Lehane, D. 1973. *Political Murder in Northern Ireland*. Hammondsworth, Middlesex, England: Penguin Books.
Douglas, J.N.H. 1976. "The Irreconcilable Border." *Geographical Magazine* 49:162-68.
Deutch, R., and Magowan, V. 1974. *Northern Ireland, 1968-1973: A Chronology of Events*. Belfast: Blackstaff Press.
Fenton, J., and Hitchens, C. 1973. "Return to the Ghetto." *New Statesman* 85:225-26.
Glass, S.C., and Ober, J.L., eds. 1977. *Urban Ethnic Conflict: A Comparative Perspective*. Comparative Urban Studies Monograph Series, No. 3. Chapel Hill, N.C.: University of North Carolina.
Graticule. 1969. "Unemployment in West Belfast." Belfast: Queen's University, Belfast Geographical Society, pp. 22-25.
Institute for the Study of Conflict. 1973. *Ulster: Politics and Terrorism*. Conflict Studies No. 36. New York.
Jones, E. 1960. *A Social Geography of Belfast*. London: Oxford University Press.
Kenyon, J.B. 1976. "Patterns of Residential Integration in the Bicultural Western City." *Professional Geographer* 28:40-44.
Kingston, W. 1973. "Northern Ireland: If Reason Fails." *Political Quarterly* 44:22-32.
Lijhart, A. 1975. "Northern Ireland Problem: Cases, Theories, and Solutions; a Review Article." *British Journal of Political Science* 5:83-106.
Litchfield, N., and Associates. 1967. *Belfast Urban Area: Interim Planning Policy*. Belfast.
Lyons, H.A. 1975. "Legacy of Violence in Northern Ireland." *International Journal of Offender Therapy and Comparative Criminology* 19:292-98.
Moore, B., and Rhodes, J. 1977. "Ulster: Economic Package Unlikely to Reduce Unemployment Levels." *The Times* (London), August 10, p. 19.
Northern Ireland Community Relations Research Unit. 1971. *Flight: A Report on Population Movement in Belfast during August, 1971*. Belfast.
Northern Ireland Ministry for Health and Local Government. 1963. *Belfast Regional Survey and Plan*. Belfast: Her Majesty's Stationary Office.

Poole, M., and Boal, F.W. 1975. "Segregation in Belfast." In *Social Patterns in Cities*, Institute of British Geographers Special Publication No. 5, ed. B.D. Clark and M.G. Cleave. Oxford, England: Alden and Monbray, Ltd., pp. 1-40.

Rose, R. 1971. *Governing without Consensus: An Irish Perspective*. Boston: Beacon Press.

Rose, R. 1972. "Ulster Politics: A Select Bibliography of Political Discord." *Political Studies* 20:206-12.

Russell, J. 1975. "Northern Ireland: Socialization into Conflict." *Social Studies: Irish Journal of Sociology* 4:109-123.

Russell, J. 1977. "Replication of Instability: Political Stabilization in Northern Ireland." *British Journal of Political Science* 7:115-128.

Sunday Times "Insight" Team. 1972. *Ulster*. London: Penguin Books.

Time. 1971. "Northern Ireland: The Powderkeg." April 5, pp. 26-32.

Times (London). 1973. "Poll Produces Overwhelming Vote for U.K. Link." March 10, p. 1.

Ulster Year Book 1976: The Official Handbook of Northern Ireland. 1976. Belfast: Her Majesty's Stationary Office.

Whalen, J., and Ryder, C. 1978a. "Ulster 1968-1978: A Decade of Despair." *Sunday Times* (London). June 18, pp. 17-18.

Whalen, J., and Ryder, C. 1978b. "Hot Line between the Hard Men." *Sunday Times* (London). June 25, pp. 17-19.

White, B. 1977. "Ulster's Deepest Troubles May Be in the Hearts of the Children." *New York Times*. April 10, Section 4, p. 18.

Whyte, J.H. 1976. "Recent Writing on Northern Ireland." *American Political Science Review* 70:592-96.

Wilson, T. 1972. "Ulster Crisis: Reformed Government with a New Border." *Round Table,* No. 245, pp. 37-54.

Winchester, S. 1975. *Northern Ireland in Crisis: Reporting on Ulster Troubles*. New York: Holmes and Meier.

11 The Lost Center: Dispersing Berlin's Capital City Functions, 1945-78

Richard L. Merritt

For most countries the development of their core areas is a matter of history. Except for certain port functions Paris has dominated France for centuries, and London has played a similar role in England if not the British Isles as a whole. Rapid social changes in the United States during the past centuries and the growth of such metropolises as Chicago and Los Angeles have failed to dislodge the corridor between New York and the District of Columbia from its premier position in most aspects of America's political, economic, and cultural life. Core areas, once established, and their relationships to their peripheries change only very slowly.

This has not been the case in Germany since World War II. Disputes among the occupying powers ultimately split Germany as well as its former capital city, Berlin, and the hopes for reunification appear more dismal as each year passes. The eastern portion of Berlin soon became de facto the capital of the German Democratic Republic (GDR). Continued adherence by the United States, Great Britain, and France to the principle of quadripartite control of the whole of Berlin has meant, by contrast, that West Berlin remained juridically apart from the Federal Republic of Germany (FRG). Nor have efforts to provide as much social, economic, and even political integration as possible been able to overcome West Berlin's physical isolation from the FRG.

One consequence of Germany's division after 1945 has been that Berlin, the former core area, has seen its main functions dispersed among a number of other German cities. To be sure, East Berlin still serves as an organizing focus for life in the GDR. West Berlin, however, has become peripheral to the vitality that characterizes the FRG. This paper examines the latter relationship, especially the growth in West Germany of a plethora of new centers to play the role that Berlin had in prewar Germany. After examining some evidence of this transformation, this chapter begins to explore long-term implications.

Isolation of West Berlin

Traditionally, and not entirely in a jocular vein, Berliners have considered their city to be the hub of the world. A review of recent history would lend support to this notion in many respects. For three-quarters of a century, from the country's unification in 1871 under Bismarck until its division into four occupation zones in 1945, Berlin was capital of all Germany. This is not to say that loyalties to regional population centers did not exist—nor even that all segments of the German people were equally willing to accept the preeminence of Berlin. Indeed, Berlin was the symbol of Prussian militarism to many, of cosmopolitan decadence to others, of rampant socialism to still others. Regardless of the cries of dissidents or the claims of other cities, however, Berlin was Germany's center, and the rest of Germany was Berlin's periphery.

The years of unity found Berlin, as core area of pre-1945 Germany, more than just the administrative center of the Wilhelminian Reich, the Weimar Republic, and Hitler's "Third Reich." The city was Germany's financial capital, its commercial capital, and its political capital. Berlin was the main node of the communication and transportation net that covered Germany. Newspapers from Berlin were daily reading matter in the provinces. Its café society set tastes and fashions for all Germany. The artistic movements that the city generated spread not only throughout Germany but throughout the entire world as well. The theater of Hauptmann, Reinhardt, and Brecht, for instance, was known and appreciated in dramatic circles everywhere. In short, by the end of the Weimar era Berlin had become *a* if not *the* leading metropolis of Europe. And after Hitler's rise to power in 1933 the city became the source of decisions that exasperated, startled, and eventually shattered the traditional international system with its traditional ways of looking at and doing things.

In the world that emerged after the ultimate defeat of Hitler in its bomb-gutted bunkers, Berlin again became a focal point of attention and tension. This time, however, the city was not the scene of the traditional German struggle between Potsdam and Weimar, between the militaristic spirit of Prussianism and the liberal, humanitarian spirit of Goethe and Beethoven. Rather, it became the scene of battle between two ideologically oriented world powers, the Soviet Union and the United States.

As Berlin was assuming a new and different role in the political system of the world, so too its function for Germany as a whole changed. In their planning for the occupation of postwar Germany, the wartime Allies divided the country into several parts. First they restored to their prewar status Austria, Czechoslovakia, and other territories overrun by the Nazis and gave to Poland and the Soviet Union, for a "temporary" administration that has proved to be permanent, those lands east of the Oder and Neisse rivers. The remainder of Germany they divided into four occupation zones and a special area comprising Greater Berlin in its 1920 boundaries, itself divided into four sectors of occupation. An Allied Control Council and, for Berlin, a Kommandatura were to ensure not only coordination but also, it was hoped, a high measure of uniformity in the policies adopted by the Four Powers.

Distrust and eventually conflict along East-West lines soon replaced the expectation of harmony that underlay the wartime agreements. The final breach occurred after the Western currency reform of June 1948. The Soviet Union countered with a separate currency reform for its own zone of occupation and all of Berlin, which lay some one hundred miles inside the Soviet zone. The West's response, including the three western sectors of Berlin, met immediately with the Soviet blockade of all land access routes to West Berlin. Before the summer was over, the city's administration was itself split and both sides were well on their way toward creating separate governments in East and West Germany.

The status of Berlin remained anomalous for many years after Germany's formal division in 1949. Despite constitutional provisions in the GDR and FRG, the Four Powers refused to permit either half of the city to merge fully with these governments. Not until after the quadripartite and inter-German treaties of the early 1970s did East Berlin (in East Germany often called Democratic Berlin) become fully integrated with the GDR. West Berlin remains an occupied city in principle but closely tied to the FRG in fact. The latter's legislation, for instance, applies in West Berlin as well—after a brief lapse of time to permit the Western Allies to examine its provisions and suspend any they consider detrimental to their occupation rights. Some West German institutions, such as the army and the federal assembly which elects the FRG's president, are nonetheless barred from the city.

West Berlin's geographic isolation from the FRG put it in a peculiarly exposed position. For one thing, the mere fact that people and goods had to travel at least a hundred miles to get from one area to the other made such transactions inconvenient at best. Added to this was a perceived political danger. The Soviet Union, after all, had blockaded West Berlin from June 1948 to May 1949. Only the Western airlift of supplies to the beleaguered Berliners, it was commonly felt in the West, had prevented the city's complete takeover by the Soviets. Soviet and East German guarantees to the contrary notwithstanding, what was to prevent the same thing from happening again? Given such a possibility, or merely the uncertainty enshrouding the city's fate, West Berlin seemed to many too fragile a reed on which to base the FRG's future. The result was a massive reorganization of German life, at least as far as West Germany and West Berlin were concerned.

Shifting Core Area Functions

Allied determination to keep West Berlin juridically separate from the Federal Republic had several consequences. First, of course, it could not serve as the FRG's political capital. This in turn meant that the wide variety of associations and institutions that gravitate toward the center of political power, such as the central offices of interest groups, would find no impelling reason to settle in West Berlin rather than in some West German city. The vacuum created by the termination of Berlin's traditional role also encouraged other areas to begin competing to capture their share of political power. Without a "natural" core area in West Germany, on which all political leaders could agree, the pressure was great both to disperse the various functions associated with a capital city and to prevent any single area from attaining the preeminent position enjoyed by prewar Berlin.

Political Core Area Functions

In the reorganization of German life, the part played by the Western Allies cannot be stressed enough. Their occupation policy rested, after all, on the principle of decentralization. The Allies were firm in their intent to prevent the reemergence of a Germany controlled from a single area and hence more susceptible, they believed, to the kind of political takeover which Hitler had effected. At the very least this called for the reestablishment of federalism—but not Bismarck's brand of federalism, which had permitted Prussia to dominate the Reich, and which had made Berlin the locus of power in Germany as a whole. Still less attractive were the Weimar Republic's centralizing attributes, such as a voting system using proportional representation based on a national list, which not only made difficult the acquisition of regional political power but also rendered it fairly insignificant as far as national or even regional political decisions were concerned. Such political systems had had a signal effect on Berlin. Budding politicians, for instance, realized in their scramble to the top of the political heap that, while someplace else might do for starters, Berlin was where the political power lay, and it was in Berlin that one had to build one's reputation and connections.

As a first step toward preventing any such centralization in postwar Germany, the Western Allies together with the Soviet Union redefined the boundaries among Germany's states (or Länder), both to eliminate what they saw as the source of aggressive militarism, Prussia, and to arrange the others so that they roughly balanced each other. They also sought to end excessive concentration in the rest of Germany's public life. Berlin's banks could thus no longer operate in Saxony or in Bavaria, nor could political or even religious organizations be formed across boundaries between occupation zones. And even after such institutions were merged in the three western zones in 1947 and 1948 the Allies made no great effort to locate their central offices in Berlin. To the contrary, as they moved toward western Germany's political reconstruction they first permitted local and then state governments and encouraged them to develop the kind of autonomy that would ensure that German politics would be competitive along regional lines and any future national government would be federal in form.

The Allies were hardly alone in pushing toward decentralization in West

Germany's political life. Some Germans, who had chafed under Prussian domination emanating from Berlin, were not unhappy to see that city's overweening political influence destroyed. Others agreed with the Allies that centralization had facilitated Hitler's takeover and the ease with which he moved Germany into a disastrous war. For them, a return to some version of Germany's traditional federalism seemed both appropriate and wise. Still others were impressed by the apparent success elsewhere of federalism in general and more specifically such decentralizing principles as single-member constituencies and strong upper houses representing federal units. Accordingly, the Allies' demand of the Parliamentary Council, which met in 1948-49 to draft a Basic Law, that it produce a federal government most assuredly did not fall on deaf ears. Even so, the Allied military governors felt constrained to intervene from time to time in the Council's proceedings to push it in a still more federal direction.

The Allies refused to countenance the prospect of a West Berlin united juridically with the Federal Republic of Germany. In part, this was to ensure that through the exercise of their occupation rights they could protect the island-city against any encroachments from the East. A continued presence underscored their insistence that all Berlin was a Four-Power city and that the legitimate status of all Germany still rested on quadripartite agreements which called for the country's eventual reunification. Some would add that the Allied presence in West Berlin also ensured their continuing influence over West German politics. But, whatever the precise cause, the effect was that the Allies suspended those portions of the Basic Law which declared West Berlin to be a constituent part of the Federal Republic.

When the FRG was established in 1949, the decision to locate its main institutions in a small university town on the Rhine River, Bonn, merely put a capstone on a process that had begun four years earlier. The starting point of the occupation was the Allied dissolution of all German governmental and political bodies. When political parties were once again permitted, Berlin's former leadership position fell by the wayside in both of West Germany's major parties—in the Social Democratic party when internecine struggles with a cold-war overtone permitted Kurt Schumacher to set up shop in Hanover; and in the old Center party's successor, the Christian Democratic Union, when the Rhenish Konrad Adenauer outfoxed his Berlin colleagues. Moreover, as state governments were making headway in the West and beginning to create a federal government, West Berliners were on the frontline of the cold war fighting for their political survival. The decision to exclude West Berlin from the Federal Republic was merely the final straw.

West Germany's development in the years since then deepened such trends. Of key importance is the fact that federalism enhanced the relative political power of the states vis-à-vis the federal government. They were increasingly prepared to fill the vacuum left by Berlin's isolation from the FRG. And through playing the federal political game they could ensure that at least some federal institutions were distributed throughout the country. The top courts, for instance, are widely distributed: the Federal Constitutional Court and the Supreme Court in Karlsruhe, the Federal Finance Court in Munich, the Federal Court of Labor and the Social Court in Kassel, and the Federal Administrative Court in West Berlin. Although the top political bodies (offices of the federal president and chancellor as well as the various ministries, and both the Bundestag and the Federal Council) are in Bonn, other federal agencies are also scattered. Of the eight leading federal agencies, three are in Bonn, one each is in Aurich, Frankfurt, Nuremburg, and West Berlin, and the remaining one has joint offices in Braunschweig and West Berlin. The passage of time has also transformed Bonn from a temporary into a permanent capital city.

A not unexpected result is that political power, once concentrated overwhelmingly in Berlin, has moved to a number of other sites in West Germany, especially but not exclusively Bonn. The ambitious young politician of today pursuing the path to the top may still see an office in West Berlin as a challenge. The person who cuts a good figure there, as Willy Brandt did in the late 1950s, has an excellent chance of rising still further. The fact that their occupied status prohibits West Berliners from voting, however, also means that establishing a regional base of power in the island-city does not automatically give the politician clout in federal politics. More generally, those anxious to play a determining role in national political decisions may see West Berlin as a way station on the road to power but certainly not the final destination.

Economic Core Area Functions

Berlin's economic outlook in the early summer of 1945 was bleak indeed. Two years of British and American aerial bombardment followed by Soviet artillery and intense streetfighting had reduced much of the city to rubble. Half its population had fled or been killed. A quarter of Berlin's dwelling units had been totally destroyed and another half partially destroyed. Main arteries were virtually impassable because of craters and rubble; the subway system lay in ruins. In short, Berlin was a scene of desolation, the kind of desolation that only modern warfare could bring. Soviet dismantling, moreover, in accord with the Soviet Union's interpretations of and expectations about reparations agreements among the wartime Allies, sharply reduced whatever industrial capacity the war had left to the city, especially those areas destined for American, British, and French occupation. Subsequent analysis estimated that wartime destruction and postwar dismantling for reparations eliminated 90 percent of West Berlin's capacity in mechanical engineering, steel and iron structural engineering, and metal goods production; 85 percent in electrical engineering; 80 percent in precision mechanics and optics; 75 percent in the printing trade; and 70 percent in vehicle production capacity (Merkatz and Metzner, 1954, p. 311).

Nor did the ensuing four years favor the reconstruction of West Berlin's economy. By mid-1948, as the currency reform indicated, the Western Allies had committed themselves to the task of rebuilding at least some sectors of the West Germany economy in order to aid reconstruction efforts in western Europe, reduce the burden of supporting a heavily dependent German population of some 50 million, and, it must be added, strengthen West Germany's potential to contribute to Western defenses against any Soviet attack. After the currency reform, economic reconstruction in West Germany proceeded rapidly. West Berlin, however, with its rail, canal, and road routes to the West blockaded, and dependent upon the American-British airlift for its mere survival, all but stagnated economically. Not until another year had passed could West Berlin begin to try to catch up with the rest of the Federal Republic.

West Berlin's delayed start toward economic rehabilitation, exacerbated by its politically exposed position, was fateful. At a time when West Germany's economic miracle was unfolding, a third of West Berlin's workers could not find employment in the city. Nor were businessmen in the west anxious to tie the future of their own enterprises to West Berlin's tenuous circumstances. Subsequent federal legislation providing a wide variety of economic incentives for businesses (including credits and tax advantages) to establish branches in West Berlin or at least to trade more with that city's firms could not repair the damage. West Berlin moved ever more into the background of the FRG's economic life.

These trends can be seen in the changing position of Berlin in Germany's occupational structure (table 11-1). In 1933 Berlin accounted for 6.4 percent of the country's population but 7.7 percent of its firms and 8.6 percent of those employed. By 1970, with only 3.5 percent of the West German population, West Berlin had 3.6 percent of the firms and 3.9 percent of those employed. One of the most important structural shifts shown in table 11-1 is in the electrical engineering field. In 1933 about a ninth (11.3 percent) of the country's firms in this field and a third (32.9 percent) of its workers were in Berlin. Relative to what we might have expected had Berlin's working population been distributed in the same way as that of the whole country, the city had 287 percent more workers in electrical engineering firms. The relative overrepresentation of Berlin workers in such firms in the FRG dropped to 130 percent in 1970—a decline of 157 percentage points. Figures for other branches in which prewar Berlin was strong showed similar declines.

Banking and insurance declined from +187 percent in 1933 to +11 percent in 1970 (a decline of 176 percentage points).

Ancillary business services (advertising, brokerage, storage) declined from +119 to +33 percent (−86 percentage points).

Printing declined from +113 to +17 percent (−96 percentage points).

Wholesale trade declined from +62 to −36 percent (−98 percentage points).

Table 11-1
German and Berlin Occupational Structure, 1933 and 1970

	Workplaces						Employees and Self-Employed					
	1933			1970			1933			1970		
Occupational Category	Reich Total	Percentage Berlin	Berlin Diff.[a]	FRG Total	Percentage Berlin	Berlin Diff.[a]	Reich Total	Percentage Berlin	Berlin Diff.[a]	FRG Total	Percentage Berlin	Berlin Diff.[a]
Agriculture, forests, fisheries	37,931	1.3	−0.83	22,084	2.0	−0.44	84,371	1.9	−0.78	96,063	3.0	−0.23
Mining	1,334	0.2	−0.97	662	0.5	−0.88	495,104	0.03	−1.00	289,751	0.01	−1.00
Stonecutting	34,407	2.3	−0.71	19,360	1.7	−0.53	409,872	1.3	−0.85	491,981	1.7	−0.55
Iron and steel	1,486	1.7	−0.77	7,863	2.7	−0.25	268,680	0.5	−0.94	716,847	0.6	−0.84
Metalworking	1,186	9.7	+0.25	1,208	5.9	+0.61	48,211	4.5	−0.48	135,874	3.2	−0.18
Iron and metal manufacturing	157,123	4.5	−0.42	32,619	1.9	−0.47	597,643	5.7	−0.34	408,796	5.0	+0.29
Machinery, tools, transport mfg.	41,944	6.3	−0.18	53,234	2.5	−0.30	613,120	7.8	−0.09	2,302,443	2.2	−0.42
Electrical engineering	27,820	11.3	+0.47	15,832	5.0	+0.38	253,806	32.9	+2.84	1,148,041	9.0	+1.30
Optics, precision mechanics	22,803	7.7	−0.002	22,817	4.6	+0.28	101,668	7.6	−0.12	703,308	2.3	−0.40
Chemical industry	7,740	10.9	+0.41	6,042	7.2	+0.99	249,949	7.0	−0.18	645,371	2.3	−0.42
Textiles	67,716	2.4	−0.69	10,827	2.6	−0.28	857,396	1.3	−0.85	521,529	1.3	−0.66
Paper goods industry	10,956	8.2	+0.06	4,153	6.9	+0.90	188,508	5.6	−0.35	227,014	2.7	−0.31
Printing	25,079	11.9	+0.54	11,775	5.1	+0.42	273,064	18.3	+1.13	303,801	4.6	+0.17
Leather goods (excl. shoes)	34,748	3.0	−0.61	4,962	3.0	−0.18	120,021	3.3	−0.61	69,767	1.1	−0.71
Plastics, rubber, asbestos	1,958	14.3	+0.85	6,518	5.0	+0.37	49,006	7.3	−0.14	338,285	1.8	−0.54
Wood and wood products	216,037	2.8	−0.63	62,922	1.3	−0.63	612,289	3.8	−0.56	536,253	1.5	−0.62
Musical instruments, toys	11,072	3.3	−0.57	6,707	3.9	+0.08	38,342	5.8	−0.33	79,878	2.0	−0.49
Foodstuffs	305,551	4.1	−0.47	101,550	1.8	−0.49	1,432,301	6.0	−0.30	971,536	3.8	−0.02
Clothing (incl. shoes)	540,505	9.3	+0.20	72,366	4.6	+0.26	1,054,811	11.4	+0.34	618,498	4.6	+0.19

Construction	263,055	5.2	−0.32	207,521	2.5	−0.32	1,025,806	6.4	−0.26	2,328,816	3.2	−0.17
Energy	8,069	1.7	−0.78	5,977	1.6	−0.55	141,679	6.8	−0.20	207,117	5.2	+0.34
Cleaning, bodily care	137,195	9.8	+0.27	104,765	4.3	+0.20	320,926	11.4	+0.34	507,275	5.4	+0.39
Wholesale trade	150,586	9.1	+0.18	131,804	2.8	−0.23	681,243	13.8	+0.62	1,239,325	2.5	−0.36
Retail trade	839,390	10.0	+0.30	506,599	4.3	+0.19	1,910,988	10.2	+0.19	2,282,388	4.7	+0.21
Advertising, brokerage, storage	201,561	15.0	+0.94	188,879	5.0	+0.38	438,938	18.7	+1.19	825,384	5.2	+0.33
Finance, banking, insurance	47,973	9.5	+0.23	74,864	2.5	−0.30	398,530	24.6	+1.87	837,072	4.3	+0.11
Transportation	124,764	6.3	−0.19	108,806	4.3	+0.20	1,325,135	8.6	+0.01	1,299,722	3.8	−0.02
Hotels, gastronomy	253,173	6.1	−0.21	206,424	2.8	−0.23	799,417	7.2	−0.16	720,981	3.5	−0.11
Other services	—	—	—	289,299	4.3	+0.19	—	—	—	3,553,743	5.9	+0.52
Total or average	3,573,162	7.7	±0.47	2,288,439	3.6	±0.40	14,790,823	8.6	±0.61	24,406,909	3.9	±0.41

Source: Statistisches Reichsamt, 1936a, 1936b, 1938; Statistiches Bundesamt, 1973.

aDifference between Berlin's actual occupational structure and what it might be expected to be if it were distributed in the same way as the national total, standardized by dividing the difference by the expected sum. Scores greater than +0.15 are underlined once, those greater than +0.30 are underlined twice.

Looking at the overall distribution, and not losing sight of the central fact that West Berlin's share of the FRG's total population and workers was less than half that of Berlin in the Germany of 1933, the net effect of the structural dislocations was to smooth out sharply those characteristics that distinguished the city's prewar economy, and to make West Berlin much more average in its distribution of firms and workers. By 1970 West Berlin's only outstanding occupational characteristic was a continued albeit reduced interest in electrical engineering.

A closer analysis of such data for postwar Germany shows where the specific economic activities previously associated with Berlin are now located (table 11-2). Electrical engineering remains strongest in West Berlin to be sure, but industrial centers in Baden-Württemberg and Bavaria are also prominent. Hamburg is a leader with respect to ancillary business services, publishing, insurance, wholesale trade, printing, and banking. Bremen is in second place in aspects of trading, Hessia (or, more particularly, its capital, Frankfurt) in banking, and the Rhineland-Palatinate and Bavaria in clothing manufactures. No single state emerges as generally dominant in the occupational structure of modern West Germany as far as the set of economic activities shown in table 11-2 is concerned. The same kind of diffusion of economic activity appears in a broader analysis of the Federal Republic's occupational structure (table 11-3).

If we turn from quantitative data on occupational structure to more qualitative estimates of the fields in which prewar Berlin excelled, then we find much the same picture. Frankfurt is clearly the banking capital of the Federal Republic and one of the most important financial centers of the world. The Federal Bank (Bundesbank), with its monetary authority, is located there, as are three of Germany's four largest private banks (Deutsche Bank, Dresdner Bank, and Commerzbank). Moreover, almost four in five (78 percent) of the 208 foreign banks in the FRG have their main offices in Frankfurt. Düsseldorf, which also houses West Germany's third largest private bank, has beaten out both Frankfurt and Hamburg to become the country's advertising center. Insurance firms have by and large concentrated in Hamburg. And rapidly growing Munich has taken over Berlin's previous role as Germany's leading women's fashion center, armaments manufacturer, and film producer.

The city's peripheral geographical position would have made it impossible at best to maintain its primacy in the field of transport. The statistics bear out this assumption. In 1937, of the 628,391 air passengers who arrived at or departed from the Reich's airports, 30.5 percent did so in Berlin. Frankfurt was in second place with 9.6 percent, followed by Hamburg (7.8 percent), Munich (7.3 percent), and Cologne (7.1 percent). By 1975, of more than 36 million passengers registered at West German airports, only 11.0 percent landed in or left from West Berlin. Frankfurt now has the FRG's largest airport and in 1975 accounted for 32.9 percent of its air passengers. The same trend describes air freight. Berlin's share of the total dropped from 35.1 percent in 1937 (11.9

Table 11-2
Distribution of Employees and Self-Employed in Selected Economic Sectors, 1970

State	Electrical Engineering	Printing	Clothing, Shoes	Wholesale Trade	Publishing	Advertising, Brokerage, Storage	Banking	Insurance
Schleswig-Holstein	−0.45	+0.52	−0.43	−0.04	−0.50	−0.08	+0.06	−0.12
Hamburg	−0.42	+0.48	−0.67	+0.66	+0.88	+1.49	+0.47	+0.73
Lower Saxony	−0.30	−0.30	−0.16	+0.06	+0.04	−0.01	+0.001	−0.06
Bremen	−0.19	−0.36	−0.64	+0.25	+0.85	+0.83	+0.02	−0.04
North Rhine-Westfalia	−0.32	−0.18	−0.15	+0.17	+0.03	−0.13	−0.11	−0.04
Hessia	−0.06	+0.23	−0.12	+0.05	+0.08	+0.20	+0.32	+0.01
Rhineland-Palatinate	−0.60	−0.21	+0.58	+0.01	−0.01	−0.28	−0.11	−0.16
Baden-Württemberg	+0.45	+0.10	−0.05	−0.18	−0.02	−0.15	−0.02	−0.15
Bavaria	+0.47	+0.14	+0.55	−0.09	−0.23	−0.14	−0.004	+0.03
Saar	−0.48	−0.34	−0.14	−0.05	−0.88	−0.22	−0.09	+0.06
West Berlin	+1.30	+0.17	+0.19	−0.36	+0.14	+0.36	−0.26	+0.48

Source: Statistisches Bundesamt, 1973.

Note: Difference between each state's actual number of workers in a sector and the number that would be expected were each state's workers distributed in the same way as the national total, standardized by dividing the difference by the expected sum. Scores greater than +0.15 are underlined once, those greater than +0.30 are underlined twice.

Table 11-3
Distribution of Employees and Self-Employed in Broad Economic Sectors, 1970

State	Agriculture	Energy Mining	Industry	Construction	Trade, Commerce	Transportation, Communication	Banking, Insurance	Services	Nonproducing Organizations	Other[a]
Schleswig-Holstein	+1.45	−0.51	−0.22	+0.25	+0.12	+0.02	−0.07	+0.14	−0.12	+0.46
Hamburg	−0.15	−0.59	−0.34	−0.20	+0.35	+1.12	+0.77	+0.33	−0.11	+.01
Lower Saxony	+0.75	−0.09	−0.09	+0.14	+0.09	−0.02	−0.05	+0.02	+0.03	+0.11
Bremen	+1.14	−0.44	−0.22	−0.11	+0.13	+1.28	+0.06	+0.05	−0.28	+0.06
North Rhine-Westfalia	−0.19	+1.05	+0.02	−0.07	+0.03	−0.10	−0.34	−0.07	+0.23	−0.16
Hessia	−0.03	−0.47	−0.03	−0.004	+0.01	+0.15	+0.25	+0.11	+0.02	−0.07
Rhineland-Palatinate	−0.39	−0.63	−0.04	+0.04	+0.01	−0.05	−0.22	−0.001	+0.21	+0.30
Baden-Württemberg	+0.17	−0.61	+0.19	−0.02	−0.17	−0.21	−0.05	−0.12	−0.22	−0.08
Bavaria	−0.47	−0.50	+0.07	+0.12	−0.08	−0.07	+0.01	−0.02	−0.20	−0.04
Saar	−0.26	+2.38	−0.06	−0.15	+0.04	−0.05	−0.13	−0.12	−0.16	+0.07
West Berlin	−0.23	−0.44	−0.16	−0.17	+0.005	+0.01	−0.17	+0.27	+0.15	+0.63

Source: Statistisches Bundesamt, 1973.

Note: Difference between each state's actual number of workers in a sector and the number that would be expected were each state's workers distributed in the same way as the national total, standardized by dividing the difference by the expected sum. Scores greater than +0.15 are underlined once, those greater than +0.30 are underlined twice.

[a]Includes those working in public corporate bodies and social insurance.

percent in Cologne and 8.9 percent in Frankfurt) to 2.4 percent in 1975, with Frankfurt leading in the latter year by handling 73.5 percent of all air freight. Insofar as the number of registered trucks indicates freight transportation, it should be noted that Berlin's share of the national total declined from 10.0 percent in 1938 (with Bavaria slightly higher at 10.5 percent) to 3.1 percent in 1975 (in contrast to 25.4 percent in North Rhine-Westfalia). In 1974 West Berlin accounted for 0.9 percent of the FRG's railway freight and 2.2 percent of its canal freight (in North Rhine-Westfalia, 46.2 and 48.0 percent, respectively).

Cultural Core Area Functions

It is rather more difficult to characterize Berlin's changing cultural role vis-à-vis the rest of Germany. Available data and impressionistic judgments are nevertheless consistent with the pattern of decentralization. In the field of higher education Berlin no longer holds the commanding position it once did. In 1937 it had 15.3 percent of Germany's university students (including those in teachers' colleges); in 1974 West Berlin's institutions of higher learning had only 8.6 percent of the Federal Republic's students. (Given changes in the relationship between the university and society, it may be added, the absolute number of students has grown dramatically in West Germany, but somewhat less so in West Berlin than in the rest of the FRG.) This trend is not solely a natural development. Other states have insisted that West Berlin should not have a proportion of students significantly larger than its share of the national population. The justification most often heard for this policy is that the reduced activity of the city's economic sector cannot accommodate an overly large number of graduates, but lurking behind this argument are the efforts of the states to protect and strengthen their own universities and the idea that a state's future employees should be products of its own educational system. A similar development characterizes the postwar growth of academic research institutes (most specifically those financed by the highly prestigious Max Planck Society).

Equally important, perhaps, is the changed reputation accorded Berlin's universities. The prewar Humboldt University and especially faculties such as medicine enjoyed immense prestige throughout the world. The division of Berlin in 1945, however, placed it under Soviet control, and before long students and some faculty members petitioned the Western Allies to set up in West Berlin a university free from Soviet domination and ideological demands. Although the new Free University of Berlin got off to a good start, in the late 1960s its students took a leading part in the unrest characteristic of those years and eventually "reforms" were instituted which caused still other problems. The highly newsworthy "troubles" by far overshadowed in the press any actual progress made by the Free University. The result of the widespread politicization exaggerated by sensationalist reporting was so damaging that, for example, a 1978 survey of personnel managers in West Germany's leading industries placed the Free University forty-ninth among fifty universities (above the "red university" in Bremen) as a favored source for recruits (Schmidt, 1978). The fact that this finding rested on very questionable methodological bases indeed did not emerge clearly in the blaze of journalistic overkill. It also overlooks the strength of individual departments, such as medicine at the Free University, as well as, more generally, the importance of West Berlin's enormous research productivity at all its universities and autonomous institutes.

Changes in Germany's newspapers are also notable. Throughout the years before 1945 it was the press in Berlin which dominated people's attention. During the Weimar era in particular Berlin newspapers, some of which appeared in several editions daily, were distributed and read throughout the land; during the Third Reich the *Völkischer Beobachter*, published in Berlin, was the voice of Nazism within and without the country. Allied decisions, however, ruined the prospects for establishing for postwar West Berlin a similar preeminence. First, most of the publishing equipment which survived the war and dismantling was located in the Soviet sector, where it was soon reactivated to print newspapers for the Soviet military government and, later, the revitalized Communist party (after April 1946, Socialist Unity party). Newsprint was also extremely scarce in the western sectors. Then, too, with the city's effective division came the loss of what is vital to the success of any metropolitan journal—its hinterland. And by hinterland is meant here not only the city's immediate environs, under Soviet and later GDR control, but also western Germany, where each of the Allies had already created its own newspaper and where the principle of decentralization meant that, even when German newspapers were licensed, they were to be aimed only at their own regions.

An independent press operating in West Berlin alone found the sledding tough. Of the several newspapers begun, only two survived into the 1950s and one, *Der Tagesspiegel*, up to the present time. Eventually the burgeoning newspaper empire created in Hamburg by Axel Caesar Springer moved into West Berlin as well, and by now four of five newspapers read by West Berliners stem from his presses. No West Berlin newspaper has much significance beyond the city's borders. A handful published in Frankfurt, Munich, and Hamburg, by contrast, are sold daily at kiosks throughout West Germany, including West Berlin.

It may be in the field of arts and letters that modern West Berlin's fate is determined. Viewing the loss of those political and economic functions associated with status as a national capital, politicians in West Berlin and West Germany alike have stressed the possibility of turning the city into a cultural center of international significance. They have also spent considerable sums to achieve this goal. But with what success?

Although judgments of artistic merit vary, few would argue that West Berlin has lived up to its cultural potential, not to speak of its dream to become once again Germany's cultural center. In part this is due to federalist pressures. Politicians in Stuttgart and Bremen, Cologne and Munich may declare publicly their sense of obligation to support the arts in West Berlin, but they are also rather reluctant to see their own cultural institutions suffer in the process. Thus it is possible to point to theaters and orchestras throughout the FRG which, usually with financial support from their state governments, have established for themselves substantial reputations.

In another part, however, West Berlin's disappointments are due to the divided views of its own political-cultural establishment. It would be incorrect to argue that the picture is uniformly bleak. There are in fact frequent high points in West Berlin's cultural life. The Schaubühne am Hallischen Ufer is widely viewed as Germany's most interesting, the Berlin Philharmonic Orchestra enjoys worldwide fame, and so do the city's museums. Its annual film and theater festivals have brought international attention to West Berlin. But all too often those officials responsible for selecting theater directors, distributing subsidies from public coffers, or determining what will be brought to Berlin from elsewhere have played it safe, shying away from originality or even brilliance if it carried with it the possibility of political controversy (compare Wirsing, 1978).

Long-term Implications

If one compares the West Berlin of today with the city called Berlin that used to exist, then the conclusion is that the former has moved to the periphery of German life. Once circumstances and Allied intervention had denied any primary political function to postwar Berlin and a Federal Republic was created which formally excluded the island-city of West Berlin, it was virtually inevitable that the other functions it served for pre-1945 Germany should also melt away. And indeed, with political power now located in Bonn and elsewhere, the centers of secondary political associations, economic organizations, the press, and still other social institutions have situated themselves accordingly.

All this is not to say that West Berlin has become a wasteland, divested of any significance for modern Germany. In fact, the city and its citizens are doing quite well. Some institutions continue to find their home base there. West Berliners for their part enjoy the same standard of living as people living in other West German metropolises, do not suffer from significant levels of unemployment, have identical guarantees of civil liberties and social security, watch the same television programs, and even have the opportunity to taste the best of modern German culture as represented by the Berlin Philharmonic Orchestra, perhaps, or the exciting playhouse, Schaubühne am Hallischen Ufer. Artists find the city's atmosphere lively (although they usually add that, if they wish to sell their paintings or sculptures, they must arrange for showings in such wealthy industrial centers as Düsseldorf or Duisberg). Visitors unaware of Berlin's bygone glory or disinclined to lament its loss will usually find themselves dazzled by West Berlin's present-day opulence and cultural attractions.

But precisely this is the city's major problem. If it is no longer to fulfill the country's major political and economic functions, and if it is able to do no better than merely compete with other West German cities in the cultural sphere, then just what is it that can set the city apart? The idea of turning West Berlin into Germany's cultural or intellectual center has simply not been realized. To the contrary, critics of the city's cultural policies argue, heavy subsidization supporting unimaginative ventures threatens to turn West Berlin's cultural program into a circus aimed at keeping an indiscriminate audience happy by not daring to do anything out of the ordinary. Mellow mediocrity may attract tourists, but it hardly speaks to Berliners' claim to being something special (Wirsing, 1978).

Another prominent possibility, serving as a political symbol, is becoming a bit threadbare. During the blockade of 1948-49 the West Berliners' steadfastness became a symbol of the West's determination to resist Soviet pressure. During the next dozen years, before August 1961, when the East Germans built their wall of concrete and barbed wire, West Berlin's existence was frequently seen as a symbol of democracy, a "beaconlight of freedom in a red sea of communism." (The GDR saw the city not as a beaconlight of freedom but rather one luring its vitally needed workers to Western factories.) The wall itself became at least in Western eyes a symbol of the intellectual and moral poverty of the communist system. The Western Allies' military presence in West Berlin and particularly that of the United States were seen as symbolic of their commitment to defend West Europe. West Berliners saw themselves as the nation's conscience, a continuing reminder of West Germany's obligations to Germans in the east and its avowed goal of German reunification.

Such symbolic functions were most useful, however, only while the cold war continued. With moves toward détente, such as Chancellor Brandt's eastern policy after 1969 and especially the various Berlin accords of 1971-73, the value of this kind of symbol declined. Nor were subsequent efforts to turn West Berlin into a bridge between East and West very successful. Although some socialist countries have sent entries to the Berlinale, West Berlin's annual film festival, for example, they have more generally been cool toward any cooperation which might shore up West Berlin's claim to be integrally linked to if not actually a constituent part of the Federal Republic. Moreover, eased relations between the GDR on the one hand and West Berlin and the FRG on the other, have taken the romance out of the image of West Berlin as an encircled and endangered outpost of freedom.

Three decades of growth meanwhile have entrenched in various West German cities the functions they took over from the old Berlin. Even if the Four Powers could agree tomorrow formally to integrate West Berlin into the Federal Republic, it would be extremely difficult to secure agreement among the West

German states on relocating the FRG's political capital in the city and possibly more difficult still to persuade other institutions performing vital functions to move there. (Such steps might be more likely in the by far more remote eventuality of Germany's reunification.)

Nor is it intuitively obvious that a recentralization of all these functions *should* take place. West Germany's federalism has worked remarkably well. Multiple centers of political, economic, and other forms of power have not prevented the FRG from becoming one of the leading industrial countries of the world. It is also possible that these multiple centers have enabled West Germans to develop new energies at the regional level that more than make up for any reduced efficiency at the national level due to a lessened ability to coordinate activities in the public and private spheres. Not least of all, the fine balance among the regions has made it difficult for any of them to attain dominance over the others. That some centralizing tendencies are evident in the FRG—pressure by the Federal Constitutional Court, for example, to create across the land uniform educational procedures—should not be taken as a sign of structural weakness in its federal system.

The result of all these trends is that West Berlin is caught in a predicament. Its leaders want it to attain a distinctiveness that will attract whatever is necessary—industry, research institutes, young people, international acclaim—to ensure the city's place in the sun. But West German states, while voicing their support for the idea of a distinctive Berlin, find it difficult in practice to give it precedence over their own needs and ambitions. Torn by internal strife over ways to attain cultural preeminence, unable to create a new symbolic function for the city and yet finding it as undesirable as it is impracticable to return to the cold-war imagery in which the city played such a central role, and all the while fully aware that the failure to do anything will only speed up the city's slide to the periphery of West German life, West Berlin's political leaders seem immobilized. The appearance of immobility or, still worse, political decay is nonetheless deceiving. In fact, changes wrought by the lost war and what followed notwithstanding, West Berlin has been able to maintain for itself a leading, if not *the* leading, position in West German life.

References

Merkatz, H.J., Metzner, W., and Ziegfield, A.H. 1954. *Germany Today: Facts and Figures*. Frankfurt am Main and Berlin: Alfred Metzner Verlag.

Schmidt, R. 1978. "Schlechte Noten für rote Unis." *Manager-Magazin*, April, pp. 146-152.

Statistisches Bundesamt. 1973. *Arbeitsstättenzählung vom 27. Mai 1970*, No. 5: *Nichtlandwirtschaftliche Arbeitsstätten (örtliche Einheiten), Beschäftigte, Lohn- und Gehaltsummen in den Ländern und deren Verwaltungsbezirken.*

In Fachseries C, "Unternehmen und Arbeitsstätten." Stuttgart and Mains: Verlag W. Kohlhammer.

Statistisches Reichsamt. 1936a. *Berufszählung: Die berufliche und soziale Gliederung der Bevölkerung in den Ländern und Landesteilen*, No. 3: *Stadt Berlin*. Vol. 454,3 in the series "Statistik des Deutschen Reichs." Berlin: Verlag für Sozialpolitik, Wirtschaft und Statistik G.m.b.H.

———. 1936b. *Gewerbliche Betriebszählung: Die gewerblichen Niederlassungen in den Ländern und Landesteilen*, No. 2: *Berlin und Provinz Brandenburg*. Vol. 463,2 in the series "Statistik des Deutschen Reichs." Berlin: Verlag für Sozialpolitik, Wirtschaft und Statistik G.m.b.H.

———. 1938. *Statistisches Jahrbuch für das Deutsche Reich 1938*. Berlin: Verlag für Sozialpolitik, Wirtschaft und Statistik, Paul Schmidt.

Wirsing, S. 1978. "Fragen nach Berlin: Zirkus-Stadt oder kulturelle Hauptstadt-Festwochen und Kulturpolitik." *Frankfurter Allgemeine Zeitung*, 7 October, p. 23.

12 County and Communal Reorganization in Western Germany

Peter H. Merkl

In the last decade and a half, governmental systems varying from unitary France and federal West Germany to the people's republics of Eastern Europe have acted with astonishing unanimity to bring about major reforms in their territorial and local government structures. In France the *communautés urbaines et rurales* movement of voluntary two-tier mergers has proceeded since 1966[1], and in the Netherlands there has been a general reorganization of local units of government. In the Communist states of Eastern Europe notions of uniformity and equality in decentralized administration have suggested the consolidation of the arbitrary scattering of hamlets in more inclusive and bureaucratically competent rural communes.[2]

In the Federal Republic considerable differences in local government structures date back to the days of the long defunct state of Prussia and to the varying local reform policies of the different occupying powers in the postwar period (Wells, 1953, pp. 57-83; Merkl, 1963). Until recently most West German states possessed an extraordinarily large number of communes including large numbers of rather small units. In 1970 West Germany had 22,500 communes, of which Bavaria alone had 7,004. There were fewer than 5,000 inhabitants in 92.6 percent of these West German communes, including 82.6 percent with fewer than 2,000 (*Statistisches Jahrbuch fuer die Bundesrepublik*, 1971, p. 34).[3] Less than a third of the total population of the Federal Republic lived in these communes under 5,000. By common consensus the vast majority of all these communes has long been considered far too small to perform even minimal communal functions.

Some time ago village schools below a certain size were consolidated in larger centers. Now the communal reorganization movement in state after state since the late 1960s has undertaken a drastic reduction of the total number of communes by mergers of all units below a certain size. In densely populated North Rhine-Westphalia and the Saar the suggested minimal size was 8,000 to 10,000 and in the less densely settled Laender (states) of Schleswig-Holstein, Lower Saxony, Bavaria, and Baden-Wuerttemberg, it was between 5,000 and 7,000. By 1975 such mergers had already eliminated some 13,000 communes, for example reducing the 2,300 communes of North Rhine-Westphalia to a mere 370. Eventually the total number of West German communes is expected to be about 9,000, of which the majority will be governed by joint administrations (Verwaltungsgemeinschaften), so that there will be only 3,500 autonomous local agencies in the country.[4] At the same time, the rural Kreise (counties) have undergone changes to bring them into conformity with an ideal size between 100,000 and 400,000 inhabitants which, for example, led to the elimination of the 72 smallest of 143 Bavarian counties in 1972. The number of towns free of Kreis control (*kreisfreie*) in Bavaria has also been reduced from 48 to 25 in a further effort to streamline German local government, which had been largely unchanged in its territorial configurations for over a hundred years.[5]

The magnitude of this reorganization at the lowest level raises many questions involving the goals and procedures employed. It also invites comparison with communal mergers in the United States and elsewhere. Of particular interest in the West German case is the question of popular participation and consent in the planning and execution of this reform. One may wonder also how the fabric of local politics will be affected by these changes. Another fruitful area of inquiry is the link between economic development planning and territorial reorganization at this level. Many related subjects await the researcher (Bocklet, 1972, pp. 81-116).

Goals of Communal Reorganization

> All the planning and the measures of administrative and territorial reform aim at the goal of adjusting the territorial-administrative structures which grew from the agrarian pre-industrial social order to the requirements of the evolving modern functional society (Bundesregierung, 1972, p. 18).

With these words, the Federal Report on Territorial Order of 1972 (*Raumordnung*) introduced its lengthy account of the territorial reorganization activities going on in the various Laender. The requirements of contemporary German society to which the governmental structures need to be adapted were characterized as follows:

1. Urban living, especially in the twenty-four metropolitan areas in which some 45 percent of West Germans live, was becoming the dominant element in German life.
2. These areas of population concentration continue to spread out, but there are also new points of concentration developing in suburban rural areas, suggesting careful planning and direction of growth.
3. Medium-sized cities have been growing rapidly too, suggesting consideration of their optimal interaction with the major centers.
4. The danger of excessive ecological damage is growing, especially near the major centers, at the same time that the increased popular desire for recreation has intensified the interaction between humankind and the environment.

5. More and more agricultural land is taken away for urban or industrial uses.

From the beginning of the scientific understanding of the *Raumordnung*, there has also been the realization in Germany that optimal economic development is highly dependent on the existing territorial distribution of population and industry and that improvement of the latter would facilitate dramatic changes in the former. Furthermore, there is a consensus that the existing geographically determined inequalities in the delivery of services make for inequality of educational and economic opportunities contrary to the egalitarian principles of a democratic society. Empirical studies overwhelmingly confirmed the impression that Germans from small-town and rural areas are far less likely to receive educational training to the best of their abilities than their metropolitan compatriots. Distance from metropolitan markets likewise implies limitations on business and professional opportunities and considerable differences in the wages and earnings of comparable occupations.[6]

To respond to these problems, the appropriate Laender and federal ministries collaborated in developing lists of goals and planning activities based on the concepts of the *Raumordnung* and culminating in the territorial reorganization plans of counties and communes and in coordinated development planning. For planning purposes the federal government divided the country into thirty-eight territorial units, which are in many ways reminiscent of the abortive territorial reorganization plans of the Laenderkonferenz of the late 1920s and similar studies of the early 1950s (Brecht, 1949; Institut zur Foerderung Oeffentlicher Angelegenheiten, 1950; Bundesminister des Innern, 1955).

The basis of the territorial reorganization scheme has been the functional definitions of population centers of varying size.[7]

1. "Small centers" must have a *Hauptschule* ("ninth grade"), kindergarten, doctor, dentist, pharmacy, stores for food and household goods, an inn, and recreation facilities. Small centers have at least 1,000 inhabitants in their core and 5,000 within a radium of 15 km.
2. "Lower centers" should have the same in a larger and more diversified form, such as several inns and stores, branches of banks, possibly an institution of secondary education, and small and medium industry. Their core area should have at least 2,000 and their 15-km circle 10,000 inhabitants.
3. "Middle centers" are defined as supporting a *Gymnasium*, vocational, special, and adult education; a general hospital with various specialists; elaborate recreational and shopping centers; diversified repair and industrial shops; and credit institutions. Their core area should have at least 7,500 and a 30-km circle at least 30,000 inhabitants. And, whereas the small and lower centers only have to have paved access roads to the outside, the middle center must have access to the federal highway system and to the railroad network (preferably as an express train stop).
4. "Upper centers" have superregional importance and are the seats of the

highest regional or *Land* governmental agencies and courts. They are also the main seats of banks, newspapers, trade associations, public theaters, orchestras, libraries, museums, and universities. Their hinterland exceeds 200,000 inhabitants.

Each center is to be determined, mapped, and developed to fulfill its prescribed functions. Whenever a development axis was found connecting several centers along bands of roads, railroads, rivers, or energy conduits, its location might be favored for the development of further industry, services, and population centers. The areas between these development axes, on the other hand, could serve as recreational areas to be kept free of settlement. Development policy would then devote its resources to (1) building up the infrastructure of the centers, (2) mapping and developing "axes" of the first and second order, (3) developing recreational opportunities, and (4) special development problem areas such as border territories or chronically underdeveloped or stagnant areas.[8] This approach is also linked to road-building and transport policy, to broad environmental concerns, and to energy and resource policies. Finally, in a state like Bavaria there are also substantial opportunities for superregional recreational development in such areas as the entire strip of land along and including the Alps, to which people come from outside the state (see Bayerisches Staatsministerium, 1973).

The county and communal reorganization is not a panacea but only one of several tools of the overall development program. Its success and fulfillment of this role, moreover, presuppose sustained economic expansion and development in the pinpointed areas. It requires very substantial public investments in the infrastructure of centers and development axes, which in turn depend on the revenues from economic prosperity and expansion. Thus the local government reform is only a link in a larger chain which might snap elsewhere under the strain of prolonged economic recessions or stagnation. The revenues available in the Federal Republic for such ambitious projects and for many other legitimate purposes have unfortunately become rather scarce in recent years. It remains to be seen how soon and to what extent the actual regional development will put some life into the reorganized shell of governmental and territorial structures.

Procedures and Timetables

Any reform of this magnitude must be planned with a great deal of attention to procedure. In some cases forerunners of the West German Laender had already begun the process of Kreis reform back in the 1930s.[9] The Laender Baden-Wuerttemberg, Hesse, and North Rhine-Westphalia enacted their first positive regional planning laws as early as 1962, followed by the Saar (1964), Lower Saxony (1966), Rhineland-Palatinate (1966), and finally in 1970-71 Bavaria and

Schleswig-Holstein. The rural Kreis reform including the reduction of fair-sized *kreisfreie* cities to the dubious status of "Kreis towns" was accomplished first, generally by state laws drawn up by the state bureaucracy with the advice of the relevant committees of the state diets and of Land planning councils and consisting of experts. Typically, the middle centers and their hinterland were used to determine the new Kreise, although several middle centers often ended up in the same Kreis. The old urban Kreise remained unchanged.[10]

Bavaria completed its Kreis reform in 1972 and followed it with communal and Kreistag elections the same year, which presumably gave the voters and their representatives a chance to respond to both the Kreis and the impending communal reorganization. Starting already in 1969, in fact, the communes were invited to carry out voluntary mergers in anticipation of communal reorganization. Special financial incentives rewarded communes that merged up until 1976. By 1 January 1975 the number of communes had already been reduced from over 7,000 to 4,186 by voluntary action although even this still left 92 percent of the communes and 40 percent of the Bavarian population in units under 5,000. To forestall the survival of very small communes under joint administrations, the state permitted this option only to units larger than 1,000 inhabitants—in other words only to small or larger centers wishing to be jointly administered with other small or larger centers.[11]

At almost the same time the state of Bavaria divided itself into eighteen planning regions and set up regional planning associations in which the Kreise and communes were represented (Bayerische Staatsregierung, 1974b, pp. 251-268). These regional committees together with the Land Planning Authority and advisory councils at all levels produced a three-volume Land Development Program (Bayerische Staatsregierung, 1974a), which still had to be submitted to the regional planning agencies and the municipal associations for comments. Hearings had to be conducted until 1975 before the Development Program was considered ready for concrete steps. As the goals of the Development Program, the Bavarian government named the following (Bayerische Staatsregierung, 1976, p. 181):[12]

1. A well balanced development of the whole state
2. Equal opportunity of living conditions in all parts of the state
3. The reduction of the existing differentials between the urban concentrations and the structurally weaker areas
4. Creation and maintenance of a sufficient and diversified supply of jobs and services within reasonable distance in all parts of the state
5. Maintenance of the natural basis of life for the population

The centers were all officially designated with the exception of the small centers which were left to the regional planning agencies. As it turned out the upper centers accounted for 43 percent and the middle centers for another 12 percent of the population. The Development Program was adopted except for the provisions on its funding and the details of the regional plans. The communes, too, were urged to prepare plans for development along certain guidelines and within this overall framework (Bayerische Staatsregierung, 1976, pp. 181-190).[13]

Inputs and Protests

Perhaps no other aspect is likely to arouse the curiosity of an American observer about this process of territorial reorganization as much as the paucity of local protests against it. To be sure there are many other enticements to researchers in this complex of planning and structural change. But to see such a fundamental change being brought about largely by state action as in the absolutist days of the European past is rather amazing, to put it mildly, considering the bitter struggles that usually accompany incorporations and annexations of local communes anywhere. In Germany, too, local annexations have always been extremely controversial and so is the question of territorial change among the Laender, as evidenced in the donnybrook over the formation of Baden-Wuerttemberg in 1951 from the remnants of the pre-1945 Laender of Baden and Wuerttemberg which had been divided by the zonal boundary between the French and American zones of occupation. Article 29 of the West German Basic Law specifically calls for such a reorganization because of the somewhat artificial nature of the new states in 1949. In spite of some feeble attempts, however, there appears to be no likelihood after twenty-five years that such a reorganization will ever take place. The resistance of the present units is far too strong to yield to a rational plan for reorganization.[14]

As for the county and communal reorganization at hand, one of the first steps taken in all the Laender involved was to modify or remove clauses from the state constitutions or communal codes (Gemeindeordnung) which required a referendum for territorial changes. Most of these clauses were not really meant to apply to a general reorganization but merely to individual cases of mergers, annexations, or secessions.[15] At any rate the state governments did not want to take chances with the courts (Klueber, 1970, pp. 243-45).[16]

The inputs from advisory councils of the planning process and, for example in Bavaria, regional planning associations may have served to anticipate some local pressures, but could do so only to a modest degree. The regional planning associations of Bavaria are limited to a membership of ten to thirty persons who represent three or four Kreise, the remaining *kreisfreie* cities, as well as the other communes. This hardly permits an individual local interests sufficient access to make a difference. The involvement of the Landtage (state diets), to which many communal officials belong, was another input of some significance, but again the number of Landtage deputies is generally too small to allow for the representation of individual local interests.[17] Most Landtage passed their reorganization laws with unanimity and little debate. In particular, partisan divisions were almost absent, although the temptation must have been great for an opposition to take advantage of such an explosive issue (Hahn and Brandel, 1974).

The long period of voluntary communal reorganization with special incentives was probably the strongest factor in facilitating the great change, even though "voluntary" has to be viewed in the context of the carrot of financial inducements and the whip of mandatory action a few years down the road. The close and generally amicable relations between the *Landrat* of the *Kreis* administration and "his" communal officials would obviously give the state ample opportunity to influence, persuade, and respond to local discontents.[18] Given the chronic lack of funds of German communes and the ambitions of communal officials, one can easily imagine that the financial incentives for early mergers also may have been rather effective.

What can we learn from the few protests reported? Guenter Golde recently described the impact of the reorganization on two small communities in Baden-Wuerttemberg where he carried out his research during the year 1971. There was an attempt to demand by popular referendum the dissolution of the state diet in Stuttgart over the Kreis reform which abolished the local Kreis and took away the status of the Kreis seat from a nearby town. The initiative failed by a wide margin although there was a lot of publicity in the papers and many people feared a loss of local income and grumbled about having to travel much farther to the new Kreis capital (Golde, 1975, p. 35).

A nearly identical story was brought to the author's attention in Upper Bavaria where in 1972 the ancient town of Wasserburg on the Inn River lost its status as *kreisfreie* city and seat of the Kreis Wasserburg which was divided between two neighboring Kreise. In their anger seven Christian Social (CSU) deputies of the city council resigned from their party, which dominates the state and was held responsible for the demotion of Wasserburg. There was a public protest rally attended by a reported 10,000 irate citizens—the town has only 7,000 souls—and then a motorcade to call on the Bavarian Minister President in Munich. Some "hard words" were said on that occasion. In the meantime a new local party was formed, the Wasserburger Block, which successfully presented a mayoral candidate and a slate of deputies. In actual fact, little Wasserburg had long been living above its means, maintaining middle center facilities at such expense to the taxpayers that there had been an exodus from the town to unincorporated areas across the river. The special state payments to cities demoted from the status of *kreisfreie* to that of a Kreis-dependent town probably have helped to salve the wounds of the local pride by now. There has also been the expectation that the communal reorganization will shore up Wasserburg's middle center character by annexing to it those newly developed areas across the Inn River to which residents and new industry had migrated. On balance, the ancient town will not have lost much more than a few Kreis offices and its perpetual deficit.[19]

By way of contrast Golde's two villages in Baden-Wuerttemberg may have suffered far greater losses. Many of these small communes had lost their "dwarf schools" not long ago to school consolidation. Now they lost their Rathaus (city hall) and native Buergermeister, an office held by an unbroken line of farmers over four hundred years, to a distant central commune. The central commune will hold the purse strings even though the old commune will still be permitted an Ortschaftsrat (council) and Ortsvorsteher (headman) of largely symbolic significance (Golde, 1975).[20] Early mergers, of course, were rewarded with larger (20 percent) state subsidies and there is little doubt that the new central commune will have a much better professional bureaucratic staff and facilities. But what price is to be attached to communal identity and to a sense of control over one's own fate?

There have been other controversies over county and communal reorganization, involving mostly annexations or reorganizations at the edge of metropolitan areas. Other cases have centered on personal or partisan conflicts rather than the issues of reorganization. A number of complaints are still before state administrative courts in several Laender (Ronellenfitsch, 1972, pp. 191-96). There is the strong impression that most of the protests are coming from officeholders whose representative positions have been or are about to be abolished by the reform. These council members and Buergermeister incumbents naturally like to claim a sizeable popular following. But there is little evidence, aside from some grumbling, that there is a real public concern over the momentous changes taking place on the local scene in West Germany.

Conclusion

The most important question about this ambitious local reorganization is what difference will it make in the long run. Leaving aside for the moment the hopes for better economic articulation and growth and for more equal opportunities, which are all dependent on economic factors beyond the control of government, will the reorganized world of German local politics be much improved or even greatly changed? It would appear, first of all, that the metropolitan areas in which most Germans live will hardly change except for some boundary adjustments and possibly better connections with their hinterland. Their immediate surroundings have been reorganized, to be sure. Government surveys in the Federal Republic have disclosed that 24 percent of the metropolitan population would rather live in a middle center or small town. On the other hand, 30 percent to 47 percent of West Germans prefer the services and proximity of a metropolis if not a home in its downtown center. An imminent major exodus from the big cities to small towns is not expected.

Of the population of rural areas (under 2,000), 80 percent express a strong preference for living where they are now, even though they admit that the availability of appropriate employment may be less in the countryside or smaller centers than in the city. These are the people who are most deeply affected by the communal reform that will bring them professional management and perhaps even better job opportunities and other services. It is in these communities also that there may well be an atrophy of traditional local politics, which in rural Germany has meant, among other things, a very high voter turnout, consensual-style politics, deference to local elites, and very little political competition. It may well be that the major parties which have a monopoly on state and federal politics will now take over the small communes too, where there used to be almost only nonpartisan voters' groups and personal factions.

The middle centers, finally, will probably be the fulcrum of the macropolitical changes that lie ahead. For they seem to be the target not only of many metropolis-weary urbanites but also of one fourth of the people living in the lower and small centers. At the same time and rather unexpectedly, only 38 percent of the people already living there express a desire to stay. Thus it is not at all clear that the newly strengthened middle centers will help to decentralize West German society in a stable way (Bundesregierung, 1972). Neither do they seem to represent the traditional stereotype of the German hometown in which people invest their whole lives and from whom they derive an important part of their identities. Only time can help to unravel the mysteries left in the wake of the ambitious local reorganization and regional development plans of today.

Notes

1. See, for example, the discussion of different types of structural and procedural arrangement in Adrian and Press (1972, pp. 294-320) and on France, in Médard (1968). See also Royal Commission on Local Government in England, 1969.

2. See, for example, Zawadzki (1976). See also Schnur (1968), who reviews Scandinavian, British, Dutch, Belgian, French, Yugoslav, Czech, Polish, Romanian, Bulgarian, and Soviet local reorganization. Everywhere the reforms include a drastic reduction in the number of communes, in Yugoslavia from 11,556 (1946) to 577 (1964), on the basis of regional planning considerations. Only in Poland where the historical units happened to be very large was there a relative increase in the number of communes. See also Rosenberg (1975).

3. In the 1950s there used to be 24,525 communes, of which all but 5 percent were smaller than 5,000. In 1925 when communes between 2,000 and 5,000 were called "rural towns" and those from 5,000 to 20,000 "small towns," Germany had 46.5 percent of its population in 62,388 communes under 5,000. (*Statistisches Jahrbuch fuer das Deutsche Reich*, 1926, pp. 6-7). Another 13.4 percent (8.36 million) lived in small towns.

4. In Bavaria, for example, there will be about 1,000 autonomous

communes and another 1,500 will be governed by 300 joint administrations. In Baden-Wuerttemberg, where the reform has already been completed, there resulted 180 autonomous communes and 900 communes administered by 270 joint arrangements.

5. In North Rhine-Westphalia, there are now only 23 instead of 37 *kreisfreie* cities and only 31 instead of 57 Kreise. The typical *kreisfreie* city in Bavaria now averages 137,000 inhabitants instead of half that size.

6. This was found to be particularly true among Catholics, South Germans, and women, all of whom are underrepresented among university graduates.

7. See the definitions, for example, in Bayerisches Staatsministerium fuer Landesentwicklung (1973, 1972) and Isbary (1965).

8. Among the frontier territories of the Federal Republic are also those bordering on the Iron Curtain, which often cuts them off from their natural hinterland. The "stagnant areas," on the other hand, may be industrial areas developed in the nineteenth century and not modernized or adjusted to new demands and markets. See Bundesregierung (1972, pp. 64-65).

9. This was true, for example, of the Kreis reform of Wuerttemberg.

10. So-called double centers required special provision for reconciling their proximity with the avoidance of duplication of services. Regarding the number of middle centers per Kreis, Bavaria was found to have seventy-six present middle centers, and another thirty-five potential ones (lower centers with some middle center functions) for seventy-one Kreise.

11. In Baden-Wuerttemberg by August of 1972, 872 voluntary annexations and mergers had occurred involving 1,400 communes and including 66 administrative unions of 348 communes. In Bavaria, however, by 1974 only 10 joint administrations with 45 communes had been formed. See Bayerische Staatsregierung (1974, pp. 235-236).

12. See also Kluepper (1972, pp. 277-293), especially regarding North Rhine-Westphalia.

13. Substantial sums (87 million German marks) had already been allocated as loans and subsidies to compensate the demoted former *kreisfreie* cities for their loss of status and centrality (Bayerische Staatsregierung, 1976, p. 174).

14. In the Baden-Wuerttemberg merger representatives of the old state of Baden were the chief opposition. On the other reorganization issues see Bundesminister des Innern, 1955. The abortive attempts at reorganization chiefly involved the dismemberment of Rhineland-Palatinate.

15. It should be borne in mind in this connection that German communes, unlike their American equivalents, are very extensive and leave hardly any land outside their boundaries (*gemeindefrei*) under the Kreis governments.

16. Klueber, a former mayor of Mannheim, stresses in particular the involuntary mergers and reorganizations, for example around the edge of metropolitan areas.

17. The Bavarian Landtag, for example, has 180 seats, about 2 for each of the present Kreise. See also Hoffman (1972, pp. 61-73).

18. The Landrat or Oberkreisdirektor (North Rhine-Westphalia) is generally elected by the Kreistag or the Kreis citizens, or at least appointed by the Land minister president with the advice and consent of the Kreistag, generally for a limited term. He or she carries out *la tutelle*, the state supervision over the communes within his Kreis. On the differences in Kreis constitutions, see Klueber (1972, pp. 472-481).

19. This information was obtained in an interview with the new mayor of Wasserburg. The precise outcome will not be known until the communal reorganization has been completed in Bavaria.

20. The merger had to be approved by the Kreis planning agency, which severely restricted the choices of the villages regarding partners for the merger.

References

Adrian, C.R., and Press, C. 1972. *Governing Urban America*. 4th ed. New York: McGraw-Hill.

Bayerische Staatsregierung. 1974a. *Landesentwicklungsprogram Bayern* Teil A, B, and C. Munich.

———. 1974b. *2. Raumordnungsbericht*. Munich.

———. 1976. *3. Raumordnungsbericht*. Munich.

Bayerisches Staatsministerium fuer Landesentwicklung und Unweltfragen. 1972. *Zentrale Orte und Nahbereiche in Bayern*. Munich.

———. 1973. *Landesplanung in Bayern*. Munich.

Bayerisches Statistisches Landesamt. 1973. *Verzeichnis der Oberbuergermeister, Landraete und ersten Buergermeister in Bayern*. Munich.

Bocklet, R. 1972. Gemeindeverfassung und Gemeindereform in Bayern. In *Aspekte und Probleme der Kommunalpolitik*, eds. H. Rausch and T. Stammen. Munich: Voegel.

Brecht, A. 1949. *Foederalismus, Regionalismus und die Teilung Preussens*. Bonn: Heymanns.

Bundesminister des Innern. 1955. *Die Neugliederung des Bundesgebietes*. Bonn: Heymanns.

Bundesregierung. 1972. *Raumordnungsbericht 1972, Federal report 1972*. Bonn.

Golde, G. 1975. *Catholics and Protestants: Agricultural Modernization in Two German Villages*. New York: Academic Press.

Hahn, J., and Brandel, J. 1974. "Die kommunale Verwaltungsreform in Baden-Wuerttemberg." *Archiv fuer Kommunalwissenschaften* 13.

Hayward, J. 1975. "The Politics of Planning in France and Britain: The Transatlantic View." *Comparative Politics* 7:285-298.

Hoffman, H. 1972. *Bayern, Handbuch zur politischen Landeskunde*. Munich: Olzog.

Institut zur Foerderung oeffentlicher Angelegenheiten. 950. *Die bundeslaender.* Frankfurt.

Isbary, G. 1965. *Zentrale Orte und Versorgungsnahbereiche.* Bad Godesberg, Germany: Institute fuer Raumforschung.

Klueber, H. 1970. "Freiwilligkeit oder Zwang bei der Gebietsreform?" *Kommunalwirtschaft*, No. 7.

⎯⎯⎯⎯. 1972. "Rahmengesetzgebung des Bundes fuer das Demeindewesen?" *Die öffentliche Verwaltung* 25:13-14, pp. 472-481.

Kluepper, U.I. 1972. "Zwischen Grosstadt und laendlichen Raum-Interessenkonflikte in der Raumordnung." *Gegenwartskunde* 3:277-293.

Leemans, A.F. 1970. *Changing Patterns of Local Government.* The Hague: International Union of Local Authorities.

Médard, J.-F. 1968. "Les Communautés Urbaines: Renforcement ou Déclin de l'Autonomic Locale?" *Revue du Droit Public et de la Science Politique en France et a l'Etranger.* July-October.

Merkl, P.H. 1963. *The Origin of the West German Republic.* New York: Oxford University Press.

Ronellenfitsch, M. 1972. "Zur Verfassungsmaessigkeit der Landkreisreform in Baden-Wuerttemberg." *Die oeffentliche Verwaltung.* March.

Rosenberg, G. 1975. "The Theory of Socialist Territorial Planning in the German Democratic Republic." *Town Planning Quarterly* 41.

Royal Commission on Local Government in England, 1966-1969. 1969. *Report*, vol. 1. London: Her Majesty's Stationery Office.

Schnur, R. 1968. "Reformen in Europa." *Der Landkreis.*

Statistisches Jahrbuch fuer das Deutsche Reich 1926. 1926. Berlin: Hobbing.

Statistisches Jahrbuch fuer die Bundesrepublik Deutschland 1971. Stuttgart: Kohlhammer.

Wagener, F. 1971. "Reform kleiner Gemeinden in Europa." *Verwaltungsarchiv* 62:97.

Wells, R.H. 1953. "Local Government." In *Governing postwar Germany.*, ed. E.H. Litchfield. Ithaca, N.Y.: Cornell University Press.

Zawadzki, S. 1976. "The Concept of Local Democracy in a Socialist State." Paper delivered at the International Political Science Association Congress, August 1976, in Edinburgh.

13 Regionalism and the Italian City

Robert H. Evans

The introduction of flexibility and diversity into an increasingly centralized and insensitive system of political and administrative controls is one of the most strongly felt needs of modern democracies. A critical issue for the state is its search for substantive and organizational solutions to the problems posed by advanced industrialization, intense urbanization, and the depopulation of rural areas. During the last decade and at present, West European states are actively grasping for new arrangements at the regional and local levels that address these problems.

Most initiatives reorganizing communal or municipal government have come from the center and led to the concentration of the smaller units with little or no modification of the powers of national governments. Though it is early to draw conclusions, compulsory concentration appears to have been quite successful (Belgium, Great Britain, Germany, Sweden), while free association, where the initiative is left to the communities (the French Syndicats Intercommunaux, the Italian Comitati Circondari), has proven to be a failure. Considerable attention has also focused on reorganizations that are evolving at a larger subnational level and that in most cases are the outcome of pressures from the periphery on the center. Belgium, in response to linguistic and economic pressures, has moved toward a semifederal structure which recognizes autonomous roles to the Flemish, Wallon, and Brussels communities; France is implementing a watered down regional division of the country; Great Britain is struggling with the concept of devolution applied to Scotland and Wales; the new Spanish government appears committed to granting some form of autonomy to Catalonia and the Basque provinces; Italy, for some thirty years, has been grappling with the problems of establishing regional states as called for by the 1948 constitution (Lambrechts, 1973; Delperée, 1972; van Impe, 1976; Baquenard, 1973a, 1973b).[1]

Regional Reorganization

The states have followed in essence a functionalist approach toward the lower levels of government (the terms local, communal, and municipal will be used

---

Much of the research for this paper was made possible by a travel grant of the American Philosophical Society, which is gratefully acknowledged.

interchangeably) and have striven for administrative reorganization in the name of greater equality and efficiency. These elements remain present in regional reorganizations, but political dimensions are paramount as the necessary decentralization requires delegation of powers to the new units that were previously in the hands of the central governments.

This is particularly true of Italy since 1972 when the regional governments became operational and the state progressively (and partially) endowed them with the powers it held over the municipalities. In the name of decentralization the state has transferred powers of decision in matters of local interest (such as city planning) to the regions which, as established by the constitution, are delegating these to the cities but retaining the powers of control that formerly belonged to the central government. As of now it is difficult to assert that local autonomies have been strengthened by regional decentralization, though of the eight thousand communes some exception may be made for the thirty-three metropolitan areas that by their sheer physical weight have a greater impact on regional administrations than they previously had over the state (Cafiero and Busca, 1970; Evans and Rizzi, 1978). Over half the metropolitan areas are regional capitals. It is in the context of regional reforms that one must address the issue of the Italian city today.

The Origins of the Regional Problem

In 1861 Italian unification corresponded to the wishes of a minority of the population, notably the northern upper bourgeoisie and the southern landowners. The Savoy monarchy held it essential to impose its principles and ideas on the ex-sovereign states that constituted the new kingdom, and on 20 March 1865 Italy was administratively unified according to the French pattern adopted by the Piedmontese. In 1919 varying degrees of regionalism were adopted in the platforms of the radical socialist, republican, and popular parties only to be swept away by fascism. Reborn more vigorously in 1945, espoused by all the political parties in the constituent assembly, particularly the Action party and the Christian Democratic party, a functional approach to regional problems— product of Catholic thought in the late nineteenth and early twentieth centuries but traceable to regionalist projects of the 1860s (Allum and Amyot, 1971; Gizzi, 1972)—called for the division of Italy into nineteen regions.[2] The new regional organization, providing extensive legislative power to the units under rigorous government control, corresponded to no other preexisting model of federative or unitary state and created on paper a regional state which became a part of the Italian heritage.

However, as in 1865, events as much as ideals determined the structure of the republic and the partial implementation of the Constitution. Separatist movements in Sardinia and Sicily and international difficulties in border areas where linguistic problems and territorial divisions were acute led to the recognition of "special" regions in the constitutional project, and their separate statutes elaborated in 1945 and 1946 were formally recognized and adopted into constitutional law by the assembly in January 1948, one month after the ratification of the constitution. The special regions corresponded to an effective need and to constitutional provisos but were the product of outside pressures rather than governmental initiative. The country's search for a new political and social equilibrium was brought to an end by the cold war which polarized the Left and the Right, leading the latter to abandon its regional policies (which might not have been very deep), only to see them adopted by the former (where they may remain shallow). Valid reasons and artificial pretexts were invoked by the government parties to slow regional implementation. Patriotism and anticommunism were summoned to prevent the creation of a red belt from the Tiber to the Adige. The cost of fifteen regional governments (though irrelevant if the constitution was to be implemented), estimated by President Einaudi at around one thousand billion lire, was invoked. The poor performance of the special regions, Sicily in particular, was cited as an indication of what the future reserved. At heart, the Christian Democratic party was only marginally interested in regionalism and reflected the position of the Italian bureaucracy, the control of which afforded the party many occasions for undivided patronage.

Optimism, changes in the international situation, and economic prosperity preceded the opening to the Left, an attempt to co-opt the Socialists into the government while further isolating the Communists. The Socialist party, which in 1948 had been among the less regionally inclined, came to the negotiating table in 1962 with a strong regionalist program and proclaimed that the creation of the ordinary regions would determine its continued presence in government. The ordinary regions which came into existence in 1970-72 were viewed as a means of making the overmanned administrative system more efficient while providing an overburdened parliament with some relief (Woodcock, 1972). While the constituent assembly had envisaged the regions as a means to answer local problems, encourage vigorous local political activities, prepare administrators for ever more important tasks, and make democratic participation in municipal government an effective reality, politicians of the 1960s did not give sufficient thought to these aims. Most parties were content to jump on the regional bandwagon in which they saw an opportunity to increase their share in the spoils of the system. The Christian Democrats felt that the issue of regionalism called for institutional and administrative solutions.

The issue was political. Local administrators and city fathers, frustrated by twenty years of government inactivity, argued that the perspective of the constituents was correct and that the regional provisos of the Constitution, notably Article 117, had to be liberally interpreted in correspondence with the needs of the country in the 1970s and 1980s. At the regional elections of June 1970, which also served as the final test for the moribund center-left experiment, the regions were presented somewhat misleadingly as key elements of future bureaucratic and tax reforms, the guiding force for advanced planning, and champions of local autonomy. Six years later, subject to the political imperatives of national politics and limited by the constitutional framework and the inertia of the central government, they had given only timid indications of their potential (Good, 1978; Putnam et al., 1977) except for their ability to control local government.

The Institutional Framework

The revolutionary step of creating a regional state rests in the Constitution and in the laws and decrees of the Italian Republic. Article 5 declares that "The Republic, one and indivisible, recognizes and promotes local autonomies;... and adjusts the principles and methods of its legislation to the requirements of autonomy and decentralization." Article 117 grants the regions powers to legislate on specific matters and also foresees the extension of their legislative competence to "matters indicated by constitutional laws." Article 118 regulates the administrative functions of the regions and their relationships with the provinces, communes, and other local bodies. Constitutional laws recognized the statutes of the special regions. In May-July 1971 Parliament endorsed the statutes drafted by the ordinary regions in consultation with the joint parliamentary committee of the Senate and the House. These statutes were presented by the government, symbol of the unitary state. This and the parliamentary endorsement that ensued implicitly recognized the constitutional validity of the statutes, though they claimed powers far more extensive than those granted in Article 117.[3] Presidential decrees in January 1972 delegated some of the powers of the state to the regions in matters pertaining to agriculture, hospitals, and health care, within the context of Article 117. Law 382 of 22 July 1975 (Article 1 a and e) instructed the government "to complete [within a year] the transfer [to the regional governments] by organic sectors, of all administrative functions related to the matters indicated in Article 117 of the Constitution, as well as all offices and personnel required" and "to provide the provinces, communes and mountain communities with the administrative functions of exclusive local interest in matters indicated by Article 117 Constitution as per Article 118 Constitution." On 23 July 1977, under heavy pressure from the left, the government finally agreed that such functions and powers would effectively be transferred to the regions by 1 January 1978. However, while agreement on the principle might have been reached, until detailed framework and financial laws are elaborated, regional autonomy remains considerably limited, as it has been since 1972. In brief, regional order in Italy provides a prime example of incomplete and piecemeal legislation, reflective of the complexities and consequences of the issue, but also of the reluctance of the government and the

Christian Democratic party to divest themselves of the powers of the state and transfer them to the regional bodies.

The Structure of Regional Government. Minor variations notwithstanding, the institutions of the special and ordinary regions can be considered together: their structures are similar, regional entities are now the rule and no longer the exception, and the exercise of regional functions is determined in a uniform manner with regard to the ordinary regions (Palladin, 1973, pp. 28-31). The institutions consist of a council, a junta, and a president of the region (Article 121).

The council (Consiglio Regionale) is a politically autonomous, yet not sovereign, unicameral legislative body. It is elected for five years by direct universal suffrage. The number of councillors is proportional to the size of the population and varies between thirty for regions with less than 1 million inhabitants and eighty for those with more than 6 million. Elections are held under a list system of proportional representation and constituency boundaries coincide with those of the provinces. The final selection of representatives is based on list votes received by the parties and, within these lists, on preferential votes received by the candidates. Leftovers are tabulated at the regional level. Elected councillors represent the region and not the province in which they were elected. The councillors are predominantly recruited from the middle class (Allum, 1973, p. 227). The council elects its president by secret vote, preferably by an absolute majority.

The junta is the executive branch of the council, and its members (*assessori*) are held responsible for specific departments in the five special regions, while responsibility is collective in the ordinary ones. The council elects the president of the junta, who is president of the region. Disposing of notable prestige and supported by majorities subject to rigid party discipline, the president is the leader of the executive and has proven quite able, notably in the red belt, to manhandle the council and modify the composition of the junta. While some authorities (Gizzi, 1972, p. 143) have noted that the council participates in the determination of regional policies and in their implementation through the junta, in practice it appears that president and junta have acted quite independently where their majorities have been homogeneous.

The Powers of Regional Government. The legislative powers of regional governments fall into three formal categories: exclusive, complementary, and integrative (Gizzi, 1972, pp. 28-35). While only the special regions hold all three (ordinary regions were not granted exclusive legislative power), the broad interpretation by the regional statutes of Article 117 ratified by parliament and the restrictive view taken by the constitutional court in relation to exclusive power establish a de facto equality between the special and the ordinary regions (Ottaviano, 1971, pp. 29-34; Piras, 1971, p. 36). Rather than examine the regional powers in detail I shall emphasize those that have an impact on municipal administration, namely the ones the regions are to delegate to local governments, the powers of control the regions inherited from the state, and the financial status of the regions.

Regional delegation to local administration falls essentially in the broad category of complementary legislation by which the regional council must comply with the principles underlying national legislation as established by framework laws or deduced by the regional legislator from the existing body of national law. This applies to all the areas enumerated in Article 117, namely, "Organization of the offices and the administrative bodies dependent on the region; communal boundaries; urban and rural police; fairs and markets; public charities and health and hospital assistance; vocational training, training of artisans and scholastic assistance; museums and libraries of local bodies; town planning; tourist trade and hotel industry; tram and motor coach services of regional interest; roads, aqueducts, and public works of regional interest; lake navigation and ports; mineral and thermal waters; agriculture and forestry; artisanship."

In these matters the region is a legislative body in charge of programming and coordinating the activities of local-government dealing with the administration of its territory, the development of productive activities, and the supply of fundamental services, except public education. This is strengthened by Article 1, Law 382, 1975 which, with regard to Article 117, recognizes that the state can delegate to local governments those functions of exclusive local interest and must transfer all other functions (such as public health, tourism) to the regions which in turn may and normally should delegate these to local governments. At the discretion of the state elements that are not covered by Article 117 may be attributed to local governments or delegated to the regions, which, again, may assign these to the local governing bodies (Bassani, 1976, pp. 316-321; Berti, 1971, p. 45). Thus the region as much as the state becomes the true source of local administration (Lambrechts, 1973, p. 285).

The transfer of powers to the regions and the delegation of these powers to local administrations presupposes, to be successful, some degree of financial autonomy as foreseen by Article 119 of the constitution. Unfortunately it remains limited, pending the implementation of tax reforms which will allow the regions to levy a 2 percent income tax (Law 281, 16 May 1970). In the meantime 60 percent of regional funds come from a state common compensation fund, 30 percent from specific state contributions earmarked for housing and hospital services, and 10 percent from regionally generated funds. In 1975 totals amounted to some $5.2 billion and had tripled since 1973. Decrees of 1977 could well double the amount.

However, a large share of the central government disbursements remain unspent appropriations (*residui passivi*) and the limited amounts of regionally generated income (most in the north) allows the central government to limit regional initiatives and policies, notably in the south which is almost exclusively dependent on Rome. Furthermore, while the sums appear substantial, the tasks to be accomplished are greater, thus effectively hindering the operation of municipalities, which may well receive delegated regional powers (health services for instance) without the means to accomplish their mandate.

In a further limitation of local autonomies the regional bodies and the president in particular appoint, and to an extent control, three out of five members of the provincial control committees which supervise the operations of municipal governments and provinces, with powers roughly equivalent to those previously held by the prefect and the GPA (Giunta Provinciale Amministrativa). Committee authority extends to all acts performed by local governments, either on the basis of their own rights or on those resulting from regional delegation. In the first case control is exercised in terms of the legitimacy (abuse of power) as well as of the merit of the act itself; the only recourse against the committee's decision is through the notoriously slow court system. In the second case all municipal acts that evolve from delegations based on Article 117 (in spite of the ambiguities contained in the transfer decrees of the central government) are subjected to the review of the committees. One may speculate that their power could extend to the appointment of a regional commissioner in the case where local governments would not legislate after having received a delegation from the regions (Gizzi, 1972, pp. 373-389).

In brief, from a legal point of view, towns and cities that previously had to contend only with the prefect as representative of the state are now caught in a network of controls that duplicates and enhances the one they consistently fought prior to 1970. Politically the matter is slightly different in that the committees are appointed by the regional president, provided that regional and local administrations are of the same political leaning. But even in this case the degree of flexibility granted the provincial control committee remains limited, as its two "nonpolitical" members are an appointee of the government commissioner and a judge of the regional administrative courts. Through the regions the central government continues its domination of local government. Such a complex system suffers from many ambiguities which provide some margin for local autonomies, but the ambiguities are product of the halting implementation of the regional order to which we now turn.

The Implementation of Regional Order

The Relationship between Central Government and Regions

Italy has been characterized as a "republic without government" or as "surviving without governing" (Allum, 1973; diPalma, 1977). The overall Italian situation and the progressive weakening of Italy's leading party, the Christian Democrats (DC), does much to explain the reluctance of the central government to surrender its powers to the regions and local governments.

The Politics of Regionalism. Two conflicting views compete for preeminence. In a manner coherent with policies it developed for city government in the late 1940s, the Left, notably the Italian Communist Party (PCI), envisages the regions as political legislative bodies that will offer a "dynamic, modern and open interpretation" (Modica, 1974, p. 26) of Italian society and will bring about "a rupture of centralism, ... of provincialism, a pluralistic state, articulated in spheres of separate powers, coordinated and guaranteed by reciprocal autonomy" (Fanti, 1974, p. 78). This position is partly supported by the Italian Socialist party, which emphasizes the need to give more powers to local government. The views of a large share of the DC are not radically different though greater emphasis is laid on the coordinating and controlling role played by the central government. The Right, from the neo-Fascists to the more traditionalist groups of the DC, envisage the regions as mere administrative bodies of a decentralized state. Local politicians of all parties (with the exception of the neo-Fascists) espouse the more progressive view, calling for the transfer to regional assemblies of greater powers than those outlined in the Constitution and the governmental decrees transferring responsibilities to the regions. They regard the regions as the central component in the reorganization of local government, the active and most dynamic elements of the state, and the focal point of all social services required by an advanced industrial democracy.

Regional politics have become a thermometer for the state of health of the central government; the regional issues and regional alliance policies are carefully followed. Regionalism has become inextricably linked with national politics and can easily be perceived as the forerunner of new alignments. In the period 1970-75, which saw the end of the center-left experiment, regional governments were viewed as the testing grounds for the *rottura degli equilibri*, the "breaking of equilibria," and a search for more advanced ones. The DC insisted that regional alliances were to reflect national ones, while the Socialists believed regional and national politics could be dissociated; the PCI, following its offers of "compromise," defended the idea of broad alliances that reflected local conditions and provided for the most effective regional and local governments. The regional elections of 1975 and more so the political ones of 1976 have changed the picture further. With a minority DC government dependent on PCI votes for survival, the situation is even less clear and regional alliances reflect the ambiguities of DC politics at the center. By way of illustration, the DC and the PCI have reached agreements on common regional programs in Abruzzi, Basilicata, Calabria, Campagna, Lombardy, Marche, Sardegna, and Sicily, while "institutional accords" in Emilia-Romagna and Lazio have elected Christian Democrats at the head of regional councils with the open support of the

Communist party (Corriere della Sera, 1977, p. 2).[4] The national DC argues that such agreements are not to be viewed as leading to broader solutions, but local politics seem to follow their own ways. It is in fact difficult not to see parallels between the regional arrangements and the July 1977 and February 1978 pacts between the six major parties to support the minority DC government in its attempts to solve the Italian crisis. Though one may not view limited accords as compromises, without doubt the Socialist party feels seriously threatened, the loser in the game, and rightly so. The agreement between the PCI and the DC in the joint parliamentary committee, dealing with the enabling decrees of Law 382 on 23 July 1977, was reached against the explicit will of the Socialists. The regional order established by the Constitution and developed during thirty years of political struggles between government, parties, regions, and cities calls for radical changes in the Italian state: a century-old tradition of centralization with all the mechanisms it implies has to be abolished. The task of reform is simply immense and is rendered ever more complex by the vicissitudes of the overall political situation.

At the national-regional level the reforms call for a partial overhaul of the elephantine Italian bureaucracy, the decentralization of as much as 10 percent of its personnel, the abolishing of ministries now redundant, such as Tourism, and the reorganizing of others such as Agriculture into planning and supervising bodies. The regional order requires modification of the tax laws, not to say the entire tax system, if the regions are to obtain specific taxation powers as their statutes proclaim and if the state is to dispose of sufficient revenues to grant the regions enough monies to cover the costs of programs they have been entrusted with—notably the health care delivery system. At the local level the necessity of addressing the problem of the insolvency of city governments appears fundamental. Regional delegations of power can be effective only if municipal budgets are not subject to overwhelming liabilities and if local administrations are to function effectively. In 1976 the total local debt amounted to some $28.5 billion; 82 of 94 provinces, 81 of 94 major cities, and 3,966 of 8,053 communes were debt-ridden; 91.1 percent of southern communes, 88.2 percent of central ones, but only 12.2 of northern ones ran heavy deficits. In 1970, 47.5 of the municipal debt was used to balance budgets (Dente, 1977, pp. 219-221); in 1973 six cities of over 500,000 population accounted for two-thirds of the total debt, while the annual debt ($1.5 billion) was doubling every three years (Cazzola, 1978, pp. 306-308).[5] One may doubt that the national improvement fund for the municipal debt, the financing of which is dependent on a successful tax reform, will suffice.

The magnitude of the problems is rendered evident by a survey of the consequences of the enabling decrees of Law 382 decided on 23 July 1977 (*Gazzetta Ufficiale*, 1977). At the central level fifteen ministerial directive bodies (Direzioni Generali) will be abolished: three in Public Works, two in the Ministry of the Interior, two in Public Education, three in Agriculture, one in each of the ministries of Health, Transport, Tourism, Industry, and Employment. Many departments will be reorganized. The relocation of personnel to the regions and the salaries of those no longer needed may cost the state up to $2.3 billion (*Il Giornale*, July 17, 1977, p. 2). On a local level up to 22,000 local bodies (*enti pubblici a carattere locale*) could be abolished, while the existence of 62 national ones will be questioned (*Il Resto del Carlino*, 1977, p. 2). These organizations are so different that it is nearly impossible to summarize the extent of change except in the broadest terms: urban, rural, and administrative police are now the responsibility of the municipalities; the regions will take over charitable institutions (with a budget of $20 billion), health care, public assistance services for school children and university students, tourism, environmental protection, urban planning, regional transportation, forestry, artisanship, and agriculture. Charitable institutions, health care, student assistance, and tourism will be delegated to municipalities.

The Central Government and the Regions. While changes of such magnitude will have a heavy impact on the operation of local and regional government, the state retains the upper hand in the seesaw game that has been played since 1970. On the one hand, the regions have enthusiastically exploited the ambiguities of the constitutional text, and their statutes diverge considerably from a strict constitutionalist interpretation. (For example, the statutes claim a directing and coordinating power over public economic bodies and corporations, although Article 117 does not grant the regions competence in industry or commerce; it is difficult to find in Articles 117 and 118 any justification for the establishment of regional television networks.) On the other hand, the constitutional court has a rather consistent record of ignoring the regional context and the theory of implicit powers and of rejecting the teleological interpretations the regions have set forth (Barile, 1973, p. 88). While the new framework laws and the pressures of public opinion may influence the court in favor of the regions in the future, one is entitled to doubt this will be the case.

In matters of regional and, indirectly, local control, the means available to the central authorities are clear. A state-appointed commissioner, normally a prefect, may dissolve the regional council (Article 126), and constitutional and administrative supervision of all regional acts is exercised by the government (Articles 124, 125) which is entitled to reject a law on the grounds of legitimacy or merit (Article 127). While the right of veto has been exercised without antiregionalist feelings and essentially on technical grounds due to regional errors, with the highest rate of vetoes applying to the south (30 percent, 1970-75), the state does control the regions, and these, the communist ones in particular, have been shy in innovations and have given the government few reasons to veto laws (Good, 1978, pp. 13-15). Their defense of local, as opposed to regional, autonomies has been essentially rhetorical.

More important than the formal powers of control is the ability of the state to slow reform, to exploit its power of inertia, in brief to prove unable to deliver on its promises. Thus, the transfer of personnel to the regions in 1970-72 was a token gesture (14,443 people were involved) and effectively prevented them from spending a large amount of the funds they had been assigned. However, in 1978 the regions had to assume personnel from the central ministries in consequence of the decrees of Law 382; more often than not, these persons will now be redundant and weigh heavily on budgets. Finally, the transfer of local bodies dealing with welfare and public charity, many of which are church administered, will take place in 1979 at the earliest, after a commission has examined each of the 22,000 organizations to exempt from the transfer those whose main functions is educational or religious.

The essence of the question is not administrative but political and is characterized by the contrasts that exist between the DC-dominated central government and the regional governments supported by the Left and by the ability or inability of the government to make good on somewhat unrealistic promises dictated by the vagaries of the political moment and the presence of frustrated regional politicians who claim more power than the Constitution calls for and more responsibilities than they can handle.

The Relationship of Regions and Local Governments

The constitutional limitations on the regional governments in their relationships with local governments are severe, and earlier the chapter referred to the powers of control the regions can exercise over city governments. Article 117 refers only to the modification of communal boundaries, while Article 118 mentions that "the region normally exercises its administrative functions by delegating these to the provinces, communes and other local bodies." The regions, while they acknowledge their responsibilities of coordination, have interpreted this proviso to mean that delegation will go beyond the mere exercise of administrative responsibilities and that local governments should be entrusted with powers of decision. There is general agreement among regionalist politicians that the representative of the central government in the provinces, the prefect, should be done away with—in other words, that the essential relationship should be local government-region rather than local government-state. Local autonomy, a leitmotiv of the Left, has become an essential component of regional politics. Provinces and communes are to be seen as "autonomous political-institutional expressions of the local collectivity, organizations that can translate basic political demands, and . . . play an effective government role" (Istituto di Diritto Pubblico, 1976, p. 16). Many ambiguities survive, and as the past president of Lombardy has said about the relationship between regional and local governments, ". . . we cannot say that all has been good, but the natural alliance between decentralized powers has had the best over the difficulties encountered...." (Bassetti, 1974, p. 24).

The regions envision as their main task planning, legislating, and controlling decentralized units that will encompass all local governments and to which regional personnel will be transferred and specific powers will be delegated. Ideals, however, are often far removed from realities. Generally speaking such delegations can be successful only where adequate structures and personnel exist at the local levels (for instance, in the case of city planning), which essentially limits such transfers to large metropolitan areas in the northern part of the country or to areas that are socially integrated such as Emilia-Romagna (Putnam et al., 1977). And even in regions such as the latter, which is viewed as one of the most successful, the personnel remains overpoliticized (Evans, 1977) and lacks preparation notably in the categories of "administrators, accountants, engineers, architects, geologists, forestry experts, doctors, veterinarians, statisticians" (Regione Emilia-Romagna, 1977). Last but not least, the three-year hiatus between Law 382 on the delegation of powers from the central to the regional governments and the enabling decrees of 1977 perforce limited regional intervention in all the areas where powers to the municipalities were to be delegated.

In their relationship with local governments the regions have followed four main lines of action: planning, delegation, financial support, and institutional reform. In spite of numerous handicaps the balance sheet is not entirely negative and reveals a considerable potential for the Italian cities, if one excepts the area of local autonomies. The area of greatest success has been planning, which calls for limited expenditures and is entrusted to central regional offices in cooperation with the municipalities. While indicative, it has made its impact felt through the quality of the arguments advanced. Thus Emilia-Romagna disposes of extremely detailed maps (1:100,000 and 1:25,000 scales) of its territory divided into units of sixty acres: these physical maps (continuously brought up to date using the latest techniques, including satellite photography in cooperation with NASA) and population maps certainly allow for more precise planning than has ever been the case before. Similar observations are feasible in the area of town planning, where the regional offices have been particularly effective.

Delegation of powers during the first five years of regional activity has been limited as the regions waited to see exactly what powers they would effectively be entrusted with by the central government. The decree of July 1977 will undoubtedly foster a greater activity when it is effectively implemented in 1978-79. In those cases where delegation was possible it usually involved matters of limited consequences. Six regions delegated some of their powers dealing with social security, and six addressed themselves to the problems of agriculture, forestry, and fishing. More significantly, the delegations tended to be granted to the provinces rather than to the communes (at least this is the case for seventeen of twenty-three delegating laws dealing with artisanship and scholastic assistance) and preferably to associations that foster collaboration among local governments such as chambers of commerce (Dente, 1977, p. 269). On the one hand, there existed considerable doubt as to how far the regions could go in delegating powers they were not certain to possess, while on the other hand, and more seriously, local governments, with the exception of metropolitan areas, were either poorly equipped to receive such delegations or reluctant to share in them because of financial limitations.

The information regarding financial transfers from the regions to local governments is limited and has not been updated since 1972, so the flow undoubtedly has increased and gone beyond the simple concession of subventions. In Lombardy, for example, 3 billion lire ($5 million) were transferred to local governments, but 2.3 billion were to balance current accounts and only 0.7 billion dealt with capital investments. While this represented 7 percent of all regional expenditures, it corresponded to only 0.5 percent of communal expenses (Dente, 1977, p. 263). It is thus difficult to consider regional financing decisive even if it has increased considerably over the last five years. One must also distinguish between appropriations and monies effectively spent: in Lombardy 350 million lire were deliberated for the protection of flora, 1 billion for local museums, 1 billion for environmental protection, 2 billion for town planning, and only 150 million were effectively spent (Dente, 1977). Much of this results from the extremely specific qualifications and restrictive claims that regional legislators write into the laws. Financial contributions are seldom generous and more often than not are insufficient with regard to the aims they wish to accomplish. Hence, the communes do not file requests for financial support either because they feel there are too many strings attached or because the contributions would oblige them to other investments they cannot afford.

More interesting and far-reaching are the regional experiments at an institutional level. Depending on the political color of the region, more or less bold experiments have been attempted. In Piedmont, a moderate region, the Circondario has been brought back to life, corresponding roughly to a subprefecture in terms of extension. They appear, however, little more than decentralized offices for the regional control bodies and while they may encourage localism in the cities that have been promoted to such status, their main function appears to have been the creation of somewhat redundant administrative posts (Dente, 1977, p. 277).

In the wake of Emilia-Romagna, the regional assemblies of Piedmont, Lombardy, Venetia, and Lazio had passed laws establishing Comprensori by the end of 1975 and projects of law had been deposited in Tuscany and Puglia. The Comprensorio can be defined as the optimal geographical unit for territorial planning. It derives from the experiences of urbanists rather than politicians who at first were reluctant to accept the notion. In Emilia-Romagna, which is divided into twenty-eight Comprensori, these are viewed as participating instruments for the elaboration and application of regional development and urbanization plans (Assessorato Affari Istituzionali, 1977). They serve as a link between the region and the communes, act as selecting bodies at the subregional level as well as political administrative coordinating bodies for the regional functions delegated to the communes, and encourage the formation of associations between local governments. The directive bodies of the Comprensori are chosen by second degree election among municipal and provincial councillors of the areas concerned. They are functional bodies aimed at superseding the imbalances that exist in the territory they cover while increasing "the process of democratic participation in determining choices and deciding upon necessary interventions" (Regione Emilia-Romagna, 1976, p. 153). Participation in Comprensori is compulsory for the communes although they cannot be obliged to accept its decisions. Financial appropriations being granted to the Comprensorio rather than to cities (such as for processing urban refuse) may well make it difficult for a recalcitrant commune to escape the regional embrace. The impact of the Comprensorio on smaller cities cannot be ignored, as it will effectively provide greater weight to the larger towns which, in metropolitan areas in particular, can force smaller communities into submission. In consequence, the Comprensorio is a regional instrument, which rather than developing local autonomies, if not in the most formal sense, limits them and could lead to a de facto concentration of communes.

The Comprensorio must be viewed as an experiment (only fourteen of twenty-eight were operative in Emilia-Romagna in 1977) that has a potential for considerable impact, but whose legality is doubtful, as the regions have no authority to establish new units of government. That they would go so far as they have, without encountering major grass-roots resistance, is indicative of the strongly felt need for reform of local government. In July 1977 the six major parties agreed this would be a priority item for the Andreotti government, and such a commitment was reaffirmed in February 1978. While little has been said, it appears that PCI has accepted the DC argument that provinces rather than Comprensori would be the key element of the reform, which in turn could mean less influence of the regions over local governments[6] and a reassertion of the power of the central government.

Municipal government has plainly suffered from the uncertainties of the overall Italian political situation. Until the establishment of the regions in 1972 and the subsequent transfers of state powers in 1975 and 1977, local governments were subject to the 1934 municipal code which hardly represented an improvement over the one of 1915; they were granted only the most elementary powers. While over the years the Italian parliament extended or imposed other duties on the communes such as social welfare activities, these were subject to prefectoral review. Under such conditions it is not surprising that local politicians became ardent regionalists in the hope of wresting some independence from the regional bodies which appeared committed to the development of local autonomies.

The controlling mechanisms set up by the central government and entrusted to the regions (provincial control committees) and the assent by the regions to the province rather than the Comprensorio as the major organ of decentralization cast doubts on the level of autonomy that local governments might dispose of. The precarious financial situation of the towns and regions, which are both totally dependent on the national government for their survival, add to this.

While the regions have not truly had the opportunity to exercise the full extent of their powers, they have given some indications of autonomy. If the national political situation were to evolve further to the left, local governments may try to obtain the independence they have been seeking. But would they succeed? At present one must conclude that until a new municipal code is produced, little will have changed. With regional reforms, local governments remain between Scylla and Charybdis.

Notes

1. In addition, see van Impe (1973), Gunlicks (1977), Brand (1974), Richards (1975).

2. They are Piedmont, Lombardy, Venice, Liguria, Emilia-Romagna, Tuscany, Umbria, Marche, Lazio, Abruzzo, Molise, Campania, Puglia, Basilicata, Calabria, and the five special regions of Valle d'Aosta, Trentino-Alto Adige, Friuli-Venezia Giulia, Sicily, and Sardinia. The latter, in accordance with Article 116, were granted "particular forms and conditions of autonomy." In 1963 Abruzzo and Molise were separated (Constitutional Law 1, 31-12, 1963).

3. The regional bodies were established by Law 62 (10 February 1953) modified by Law 1084 (23 December 1970); electoral norms were spelled out in Law 103 (17 February 1968) and financial provisions by Law 281 (16 May 1970) modified by Law 1084 (23 December 1970).

4. In 1970 three regional governments were dominated by the PCI; in 1975 it controlled seven, though it had allowed the election of a Socialist president in four of these. In 1977, in the context of historical compromise thirteen regions are presided over by Christian Democrats, four by Socialists, and three by Communists; however, nine regional councils are presided over by Communists and seven by Socialists; altogether, at least ten regional governments have witnessed some form of agreement between Christian Democrat, Socialist, and Communist regional politicians. In 1978 the agreement in the Marche appeared to be breaking.

5. The cities are, in order, Rome, Naples, Milan, Palermo, Torino, and Genoa.

6. In Emilia the Comprensori were shelved until 1980 (*Il Giornale*, 29 July 1977, p. 6).

References

Allum, P.A. 1973. *Italy, Republic without Government?* New York: Norton.
Allum, P.A., and Amyot, G. 1970-71. "Regionalism in Italy: Old wine in new bottles?" *Parliamentary Affairs* 24:54.
Assessorato Affari Istituzionali. 1977. *Il Comprensorio in Emilia Romagna.* Bologna.
Baquenard, J. 1973a. "L'Organisation Régionale (Loi du 5 Juillet 1972)." *Revue du Droit Public et de la Science Politique en France et à l'Etranger.* November-December, No. 6, pp. 1405-1487.
———. 1973b. "La Region." *Cahiers Francais* No. 158, 159, January-April, pp. 1-96.
Barile, P. 1973. "Corte Costituzionale e Regioni a Statuto Ordinario." *Le regioni: Politica o amministrazione?* Milan: Edizioni Comunità.
Bassani, F. 1976. *Le Regioni fra Stato e Communità Locali.* Bologna: Il Mulino.
Bassetti, P. 1974. "La Crisi del Sistema del Potere Locale." *A Che Punto Siamo con le Regioni, Quaderni di Ulisse* 13:24.
Berti, G. 1971. "Les Nouvelles Tendances dans l'Organisation des Administrations Locales en Italie." *International Review of Administrative Sciences* 37:45.
Brand, J.L. 1974. *Local Government Reform in England 1888-1974.* Hamden: Archon Books.
Cafiero, S., and Busca, A. 1970. *Lo Sviluppo Metropolitano in Italia.* Rome.
Cazzola, F. 1978. *Il Sistema Politico dell'Italia Contemporanea.* Torino: Loescher.
Delperée, F. 1972. "La Belgique, Etat Federal?" *Revue du Droit Public et de la Science Politique en France et à l'Etranger.* May-June, no. 3, pp. 607-660.
Dente, B. 1977. *Il Governo Locale in Europa.* Milan: Comunità.
diPalma, G. 1977. *Surviving without Governing: The Italian Parties in Parliament.* Berkeley and Los Angeles: University of California Press.
Evans, R. "Recent Reforms in European Sub-National Politics, the Italian Case." Paper presented to the Southern Political Science Association, November 1977, in New Orleans.
Evans, R.H., and Rizzi, F. 1978. "Italy's Regional Governments." *The Review of Politics* 40:72-73.
Fanti, G. 1974. "L'Esperienza Emiliana." *A Che Punto Siamo con le Regioni, Quaderni di Ulisse* 13:78.
Gazzetta Ufficiale. 1977. No. 234, August 29.
Gizzi, E. 1972. *Manuale di Diritto Regionale.* Milan: Giuffré.
Good, Martha H. 1978. "Policymaking Autonomy of the Italian Regions: A Study of Legislation and Central Controls 1970-1975." *Planning and Administration* 5:7-19.
Gunlicks, A.B. 1977. "Comparative Local Government Reform: United States

and Germany." Paper presented to the American Political Science Association.
Istituto di Diritto Pubblico. 1976. *Nuova Legge sull'Amministrazione Locale.* Pavia.
Lambrechts, W. 1973. "Régionalisation et Administration: Conséquences et Perspectives." *International Review of Administrative Sciences* 39:271-287.
Miele, G. 1973. *Le Regioni: Politica o Amministrazione?* Introduzione. Milan: Communità.
Modica, E. 1974. "Struttura Istituzionale Delle Regioni." *A Che Punto Siamo con le Regioni, Quaderni di Ulisse* 13:26.
Ottaviano, V. 1971. "Tendances dans l'Evolution des Régions à Statut Spécial." *International Review of Administrative Sciences* 37:29-34.
Palladin, L. 1973. "Problemi e Prospettive dell'Autonomia Normative Regionale." *Le regioni: Politica o Amministrazione?* ed. G. Miele. Milan: Comunità.
Piras, A. 1971. "Les Régions à Statut Ordinaire." *International Review of Administrative Sciences* 37:36.
Putnam, R.D., Leonardi, R., and Nanetti-Leonardi, R. 1977. "Decentralizing Power: Initial Findings from an Italian Case Study." Cambridge, Mass.: Italian Studies Seminar, Harvard University, mimeo.
Regione Emilia-Romagna. 1977. *"Progetto Sulla Organizzazione degli Uffici."* Bologna.
Richards, P.G. 1975. *The Local Government Act of 1972: Problems of Implementation.* London: George Allen and Unwin Ltd.
van Impe, H. 1973. Belgique: "La révision Constitutionelle et les Problèmes Communautaires." *La Documentation Française, Problèmes Economiques et Sociaux.* January 5-12, pp. 1-67.
———. 1976. "La Belgique sous une Constitution Révisée." *Revue du Droit Public et de la Science Politique en France et à l'étranger.* November-December, No. 2, pp. 1405-1487.
Woodcock, G. 1972. "Regional Government: The Italian Example." *Public Administration* 45:403.

Index

Abruzzi, 222
Achievement, 29
Acquaintances, 71
Activity Spaces, 172
Adjustment, 28; cultural, 12; social, 12
Affiliation, 29
Age cohorts in Danish population, 59
Aged, care for, in Denmark, 60-61
Air conditioning, 84
Air humidity, 84, 88, 96, 99
Air temperature, 84, 85, 86, 88, 98, 99, 100
Alienation, 67-68
Allegiance, community, 62-63, 64, 65
Amsterdam, 127-134
Anomie, 21, 24, 25
Anonymity, 21, 22, 23, 24, 26, 68
Arbus, 59
Architecture, 83, 95, 99, 100
Athens, 11, 21
Attitudes, 29; urban, 71
Attitudes or urban residents, 47-55, 61-63, 63; toward poverty, 52-54; toward social change, 52-54, 61-62; toward women's rights, 52-55, 64
Austria, 13, 69, 97, 98
Automobiles, 84, 86, 100, 155, 159-160
Autonomous Institutes for Public Housing (IACPs), 136, 137, 139, 140, 145; in Milan (IACPM), 136, 138, 144-146, 149
Auto restricted zones (ARZ), 155

Basilicata, 222
Basque provinces, 215
Bauhaus, 105
Belfast, 165-184
Belgium, 21, 49, 50, 53, 63, 97, 98, 215
Berlin, 88, 105, 185-202; as core area of pre-1945 Germany, 186; East, 187; Quadripartite control of, 185

Berlin, West, 185-202; as a cultural center, 200; as a political symbol, 200; arts and letters, 198; decentralization of functions, 185-202; electrical engineering, 194; higher education, 197-198; reconstruction of its economy, 191; ties to Federal Republic of Germany, 187-189, 199
Blackouts, urban, 83
Bologna, 149
Bonn, 189; as capital of the Federal Republic of Germany, 189; ties to Federal Republic of Germany, 187-189, 199
Border Zone, 167-169
Bornholm, 64
Borrowing. See loans
Bremen, 62
Britain, 149
Brussels, 215
Bundesgartenschau, 62

Calabria, 222
Campagna, 222
Capital grants, 136, 137, 138, 139-140, 146-148
Careers, opportunities for, 26
Catalonia, 215
Catholics, 165-184
Central cities, 26
Central city, 62, 64; of Copenhagen, 56-59
Central countries, 26
Christian Democratic Party, 138, 139, 141, 145
Circondario, 215, 227
Citizens' groups, 153, 155-159
City planning, 154-156
Civic affairs, involvement in, 24
Civil Rights, 169
Climate, 83, 84, 86, 96, 98, 99, 100
Combatants in N. Ireland, 170
Communal reorganization: Baden-

233

Communal reorganization (cont.)
Wuerttemberg, 203, 206, 209-210, 212; Bavaria, 203, 204, 206-209, 211, 212; Eastern Europe, 203; France, 203, 211; Hesse, 206; Lower Saxony, 203, 206; Netherlands, 203; North Rhine-Westphalia, 203, 206, 212, 213; Rhineland-Palatinate, 206, 212; Saar, 203, 206; Schleswig-Holstein, 203, 207
Communication, 21, 24
Communist Party, 139, 141
Community disintegration, 14, 15
Competition, 27, 29
Comprensorio, 227-228
Concentration, urban, 8
Conflict, 165-184
Contacts, among individuals, 68
Copenhagen, 56-61
Core area, 185; functions of, 185, 187, 190, 194
Cosmopolitan, 23
County reform (Kreis), 206-207
Crime, 26, 27, 37, 40
Crowding, 23, 24

Day-care, Denmark, 60-61
Denmark, 47-51, 55-56, 58-59, 61, 63, 64, 97, 98; care for the aged, 60-61; growth of urban population, 56
Density, 26; population, 98; urban, 8
Development axis, 206
Dissatisfaction among urban residents, EC nations, 47-52, 56, 61-62, 63
Divorce, 27
Düsseldorf, 194

Education, 24, 35, 37
Educational opportunities, 56, 61-62
Elections, 169, 174-177
Emigration from Northern Ireland, 180
Emilia-Romagna, 222, 226-229
Energy consumption, 99
Environment, 153, 155; physical, 21, 28, 83, 84; rural, 28; social, 21, 28, 83; social complexity of, 23, 24; urban, 29
European Community (EC), 47-55, 63, 64
European Economic Community, 17
Extended family, 22

Factor analysis, 33, 34
Factory experience, 24
Family: in Denmark, 56; structure, 59-61
Farm labor, 14
Farm land, abandonment of, 15
Federalism, 188-189; in the Federal Republic of Germany, 189, 201
Finland, 97, 98, 103
Florence, 27
Fog, London "Pea Soup," 101
Forced emigration, 172
France, 4, 7, 13, 49-51, 63, 97, 98, 215
Frankfurt, 194; as FRG's banking capital, 194
Frederiksberg, 56, 59
Friends, friendship, 71, 72-76
Frustration, 27
Fuel use, shortage, 99-100
Funen, 64

Genoa, 229
German Democratic Republic, 185
Germany, 4, 6-7, 13, 17, 21, 103, 105, 215
Germany, division of, 186
Germany, Federal Republic of, 48-51, 53, 63, 64, 65, 97, 98, 185, 189, 203-214; courts in, 190; culture, 199; economic functions, 200; Federal Report on Territorial Order, 204; multiple centers, 201; newspapers, dominance of, 198; occupational structure, 191-192, 194, 195, 196; political power in, 190, 200; postwar, occupation of, 186
Gescal, 140, 142-143, 145-149; investments, 142-143

Index

Great Britain, 4, 6-7, 9, 13, 17, 49-51, 63, 97, 98, 107, 165-184, 215
Greece, 6, 8, 11, 15, 21, 25-26

Hamburg, 153, 154, 156-158, 160, 194
Health care, 33, 37, 40, 56, 62
Heat, 85
Heat island, urban, 86
Heterogeneity, 23, 24, 26
Highways, 155, 157
Holiday activities, 57-58, 61
Holland. *See* Netherlands
Hostility: indifferent, 22; involved, 22
Housing, 62, 103; architectural theories of, 104; communication view of, 106; conservation and rehabilitation, 127, 134; shortage, 11; urban, 9
Housing crisis, 178
Housing indicators, 37, 40
Housing needs, 103, 124
Housing policy, 135-152
Housing quality, 104, 127
Housing research: findings, 111; usefulness of, 124
Housing satisfaction, 107
Hungary, 6

Illegal settlements, 9, 11, 17, 18
Image-building, 62-63
Impacts, economic, 37
Impacts of urban services, 33
INA-Casa, 140-143, 145-148
In-group, 35
Income, personal. Rural-urban differences, 52, 61
Index of Religious Voting, 174
Indicators, 32, 49, 60
Industrial Heat, 84, 89; areas, 89, 95
Inequality, 39
Innsbruck, 78
Insurance claims, 83
Integration levels, 170
Interest subsidy, 136, 137, 139-140, 144-146
Ireland, 6, 49-51, 53, 63, 64

Irish conflict, federal solution to, 181
Irish Independence, 169
Italy, 4-6, 14-15, 21, 49, 50, 53, 63, 64, 135-152, 215, 231

Joint administration, 204, 209

Karlsruhe, 88
Kin, kinship, 71, 76

Land use, 98; impacts on, 6; parks, 98, 99
Lazio, 222, 227
Legal issues, 83
Leisure, 56-57, 61-62, 64
Limits, spatial, 64
Loans, 136, 137, 140, 146-148
Local autonomies, 221-222, 225-226
Lombardy, 222, 227
London, 9, 23, 86, 87, 88, 90, 92, 100, 101, 112, 124, 170
Loneliness, 23
Longitudinal data, 34
Ludwigshafen, 93, 94
Lund, 88
Luxemburg, 49, 50, 63
Luzzati Law, 135, 136

Malmö, 88
Mannheim, 62, 93, 94
Marche, 222
Marseilles, 26, 27
Mass media, exposure, 24
Media sources, 172
Messina, 141
Metropolitan areas, 204, 210
Mezzogiorno, 14
Migrants, 136, 137, 139, 141-142
Migration, 3, 4, 16, 17, 21, 26, 28; impact of rural, 6, 13; internal, 4; international, 6; Italy, 4; rural, 4, 12;
Milan, 27, 136, 138, 143-148, 149, 150, 229; public housing policy, 136, 138, 143-146
Modernity, 24
Movies, attendance at, 24

Munich, 88, 90, 194
Municipal debt, 223

Naples, 27, 149
National controls, 224-225
Nationalism, 165-184
Neighborhoods, 165-184
Neighborhood growth, 167
Neighbors, 71, 72, 74-75
Netherlands, the, 13, 48-51, 63, 64, 97, 98
Networks, personal, 69
New York, 83
Norms, 24
North Rhine-Westphalia, 65
Northern Ireland, 165-184
Norway, 97-98
Nuclear family, 23
Nursing homes, Denmark, 60

Occupational demands, 28
Openness, 24
Opportunities, urban, 27
Organization for Economic Cooperation and Development (OECD), 95, 97, 98
Out-group, 25
Output, urban, 33, 36

Palermo, 229
Parental authority, independence from, 24
Paris, 3, 8, 26, 27
Parties and regions, 222
Peripheral cities, 26
Peripheral counties, 26
Periphery, 185
Personal safety, 173-174
Philotimo, 25
Piedmont, 227
Po Valley, 17
Poland, 6, 211
Political impasse, 180-181
Pollutants: air, 83, 84, 85; control, 92; local scale, 92; primary, 92; regional scale, 92; secondary, 92; transport of, 92-93, 95

Pollution, 26; air, 83-85, 89, 92; Clean Air Act, 92
Population, impacts on, 6; increase, 37; urban, 86, 99
Population centers, 205-206, 209, 210
Population growth, 3
Portugal, 6, 16, 103
Poverty, attitudes toward, 52-54
Power-sharing, 174-176
Powerlessness, 24, 27
Precipitation, 86, 88, 89, 91
Protestant, 165-184
Provincial control committee, 221
Public housing, 178
Public transportation, 154-155, 157, 160
Publicly financed housing: fascist, 136, 137, 138; financed by loans (borrowing), 136, 137, 138, 140, 146-148; to be rented, 136, 137, 140-141, 145-146; to be sold, 136, 137, 138, 140, 141, 145
Publia, 227

Quality of life, 31, 32, 43, 44, 47, 52, 55, 61-62
Quotas, 16

Reading, 88
Redevelopment zone, 178
Redistribution, 39
Referendum, 176
Regional: controls, 221-222; council, 219; delegation of powers, 218, 225, 227; elections, 219; finances, 220, 227; junta, 219; personnel, 225-226; planning, 154, 204-208, 226; politics and national politics, 222-223; powers, 219-226; president, 219, 221; reorganization (Law 382, July 1977), 223-224
Regionalism, history, 215-218
Religion, 165-184
Religious segregation, 162, 167
Resettlement of population, 64, 65
Residential environments, quality of, 103, 104

Index

Residents' participation, 124
Responsibility, diffusion of, 22
Rome, 149, 229
Romita Law, 139
Roskilde, 59
Rotterdam, 107
Rural decline, 56
Rural depopulation, 6, 13, 14, 17
Rural populations, 21
Rural-urban labor shifts, 3

St. Louis, 91, 101
Salonica, 11, 21
Sardinia, 14, 216, 222
Satisfaction among urban residents, EC Nations, 47-52, 55-56, 61-62, 63
Scandinavia, 6, 13
Schools, 59
Scotland, 215
Sectarian murders, 173-174
Sectarian territory, 173-174, 178
Sectarian riots, 167, 169
Segregation levels, 170-171
Services, 33; delivery of, 205, 211; economic, 37; urban, 37
Self-concept, 25
Sheffield, 88
Sicily, 14, 216, 217, 222
Smog, 101
Social Change, 94; attitudes toward, 52-53, 55-61, 64
Social class, 165
Social deprivation, 176-180
Social environment, complexity of, 23, 24
Social landscape, 177
Social norms, 21
Social spaces, 170-172
Socialist, 154, 156, 159-160; party, 136, 139, 145
Solar radiation, sunlight, sunshine, 84, 85, 86, 96
Solutions to political crisis, 181-182
Southern Jutland, 59-61, 64
Spain, 6, 21, 103, 215
Special regions, 217

Squatter settlements, 11, 17
Stockholm: city, 35, 37, 118, 153, 154-156, 158, 160; county, 153, 155
Storstrom-Zealand, 64
Strangers, 75
Stuttgart, 62
Suburbs of Copenhagen, 56-59
Suicide, 27
Sweden, 97, 98, 107, 215
Swedish government, 154, 155
Switzerland, 17, 21, 97, 98, 124

Taxation, 39
Tenements, 9
Territorial behavior, 165
Territory, 170-173, 181-182
Time, 23, 24, 28
Tirol, 69-72, 76-77, 78
Torino. See Turin
Transport, in the Federal Republic of Germany, 194
Transportation: urban, 153; Europe, 153; United States, 153, 159
Tupini Plan, 139, 140
Turin, 27, 149, 229
Turkey, 6, 18
Tuscany, 227

Ulster Plantation, 165-166
Unemployment, 176-177
United Kingdom. See Great Britain
United States, 6, 14, 17
Uppsala, 88
Urban design, 84, 95; morphology of street plans, 96
Urban surface, physical, 84, 85, 86
Urban typologies, 67-68
Urbanization, 3, 67, 69; degree of, 61; process of, 56
Utrecht, 88

Values, 29
Vejle, 59
Venetia. See Venice
Venice, 27, 222
Vienna, 88

Wales, 215
Water, 84, 85, 86, 89; acidity of rain, 96; clouds, 88, 89; vapor, 84, 85
Weather: related to urban areas, 83, 84, 96; severe storms, 83, 86, 91, 100

West German Government, 154, 157
Wind, 84, 85, 91, 96, 99
Women's rights, attitudes toward, 53-55, 64
Workers, migrant, 13

Yugoslavia, 211

About the Contributors

Frank C. Colcord, Jr., received the A.B. from Middlebury College and the Ph.D. in political science from the Massachusetts Institute of Technology in 1964. He spent nine years in Washington with the State Department, the Foreign Aid Program, and the Bureau of the Budget. He taught at the Massachusetts Institute of Technology for several years before coming to Tufts University in 1969 as chairman of the Department of Political Science. He was involved with several sponsored research programs at MIT in the field of urban transportation; and under contract with the Department of Transportation he has written numerous monographs on urban transport policymaking in cities such as Hamburg, Manchester (England), Amsterdam, Toronto, San Francisco, and Minneapolis-St. Paul. He is coauthor of *Rites of Way: The Politics of Transportation in Boston and the U.S. City* (Little, Brown, 1971).

Patricia Ward Crowe received the Ph.D. in anthropology from Stanford University in 1978. She also holds the B.A. in English from the College of William and Mary and the M.A. in English, social anthropology, and anthropology from Boston University, Northeastern University, and Stanford University, respectively. She spent two years working for an urban planning agency and a government program to improve urban housing. In addition to the Tirolean research on social networks at different levels of urbanization and among different socioeconomic groups, she has done fieldwork on complainant reactions in the Massachusetts Commission against Discrimination in Boston and is currently investigating the relationship between women's occupational roles and social stratification. She has taught individual courses at Stanford University and Northeastern University and is currently an assistant professor of anthropology at the College of William and Mary. She belongs to several professional and honor societies and is the author of several papers and articles relating to her research.

Robert H. Evans received the bachelor's degree in political science at the Institut d'Études Politiques in Paris, studied at the Johns Hopkins School of Advanced International Studies in, Bologna, Italy, and received the M.A. and Ph.D. from the University of Denver. Professor Evans has taught at the Universities of Notre Dame and Denver and is presently professor of government and foreign affairs at the University of Virginia. He is the author of *Coexistence: Communism and Its Practice in Bologna, 1945-1965* (University of Notre Dame Press, 1967), *Life and Politics in a Venetian Community* (University of Notre Dame Press, 1966), several works in Italian, and articles dealing with Italian politics.

Guido Francescato studied architecture at the University of Buenos Aires and at the University of Illinois at Urbana-Champaign, where he earned the B.Arch. degree in architectural engineering and the M.Arch. degree in urban design. He has designed various residential, commercial, and industrial buildings in Argentina, the United States, Canada, Italy, and Ethiopia. Between 1966 and 1978 he taught urban design and architectural criticism and theory at the University of Illinois. He is presently a professor and chairman of the Department of Housing and Applied Design at the University of Maryland, College Park. Professor Francescato has done extensive research in housing for low- and moderate-income families for the Ford Foundation, the U.S. Department of Housing and Urban Development, and the National Endowment for the Arts. He is the author of several articles, papers, and monographs on residents' satisfaction and on housing quality.

William P. Lowry experienced many landscapes and climates during his youth as the son of a career army officer. His own army service was in Alaska, where he became fascinated with the conflicts between self-centered man trying to control nature and bend her to his will, and nature's gentle, often forgiving, yet inexorable and prevailing resistance. With the A.B. in mathematics from Cincinnati and the M.S. in meteorology from Wisconsin, he worked for the State of Oregon Forestry Department before receiving an interdisciplinary Ph.D. at Oregon State in 1962. Combining meteorology and climatology with different aspects of the life sciences, he calls himself a bioclimatologist. A research specialty is the study of man's impacts on weather and climate through the processes of urbanization. He is professor of ecology and a member of the Institute for Environmental Studies at the University of Illinois, Urbana.

Peter H. Merkl has been a professor of political science at the University of California, Santa Barbara, since 1968. He received the Ph.D. at the University of California, Berkeley, in 1959 and the M.A. in international relations at the University of Minnesota in 1953. He has been involved in the study of local government reform in Germany since 1974 and is the author of *Modern Comparative Politics* (Holt, Rinehart, 2nd ed., 1977) and *Political Violence under the Swastika: 581 Early Nazis* (Princeton University Press, 1975).

Richard L. Merritt is professor of political science and communications at the University of Illinois at Urbana-Champaign and head of the Department of Political Science. After receiving the Ph.D. from Yale University, he worked in the fields of international communications, quantitative cross-national research, and political integration, with special reference to Berlin and Germany. His publications include *Symbols of American Community, 1735-1775* (Yale University Press, 1966), *Systematic Approaches to Comparative Politics* (Rand-McNally, 1970), and, together with Anna J. Merritt, *Public Opinion in Semisovereign Germany: The HICOG Surveys, 1949-1955* (University of Illinois Press, 1979).

John O'Loughlin a native of Ireland, earned the B.A. (Hons.) degree from the National University of Ireland (University College, Dublin) in geography and history. He received the M.S. and Ph.D. degrees in geography at the Pennsylvania State University. Since 1973 he has been assistant professor of geography at the University of Illinois, Urbana. He is presently on leave as an Alexander Von Humboldt Fellow at the University of Düsseldorf, West Germany. Professor O'Loughlin is the author of several papers on electoral behavior of black Americans, malapportionment and gerrymandering of electoral districts, housing rehabilitation in inner cities, and geography as social science.

B. Guy Peters is currently director and associate professor of the Center for Public Policy Studies, Tulane University. He has also taught at Emory University and the University of Delaware, and he has been a Fulbright Professor at the University of Strathclyde, Glasgow, Scotland. He received the M.A. and Ph.D. in political science from Michigan State University. Professor Peters is the author of *The Politics of Bureaucracy: A Comparative Perspective* (Longmans, 1978) and coauthor of *Can Government Go Bankrupt?* (Basic Books, 1978) as well as of a number of articles in scholarly journals.

Alberta Mary Sbragia received the Ph.D. in political science from the University of Wisconsin, Madison in 1974. She studied at the Sorbonne in 1967-68 and spent 1972-73 in Italy as a Fulbright scholar. Since 1974, she has been an assistant professor of political science at the University of Pittsburgh. Professor Sbragia is a member of several professional organizations and is also the author of several articles and papers on public housing and land-use policies and on the political economy of local government capital investment.

Harry C. Triandis studied engineering at McGill University in Montreal, business administration at the University of Toronto, and social psychology at Cornell University, receiving the Ph.D. in 1958. He has been professor of psychology at the University of Illinois in Urbana since 1966 and is a member of many professional psychological associations. He has served as chairman of the Society of Experimental Social Psychology, president of the International Association of Cross-Cultural Psychology, president of the Society for the Psychological Study of Social Issues, and president of the Society for Personality and Social Psychology. He has been on the editorial board of the leading social psychology journals for various periods of time and is the author of *Attitude and Attitude Change* (Wiley, 1971), *The Analysis of Subjective Culture* (Wiley, 1972), *Variations of Black and White Perceptions of the Social Environment* (University of Illinois Press, 1976), *Interpersonal Behavior* (Brooks/Cole, 1977) and the editor of the six-volume *Handbook of Cross-Cultural Psychology* (Allyn and Bacon, 1979-80, forthcoming).

Zelime Amen Ward received her secondary education in West German and French schools and thereafter continued her academic training in the United States, with the exception of one year spent in Europe as a Fulbright scholar. After receiving the Ph.D. degree, she was employed as an assistant professor at the University of North Carolina at Charlotte and later at the University of Texas at Austin. Professor Ward has conducted periodic research in West Germany, primarily in Bonn and at the Universities of Mannheim and Cologne. Her contributed chapters to books and articles in professional journals have focused on policy priorities in postindustrial societies, European urban reform, European party systems, the women's movement in West Germany, and nationalism in East Germany. She currently is completing a book, *Consensus and Conflict in Postindustrial Western Europe*.

About the Editor

Michael C. Romanos received the Diploma in Architectural Engineering from the National Technical University in Athens, the M.S. in urban and regional planning at the Florida State University, and the Ph.D. in regional science from Cornell University. Before coming to the United States as a Fulbright scholar, he worked for several years in the Greek Ministry of Coordination and Planning. Between 1973 and 1975 he taught at Cornell University, and he is presently an associate professor of urban and regional planning and civil engineering at the Urbana campus of the University of Illinois. He is the author of *Residential Spatial Structure* (Lexington Books, D.C. Heath, 1976), *Community Planning for Energy Conservation* (U.S. Department of Energy, 1977), and several articles and monographs dealing with urban and regional analysis.